LIVING ON THE EDGE

Living on the Edge

A GUIDE TO INTERVENTION FOR FAMILIES WITH DRUG AND ALCOHOL PROBLEMS

Katherine Ketcham and
Ginny Lyford Gustafson

BANTAM BOOKS
NEW YORK • TORONTO • LONDON • SYDNEY • AUCKLAND

To our children

**Robyn, Alison and Benjamin
Heidi, Leif, Erik and Ryan**

LIVING ON THE EDGE

A Bantam Book / April 1989

Library of Congress Cataloging-in-Publication Data
Ketcham, Katherine, 1949–
    Living on the edge.
    Bibliography: p.
    Includes index.
    1. Co-dependence (Psychology)
    2. Co-dependence (Psychology)—Case studies.
I. Gustafson, Ginny Lyford.   II. Title.
RC569.5.C63K47   1989   616.86   88-7723
ISBN 0-553-34606-7

Published simultaneously in the United States and Canada

Bantam Books are published by Bantam Books, a division of Bantam Doubleday
Dell Publishing Group, Inc. Its trademark, consisting of the words "Bantam Books"
and the portrayal of a rooster, is Registered in U.S. Patent and Trademark Office
and in other countries. Marca Registrada. Bantam Books, 666 Fifth Avenue,
New York, New York 10103.

PRINTED IN THE UNITED STATES OF AMERICA

CWO   0   9   8   7   6   5   4   3   2   1

ACKNOWLEDGMENTS

Special thanks to James R. Milam, Ph.D.;
Dr. Gary Connor; Dr. Ann Mueller; Joyce Sundin;
Michael Kirkland; Father Tim Sauer; Nikki Moore;
Mary O'Cleary; and Carole Abel.

Contents

III OVERCOMING

Personal Introduction

I began working as an intervention counselor ten years ago, just a few years after Vernon Johnson introduced the concept of intervention in his book *I'll Quit Tomorrow*. Johnson argued eloquently against the then-prevalent belief that alcoholics have to hit bottom before they can be helped, and he suggested a method for "bringing the bottom up"—intervention. Intervention, as Johnson defined the term, is a "therapy designed to bring the patient back to reality"; its purpose is to create a crisis by bringing together the meaningful people in the alcoholic's life and having them present to him, in a caring and concerned way, the desperate reality of his situation.

Intervention revolutionized the alcoholism treatment world. Now, finally, we could help alcoholics and drug addicts before they had lost everything of value in their lives. Now we could save the families before they, too, were destroyed.

But it was a rough and rocky road, still. There was so much ignorance to combat, so much fear to dispel, so much anger and bitterness to change back into love, caring, self-respect. It felt, at times, like standing on the earth and trying to blow the clouds out of the sky.

Then, in 1981, *Under the Influence*, by James R. Milam,

Ph.D., and Katherine Ketcham, was published. I had worked with Dr. Milam, a psychologist and researcher, at his innovative treatment center in Kirkland, Washington, and I was to meet Katherine Ketcham several years later, when she asked for my help on a section on intervention in another groundbreaking book, *Recovering: How to Get and Stay Sober.* From that collaboration evolved the idea for this book on intervention.

But back to 1981. *Under the Influence,* painstakingly researched and beautifully written, took all the information about alcoholism, welded it together in new ways, and made it understandable for the first time. Now I had a foundation to build on, a common base of understanding that would help alcoholics and their families understand what, exactly, had torn their world into so many bits and pieces.

It's hard to imagine now, but when *Under the Influence* was published most people in this country still believed alcoholism was a moral weakness, a disease of willpower. And back then the terms *codependency* and *adult children of alcoholics* were virtually unknown. Like most people working in the alcoholism treatment field in the early 1980s, I focused my attention on the alcoholic and his needs. And I would find myself getting frustrated with family members who gave up and left the alcoholic because they couldn't take any more, they had "had it."

But as I worked with more and more families and came to know the disease from their perspective, my allegiances gradually began to shift. When I saw whole families destroyed by the disease and by the "fallout" emotions of grief, anger, shame, and guilt, I realized how desperately families need an advocate: someone to understand their special needs and concerns, someone to fight on their side against the disease.

As an intervention counselor, I have become the family's advocate. My primary concern is to get help for the family members *before* they are destroyed, before they've "had it." Then we have a chance, working together, to save not only the alcoholic but the family as a whole. I believe that if I can help the family, I will have a much better chance to help the alcoholic. Rather than trying to help the alcoholic and then hope the family will adjust to his recovery, I believe the better way is to help the family members change *their* lives. When they become committed to a healthier, saner way of life, the alcoholic will be forced to change, too.

In the last ten years, working with treatment centers and as an independent intervention counselor, I have had the privilege to serve many, many families. In more than five hundred interventions I have witnessed the incredible power of this relatively simple technique that is designed to change the structure of a dying family. I think of intervention as a human particle accelerator, an atom smasher in which old particles are destroyed and new ones created. Intervention brings all the players together and forces them to collide and create new structures. After participating in an intervention, the family will never again see things as they used to see them. As their perspective changes completely, nothing in their lives will ever be the same again.

A few months ago, I left an intervention at a house where they'd had a major problem with bees. That morning, the family had sprayed the bees' nest. As I stepped onto the porch, the bees were falling out of the nest and writhing in agony on the ground. One huge can of Raid had ended everything for them.

During the intervention I'd been controlled, unemotional, dry-eyed. But afterward, as I stood on the porch and watched those dying bees—a whole family unit, generations, an entire tribe of bees wiped off the face of the earth—I cried my heart out. The bees, of course, were a reminder of the families who don't get help. The disease of addiction will tear a family apart just as that big can of Raid wiped out generations of bees. The family members all die off, one at a time, apart from one another, isolated in their agony, unable to reach out and console one another, their hearts and spirits broken by this disease.

But at the other end of the spectrum are the families who work so hard to put an end to the agony. When I see them together and witness the commitment they make in the name of love, I am overwhelmed. Grandparents, parents, children, aunts, uncles, cousins, brothers, sisters—all come together because they believe they can make a difference.

And they can. They do. These families have decided that they will not die without a fight. They learn how to disarm the disease before it destroys them. They learn how to fight for love.

It is a grand fight. No matter what the outcome, it is a fight worth waging. And once you have decided to enter the arena, you cannot lose. If you are willing to fight for love and for your own future, you are already a winner.

PART I

Identifying

If you are like most people who live with or love a Dependent—someone who is addicted to alcohol, cocaine, heroin, or prescription pills—you want to get right to the "action" part of intervention. You want to find a way—quickly, if possible—to fix your "problem." You don't want to do any more soul-searching. You don't need to hear again that you are part of the problem. Your patience and understanding are all used up, and you're ready to hand this problem over to the professionals and have them fix it. Then, you hope, all will be well, and life will be worth living once again.

We wish we could offer you easy answers and fast solutions. But we can't. We'd be deceiving you if we did. Addiction to alcohol and drugs affects not only the body but the mind and even the soul; it affects not only its victims but its victims' families and friends. The addiction has entrapped *you*—an innocent bystander—in its tentacles, and it has blinded you to your own imprisonment. You know that things are not right, but the reasons escape you, and you blame yourself for the joylessness of your life.

Intervention—stepping in and stopping the addiction—must begin with self-assessment and self-discovery. As a process of education and enlightenment as well as action, intervention must take into account the depth and power of the addiction's tenacious hold on both the Dependent and the Dependent's family. Thus, we must start at the beginning, by identifying *what* has happened to your life and *why* it happened.

In the next seven chapters, we will lead you gradually into understanding the disease of addiction. Our goals are to help you:

- *Identify* the addiction so that you know what it is and how far it has progressed.
- *Identify* common misconceptions and stereotypes about alcoholism and drug addiction so that you will understand why you and your family became its victims.
- *Identify* how your behavior has been manipulated by the addiction so that you can begin to see how certain of your thoughts, feelings, and actions are actually a product of living with this disease.
- *Identify* the addiction-related behaviors in your Dependent so that you can learn to separate the person you love from the person controlled by the addiction.
- *Identify* your losses—love, affection, self-esteem, confidence, inner strength, control over your life—so that you will know what it is you intend to fight for.

ONE

Living on the Edge

If you love a chemically addicted person, you are living on the edge: the knife-sharp precipice between hope and despair, anger and fear, love and hate, sanity and insanity. You teeter there, swaying back and forth: your concern for the person you love makes you incapable of acting or making a decision. Because of your love, you have not been able to move, for you have feared letting go, losing your love, and, ultimately, destroying your life.

Because of your love and increasingly because of fear, you have not been able to free yourself. You have come to believe that your only hope is to wait things out, to hide your pain, to mask your feelings. You have become emotionally anesthetized, afraid to acknowledge your feelings to yourself or to anyone else.

But waiting things out, keeping silent, and hiding your pain haven't worked. Over the years, love—that precious starting point—has eroded. Despite all your best efforts to love deeply and well, to love so much that your love itself will work miracles, nothing works for very long. Slowly, almost unnoticed, your love is consumed by anger, shame, guilt, remorse, and fear—all the emotions that come with the territory of living on the edge.

When love is gone, what's left? In the beginning, there is the effort of trying to survive within the relationship. You adapt, hide your feelings, cover up, protect, smooth things over, and pretend everything will be all right. But if you're just surviving—if you're so consumed with worry and fear about falling off the edge that you've become paralyzed and incapable of stepping away from it—you've accepted a life of joylessness. You may not even remember, now, what it was like to feel joy or happiness, to act spontaneously, to smile or laugh without an effort. Now your days are spent in a state of free-floating anxiety about what might happen next. Your fear of the unknown—what will happen if I leave? what will happen if I don't leave?—has caused you to react with extreme caution. You find it very difficult to take risks or express opinions. "I don't care," you respond when someone asks what you'd like for dinner or what movie you'd like to see. And you really don't care. You can't afford to care, because caring hurts too much.

All of us who live on the edge spend our time waiting, anxiously, for things to happen; if nothing happens, that's just fine with us. Because when things happen these days, they are almost always stressful, anxiety-provoking, and emotionally painful. Better not to have anything happen—better to stay right where we are—than to risk the pain and uncertainty of even the slightest movement. Living as close as we do to the edge, we know how quickly the earth can give out beneath our feet. We've become experts at maneuvering slowly along the precipice, holding our breath, not daring to step away from the well-traveled path we have worn down through the years, fearing even to look to either side. As bad as the pain is now, the unknown is simply terrifying.

Eventually the pain will give way to numbness, and survival will metamorphose to apathy: the emotional end of the line. Thirty-eight-year-old Jessica explains what happened to her emotions after years of living with her alcoholic father:

I remember the one and only present my father ever gave me—a bottle of Chanel No. 5 perfume. I was thirteen, and I hated perfume. It seemed that I'd been spending my whole life trying to get my father's attention by doing "boy" things—playing baseball and football, flying a plane—but he paid no attention at all. I qualified for the Olympics in swimming, and, do you know, he never once came to one of my swim meets?

Jessica smiled, with no trace of sadness or other emotion, as if the bittersweet childhood event was too far back to have any meaning for her now.

Dad drank every day, all day—I never remember him not drinking. But I never saw him drunk. He always went to work, he was always in perfect control.

When my brother and I were little kids, maybe five and seven years old, we would all go out on our little fishing boat, early in the morning. Dad would take out the jelly glass and pour himself half a glass of bourbon, and then he'd let us pour him a chaser of water. After he drank the bourbon, we'd hand him the water to wash it down. We always thought that was great fun.

I got married when I was nineteen, and by that time I just didn't care what my father thought or did. I remember introducing him to my husband and thinking, *I don't even care if they like each other; it just doesn't matter.*

I had to learn to love people because I had no practice with it. My parents never hugged or kissed me. They never told me they loved me. Even when I had my own children, I had to make a conscious decision to love them—I had to learn *how* to love them. Love was like a new language for me.

I ran into Dad on the subway last year. I walked up to him and said, "Hi, Dad, I'm Jessie." I shook his hand. It had been ten years since I'd seen him. He said, "Well, for heaven's sake." After that, we had nothing to say to each other.

My brother called me three months ago to tell me Dad had had a mild heart attack. "That's too bad," I said. It simply didn't touch me.

I have as much emotional connection to my father as I have to the person at the checkout stand in the grocery store.

Jessica, like so many of us who have lived with or loved a Dependent, is past anger; she is even past fear. She simply doesn't care anymore. It doesn't matter to her where, how, or with whom her father lives; his death would cause no feeling in her, not even one of relief.

Living on the edge for too long inevitably leads to the absolute death of feeling, which is called apathy. As Jessica puts it, "I just didn't feel anything when I finally left home. It was like the flat line on an EKG—my emotions were absolutely dead." Apathy is a natural phenomenon, the result of caring and feeling too much and not having the caring or the feeling change anything. It is not a conscious choice, but a consequence of living for too long with someone who is chemically addicted. The feelings that once were so alive are now dead, beyond resurrection.

Somewhere between survival and apathy a choice must be made: to stay and continue living on the edge, or to begin to break away and seek help for yourself and eventually, perhaps, help for the Dependent. Breaking away is the more immediately difficult and painful road to follow, for it is filled with unknowns, and our fear prevents us from even looking at the unknown. Furthermore, we have been greatly weakened, both emotionally and psychologically, in our struggle against the addiction. We are filled with self-doubt, we have no confidence in our ability to make it on our own, and we have been accepting the guilt for so long that we can no longer understand that the Dependent's behavior is not our fault. And then there is the desperate need to win this struggle, for only by winning do we see any hope for ourselves or our future.

And so we stay, until we, too, are wrapped up in the craziness of the addiction. At that point, we can't even recognize that we are in pain. We have lost the ability to feel good and may even have come to prefer feeling bad—because feeling bad is so familiar.

The other choice—to begin the process of breaking away—is forced on us either by a crisis or by the sudden realization that the pain is, in a very real sense, killing us. For most of us, the sheer agony will eventually overcome the fears associated with continuing to live on the edge. Living begins to become more important than simply surviving; living with the fear of the unknown becomes more acceptable than living with the continuous pain of the known.

At this point, we will be able to take the first tentative steps away from the precipice. We will begin to understand that survival is not living but simply existing, and we will come to realize that it is within our power to create our own happiness. We *can* choose to be happy. It is also within our power to refuse to be unhappy. These are not selfish or immoral choices; they are, in fact, the only choices that offer us and our Dependents any hope for the future.

TWO

How Are You Feeling?

Jane Osborne wandered from her living room to her dining room, into the kitchen, back through the dining room and living room, and back again to the kitchen. Over and over she walked this route, and as she walked she talked to herself.

"I'm worried about my husband," she said matter-of-factly. "He's an alcoholic." She stopped for a moment, staring out her kitchen window. Perhaps, she thought, I should say that I think he's an alcoholic. Or should I say I think maybe he has a drinking problem?

She resumed her circular walking, taking deep breaths every so often to steady herself. Finally, her speech carefully rehearsed, she walked into the bedroom, picked up the telephone, and began to dial. On the sixth number, she hesitated, then gently replaced the receiver. Slowly she collapsed on the bed and began to cry. "I'm a child," she sobbed. "A baby! I can't even dial the phone!" Her weakness filled her with anger; with exquisite control, she stopped the tears, steadied herself, and reached once more for the receiver. This time her shaking fingers finished dialing. A cheerful woman's voice answered.

"Hello," Jane said, clearing her throat. "I'm Jane Osborne. A friend gave me your number. I'm married to an alcoholic—at *least I think he's an alcoholic. He's drinking all the time and he's drinking more often and last night he drove the car right through the garage. He's going to kill himself if he doesn't stop drinking. My friend said you might be able to help him."*

"It sounds as if you've had a rough time lately," replied the voice on the other end of the line. "How are you feeling in the middle of all this?"

"Well," Jane answered slowly, not sure what she was supposed to say, "I want it to end."

"I can understand that. Can you tell me what else you're feeling?"

Jane was confused. Why, she thought, is this woman asking about me? I'm not the problem! She began to doubt whether she should have called at all. And suddenly she was very angry.

"I don't know how I'm feeling!" she snapped. "I haven't thought about myself in ten years. I don't think I feel anything anymore. And anyway, what does it matter? I'm not calling about me, I'm calling about my husband. What do my feelings have to do with any of this?"

"Your feelings and needs are important, too, Mrs. Osborne. Understanding how you feel will help both of us to help your husband."

"But if you can just get him sober," Jane interrupted, "I'll be fine. Look, I've done enough suffering for his sake. I'm ready to wash my hands of him."

The counselor laughed gently. "I know how that feels," she confided. "I have clients who are so tired of suffering that they look for any way to get out of the relationship. I often hear from them that they wish their husbands or wives would get hit by a truck or a train, just to end the misery. Then they struggle with the terrible guilt of wishing a loved one dead."

"They wish they'd die," Jane said softly. It was a confirmation, not a question.

"Yes," the counselor said. "I hear it many times."

How odd, *Jane thought.* I should be crying, but I'm fighting the giggles. *"My husband is a doctor," she said. "I can't tell you how often I've hoped that he'd catch an infectious disease from one of his patients—some mysterious, tropical disease that would kill him clean and fast—gone to the office in the morning, dead in the afternoon. I haven't even been able to admit that to my priest."*

"It helps to know that other people feel the same way, doesn't it?"

"Yes, it does." Jane took a deep breath. "Would it be possible for me to meet with you sometime soon?"

"Are you free tomorrow at two o'clock?"

"Yes, that would be fine. Thank you."

When Jane hung up the phone, she was overwhelmed with relief. She held her hands in front of her and, watching the uncontrollable trembling, began to laugh. Big tears rolled down her cheeks.

"How do I feel?" she said aloud. "Scared, neurotic, nervous, terrified, confused—and relieved! I'm not alone anymore!" Her tears came stronger now, unrestrained. Oh, my God, she thought, with a strange sense of joy, I'm not alone anymore.

■

How are *you* feeling? The honest answer to that question, for 99 percent of the people reading this book, is, "I don't know." You don't know how you feel because it's been years since you've thought about *you*, at least in any deep, searching way. You haven't had time to think about yourself, because you've been totally wrapped up in keeping the various parts of your life—and your Dependent's life—from falling apart.

Anyway, why are you important? After all, you're not the problem here—he is! As soon as he's "fixed," you'll be just fine; everything will be back to normal. That's what Jane Osborne thought, and that's what just about everyone who loves a Dependent thinks. But nothing is further from the truth.

You are not "fine." Through the years of living with the addiction, you've changed. You've learned some tricks to survive. For every left jab the addiction has thrown at you, you've developed a protective maneuver. But most of the time you avoid encounters. You hide out in the corner of the ring, waiting for the worst of it to be over with. You put on the headphones, read a book, turn up the television loud—anything to tune out the din of a fight you can't possibly win.

You don't talk about the drinking or the drugging. You change the subject when the conversation gets heated. You play down the Dependent's problems, claiming they aren't "that bad." You rationalize, saying, "No wonder he's drinking so much, his job is too stressful," or, "All the kids are doing drugs, it's a hazard of adolescence." You take the blame on yourself. You assume the responsibility for beating this "thing." "I'll stick by him," you vow, "I'll help him, we'll beat this together."

These are all survival behaviors, and they have worked just fine through the years to insulate you from the stress of your situation. But what you don't know, and can't know until you understand addiction, is that these tricks are your undoing. By closing yourself off, you have become an unwitting ally of the addiction. By refusing to talk about the problem, you deny its existence. By changing the subject, you protect the Dependent from the consequences of his addictive behavior. By keeping quiet, taking responsibility, protecting, and covering up, you allow the disease to strengthen its reign of terror over your family. You have learned to live within the rules that the addiction has established, and thus you have become its prisoner, as surely as the victim who takes the drug or the drink every day not because he wants it, necessarily, but because he thinks he can't live without it.

You, too, live your life based on the demands of the addiction, and unless you get help, you will continue to think and behave in destructive, unhealthy ways. Help means becoming educated about the disease of addiction, understanding why it has nearly destroyed your family, acknowledging its widespread impact on your own behavior, learning how to recognize the addiction and its symptoms, and making the commitment to begin the process of recovery, regardless of what happens to your Dependent. Unless you get this kind of help, you will stay right where the disease has trapped you: mired in fear, anger, resentment, confusion, guilt, and grief.

Unless you attend to your own needs, you will actually be a threat to any recovery attempted by the Dependent. You'll resent his absences from home to be with those "A.A. [or N.A.] people"; you'll be jealous of his friendships; you'll envy his growing self-confidence and good health; and all the while you'll wonder when and how he's going to make up to you all those wretched years. You still don't trust him, you probably don't like him, and, if you'll admit it, you are angry as hell about what *he* did to you. If he comes strutting back into your fragmented life all healthy and strong and full of enthusiasm for his new life, you may soon find yourself wishing he'd strut right back out again.

Or, if your Dependent has problems during recovery—if he's depressed or fed up with A.A., if he's constantly fighting the urge to take a drink or a drug, if he's shaky, tense, and tired—you'll be no help to him unless you understand where those problems come from and what can be done about them.

And if he does start drinking or drugging again, you won't have the strength to keep yourself from being pulled back into the maelstrom of the disease.

How are *you* feeling? The process of your recovery, and the ultimate success of your Dependent's recovery, must begin with this question. You, as someone who cares deeply about the Dependent, can be the greatest single weapon against this cunning and insidious disease. You can also, without realizing it, be its greatest ally.

THREE

—

Whose Problem Is This, Anyway?

"I'm not part of this disease," you say. "I'm just trying to cope with it." But consider the following situations.

- Carefully measuring each of your husband's drinks, hoping against hope that as long as he drinks just that much and no more, he'll be okay.
- Adding water to your parents' bottle of scotch, thereby hoping to water down their nightly arguments.
- Excusing your teenager's plummeting grades, rebellious behavior, and refusal to communicate as "typical adolescence."
- Trying to get the Thanksgiving turkey ready early so Dad won't be too drunk and embarrass all the relatives.
- Putting gates on the stairs so that Mom doesn't fall and break her leg again.
- Removing all the clothes and lining the closet with plastic so that when Dad mistakes the closet for the bathroom, cleanup is a breeze.
- Making up excuses why the grandchildren can't visit when the real reason is that Granddad gets plastered every afternoon.

- Playing racquetball every morning to have an excuse for the bruises inflicted the night before by a drunken spouse.
- Never mentioning the drinking and the drugging when they are what is tearing everything apart. If you just don't talk about it, the crazy thoughts go, maybe it will all suddenly go away.

It's impossible to "cope" with an addiction without becoming wrapped up in its lunacy. In order to cope, you have to adapt, and by adapting you will begin to lose progressively larger chunks of yourself. You will begin to think, feel, and behave in "crazy" ways: ways that are dictated by the demands of the addiction.

It's as if a violent storm came along, blowing gaping holes in your home's roof and walls. At first you try to plug up the holes with plastic, old sheets, pieces of wood—but the wind and the rain keep hammering away, eventually tearing down your puny efforts. So you give up trying to fix things and instead put all your energy into accepting the house as it is and attempting to keep things from getting worse. When it rains, you put on a raincoat; when it snows, you bundle up. You hammer and saw, patch and mend, spending most of your time trying to protect yourself from the periodic downpours and then cleaning up after the mess. You have ceased to think of this as inconsequential work; in fact, you get a strange satisfaction from your efforts. You can win, you think, if only you work harder. And you become obsessed with your task, thinking of little else.

Anyone who would live such a life has to be crazy, right? And so is twenty-five-year-old Mary, whose husband is a cocaine addict and whose two young children go to bed terrified every night. For years Mary resisted asking for help for her husband because she believed if only she tried harder, life would get better. She tried and tried, and sure enough, one day things did seem a little better. That day Mary called her therapist and happily reported that her husband was making progress. He used to sleep with a loaded .44 Magnum under his pillow, she admitted; but he finally heeded her protests and in the past month he'd been satisfied with bringing a large hunting knife to bed. The pistol, still loaded, was stuffed behind some books in the bedside table.

Furthermore, Mary confided, he was beginning to see the insanity of his behavior. Just last week he woke up in a sweat, convinced that someone was trying to break into the house. Mary reached for the knife, her husband tried to grab it from her, and she accidentally took a three-inch slice out of his arm.

That brought him to his senses, she said. He began to cry and apologize for all his weird behavior. So Mary comforted him, dressed his arm, and whispered that everything would be all right, that they would work together to change their lives. "We can make it," she soothed him, holding him in her arms like a baby and feeling her power as a woman. This one moment, she told the therapist, gave her confidence and hope. She felt sure she could turn things around; she just needed time.

What are the symptoms of Mary's craziness? She is living with an emotionally unstable, paranoid, delusional drug addict. She has come to accept a hunting knife in her bed and a three-inch slice out of her husband's arm as "progress." She believes that if only she loves her husband enough, she can help him to overcome his "problems." She has given up thinking about anything but the most basic of her own needs, focusing all the rest of her energy on her husband. Comforting him makes her feel needed as a woman and as a wife. The circumstances that lead to the comforting don't seem, to her, bizarre or abnormal: she has lived so long with the addiction that she has come to accept its outrageous demands as normal.

Mary wasn't always so crazy. When her husband first started using cocaine on a daily basis, she was alarmed. But her protests did no good; her tears made no difference; begging, pleading, and cajoling had absolutely no impact on her husband's drug use. Oh, he'd feel ashamed every so often; he'd break down in tears and apologize for using up their savings; he'd promise to change. But nothing changed. The drug use continued, the savings were spent, the TV and stereo were sold, and the night sweats and paranoia raged on.

In the beginning, Mary tried to talk to her friends about her husband's cocaine use and dealing. But she could talk only to those friends who were also cocaine users—her "straight" friends wouldn't understand at all. She feared their rejection of her and their shock at the circumstances of her life. She felt she couldn't handle any more criticism or well-intentioned advice about divorcing him. Besides, they couldn't understand, she reasoned; they didn't know anything about drugs. Mary never even considered confiding in her family; to them, anyone who used cocaine was as bad as someone who robbed banks or raped women. They would never understand.

Her cocaine-using friends told her not to be too concerned. "If you don't abuse it, cocaine isn't physically addicting," they assured her. "And if he deals—well, he has to try the stuff, no way around that." "But what about the free-basing?" Mary asked. "See if you can get him to cut back on the free-basing," they said. "Remember Richard Pryor?" They laughed.

Mary became more and more isolated in the tortured web of her life, which included her sick husband, her frightened children, and her disintegrating self-concept. Protecting her children, loving and helping her husband, cleaning the house, trying to keep the bill collectors at bay—these were her roles in life. She stopped confiding in family and friends. She stopped crying, laughing, fighting, or pleading. She just existed day to day, hoping that things would eventually change, believing that it was all up to her, finding comfort from those occasions when her husband turned to her for reassurance, for solace, and for strength.

What is the cost to Mary and the rest of us who continue to protect, defend, and cover up for a Dependent? A loss of self. We lose our ability to be honest and true to ourselves, to know our feelings, to act on our best instincts. Adapting our behavior to the demands of the addiction has left us no choice: we have had to stuff our feelings inside ourselves and have become experts at avoiding the emotional pain associated with these feelings. Acknowledging the feelings, bringing them out into the open, would mean acknowledging the pain. And the pain, the loss of self, is simply too much to bear.

Through the years, we have learned that our feelings are untrustworthy. At one moment we might feel sad, the next we feel mad, then suddenly everything seems better and we wonder what's wrong with us that we can't deal with life's ups and downs without jolting from one emotional extreme to another.

Mad, sad, lonely, afraid—where do these feelings get us? How many times have we begged for affection and a comforting caress—and how many times have our needs for love been thrown back at us coldly or with more selfish demands? How many times have we cried out in anger or frustration—and how many times have our cries been met with louder screams or, worse, silence? How many times have we shed bitter tears—and how many times have our grief and sadness isolated us even further? How many times have we threatened, cajoled, and pleaded—and how many times have the promises we extracted been broken?

Like Mary, we have learned that feelings don't get us anywhere. Nothing changes because we're angry, frustrated, confused, or sad. And we gradually become fed up with these feelings: they hurt too much and gain us nothing. So we stuff them deep inside, where it is dark and cold and still. There, they settle into the dull, inner ache of loneliness and hopelessness and the gradual dying of love.

Still, this pain is easier to deal with than raw anger or grief because it is so easily hidden and hurts no one but ourselves. And our pain gives us a mission. When we feel lonely, we think the answer is to keep the family together, no matter what the cost. When we feel hopeless, the trick is to lower our expectations and try to be happy with what we have. When we fear that our love is dying, we try to love harder. We can bear any pain, we think, as long as we have our family to love. We adapt because we see no other way to keep the peace.

And so we begin to direct all our attention outside ourselves, where it seems that it might, someday, make a difference. (Concentrating on ourselves certainly hasn't changed anything.) As we focus our attention on making things work, we begin to believe that whatever happens is *our* responsibility. If only we try hard enough, we can make it all work. The flip side of this thought pattern is that if things don't work, then it is somehow our fault. If only we can change, if only we can make life more comfortable, if only we can love enough, then the drinking or the drugging will stop. Through the years, we've become experts at carrying the burden.

A great deal is sacrificed in such a relationship, but a great deal is gained, too. We gain responsibility, even if it means blaming ourselves when things go wrong. We gain a measure of control, even if it means concentrating all our energies on keeping the family together. We gain a purpose in life, even though that purpose is constantly challenged. We gain hope, even if it is a mere shred, constantly battered, continually threatened. We gain a feeling of being indispensable, even if it means having to carry our Dependent to bed every night or rock our frightened children to sleep. And we gain a sense of satisfaction at performing our "duty," even though the walls of our lives are forever threatening to come crashing down.

We are survivors. We have found a way to endure the pain by adapting our behavior and trying to stay in control. Through the years, we have latched on to responsibility, hope, love, and duty, with just one loss: our selves. And because we don't think about it, because it hurts too much to think about it, that doesn't seem like too much to lose.

FOUR

How Bad Is It?

Not *that* bad. At least not yet. At least that's what we think.

Bad, after all, is the skid-row drunk passed out on the sidewalk, mouth open, drooling, an empty bottle still clutched in a blue-veined, dead-looking hand. Bad is the corpse on the mortician's table with a brain turned to mush and a liver so bloated with scar tissue it's three times its normal size. Bad is shooting heroin. Bad is spending every penny you own on cocaine and then stealing from your friends and family to keep up the habit. Bad is going crazy on PCP and driving 110 miles per hour down a residential road just for the thrill of it. Bad is sitting in your comfortable living room the morning after a bad drunk and seeing rats as big as dogs advancing on you. Bad is drinking Sterno or cough syrup or vanilla extract when you can't afford a bottle of cheap wine.

What most of us don't realize, until the realization can't be missed, is that "bad" is just the end of the line. The line has to begin somewhere, and it begins with what appears to be normal drinking or drug use. Only gradually does this line veer off into abnormal behavior, eventually rounding the bend into thoughts and actions that are bizarre, paranoid, and self-destructive. Addiction is a one-way ticket to disaster, and there's only one place the track leads: mental and physical disintegration; loss of family, career, material possessions, and self-respect; and, ultimately, death.

Where along that track are the warning signs of impending doom? How can we know, before it gets "bad," how bad it already is? *Knowledge* is our first and most important ally. We cannot hope to fight this disease without knowing exactly what it is, what causes it, and in what ways it affects the mental and physical health of both its victims and the people who love them. But knowledge is more than just information about the disease; it must also involve breaking down the myths and misconceptions surrounding addiction.

Families are fooled by addiction, in part because society misunderstands and misdiagnoses it. It takes years, we think, to become a *real* drunk or a *real* addict; if we watch carefully, it won't happen in our families.

We think of an alcoholic or addict as degenerate, out of control, and physically debilitated. We think that she lacks willpower and strength of character and has no guiding purpose in life. We think she became addicted because she used drugs to relieve her serious psychological and emotional problems.

These myths and misconceptions have confused and distorted every aspect of our thinking about alcoholism and drug addiction. Public opinion, in truth, has not changed significantly since the Roman philosopher and lawyer Seneca (4 B.C.–A.D. 65) pronounced, "Drunkenness is nothing but a condition of insanity purposely assumed."

"Purposely assumed"—the alcoholic or addict, we think, chooses his life of depravity and degeneracy. He willingly gives up his family, friends, career, and physical and emotional health for alcohol or drugs. He is basically a psychologically damaged human being, immature, selfish, and willfully irresponsible with his own life and the lives of the people who love him.

But in truth the typical alcoholic or drug addict is fundamentally no different from those who are not addicted. In the beginning, he is a decent, responsible, caring person. He doesn't drink or use drugs significantly more than anyone else does. He can handle his drug use without becoming belligerent or out of control. He doesn't suffer from any detectable withdrawal symptoms when he abstains from alcohol or drugs. In all likelihood, he still has a job, a marriage, and self-respect. And he certainly doesn't look like an alcoholic or drug addict.

But he is addicted. Inside his body, the cells are undergoing changes, adapting to the drug, laying the groundwork for the massive damage that occurs later in the disease. Slowly, gradually, the disease of addiction changes him, altering his personality, eating away at his self-confidence and self-respect, destroying his will.

The family reacts to these outward changes with bewilderment and terror. "Why is he doing this to us?" the family members wonder. It seems so obvious to us that if the Dependent would just look at his behavior, he would see what his addiction is doing to him and to those who love him. But because he doesn't see it, or refuses to see it, we begin to think that he doesn't love us, or that he's too weak to control himself, or that he's a fundamentally unhappy or depressed person. We try to think of events or situations in his life that can be changed in order to make the problems go away:

- "Maybe if we moved, he'd cut down."
- "Maybe if I stopped arguing with him, he wouldn't get so angry and drink so much."
- "Maybe if he made some new friends, he'd clean up his act."
- "Maybe if he found a less stressful job, he wouldn't need to take pills to relax."

Through the years we struggle to understand the Dependent's behavior and to find reasons for it. And we adjust and adapt to the disease by changing our own behavior, hoping that we can somehow control the disease by keeping the peace. Arguments only make things worse, so we stop arguing. Protests about the drinking or the drug use are in vain, so we stop them, too. Tears don't work, threats don't work, tirades don't work. Peace is bought only at the price of silence.

"How bad is it?" can be determined in part by the depth of this silence. Virginia Satir, a family therapist, describes the atmosphere in a troubled family in her book *Peoplemaking:*

> In troubled families the bodies and faces tell of their plight. Bodies are either stiff and tight, or slouchy. Faces look sullen, or sad, or blank like masks. Eyes look down and past people. Ears obviously don't hear. Voices are either harsh and strident, or barely audible.
>
> There is little evidence of friendship among individual family members, little joy in one another. . . . When I would see whole families in my office who were trying to live together in such an atmosphere, I used to wonder how they managed to survive. I discovered that in some, people simply avoided one another; they became so involved in work and other outside activities that they rarely had much real contact with the family.
>
> It is a sad experience for me to be with these families. I see the hopelessness, the helplessness, the loneliness. . . . There are those who are still clinging to a little hope, who can still bellow or nag or whine at each other. Others no longer care. These people go on year after year, enduring misery themselves or, in their desperation, inflicting it on others.

Satir vividly describes what the disease of addiction does to *all* families. Healthy families, trapped by an addiction, gradually become unhealthy. Through the years, the family members stop talking to one another. So few subjects are safe to discuss that we simply stop communicating. Feelings—fears, hurts, angers, disappointments, criticisms—are never shared. Our facial expressions are rigid; the lines in our faces seem carved in stone. We don't listen to one another; we look through one another and speak in strained, clipped voices. Criticisms are instantly met with anger or sullenness. Grudges are held for days, weeks, even years. We find it extraordinarily difficult to be honest and straightforward. Love is experienced not as passion, affection, or delight in one another's company, but as a duty to be dispensed, a burden to be endured.

And our children—they seem to suffer the most. In some

families, the children are ignored or even completely cut off emotionally for minor transgressions. In others, the children are overindulged and overprotected. In all drug-affected families, the children feel great guilt and shame. They feel sure the problem has something to do with them, and they try desperately to make things better.

In the very beginning of the disease, life was not so grim. In fact, in the early stages of the disease we have little reason to be alarmed, because the Dependent does not seem dependent. He drinks or uses drugs, but not all the time and not consistently in excess. All the classic symptoms associated with addiction—an overwhelming compulsion to drink or take drugs, severe withdrawal symptoms, obvious loss of control—are nowhere present in the early stages of the disease. In fact, the Dependent enjoys drinking or using drugs and is often great fun to be with at parties or social gatherings. He drinks or drugs frequently, looks forward to those occasions when he can do so, thinks up excuses to get high, and is often the last to leave a party or a bar. But all of these early warning signs can be misread as typical social drinking or drug use.

Nevertheless, even in the early stages, we may be worried. Perhaps he is a little too involved with drugs, we think. But if we bring up the subject, the Dependent laughs it off; if we keep at him, the Dependent becomes hostile and defensive. Here's a typical reaction to any attempt to discuss his drinking or drug habits: "Come on, give me a break! I don't use any more than Bob or John, I haven't missed a day's work because of drugs, I'm not sick or deranged, I'm always in control, and I've never been belligerent or violent. What's wrong with *you*, anyway?"

We are swayed as much by the logic of the argument as by a fierce resistance even to thinking about the possibility of a drug problem. And the seed of doubt is planted early with the Dependent's accusation: "What's wrong with *you*?" Right in the beginning, we suspect that the problem might be in our own heads. "Am I overreacting?" we wonder. "Am I making mountains out of molehills?"

It doesn't take too long for us to assume the heavier mantle of responsibility: perhaps by making too big a thing of the "problem," we are actually contributing to it. The focus is subtly being taken *off* the drug and put *on* the family members themselves. Which is just where the addiction wants it.

As the addiction gains strength, the family begins to realize that they are in trouble. But they also become increasingly uncertain about exactly what the source of the trouble is. The Dependent hotly denies he has a problem and becomes adept at blaming his increasing preoccupation with drugs or alcohol on his job, external stresses, financial concerns, family obligations, his boss, his wife, his parents, or his children. The family learns to accept the excuses and shoulders the burden of helping the Dependent to work through the stress and strain of his life. Mood swings, personality changes, irritability, depression, nervousness, and anxiety are all seen as symptoms of psychological upset, and the family tries to insulate the Dependent from additional stresses that might make things worse.

Love is the motivator here; it is the reason why most families so patiently and willingly endure the loneliness, misery, and shame of the later stages of the disease. By continuing to love and protect our Dependent we hope to defeat whatever it is that is tearing us apart, and this is our tragic mistake. Love is powerful, but when pitted against an active addiction its power is useless. The addiction will subvert love, taking its best qualities—patience, commitment to devotion and duty, the need to protect at all costs—and using them to render the family helpless.

After living for too long with the disease, we stop caring because we see, finally, the power of what we are up against. And it all seems so hopeless. In the later stages of addiction, the only thing that really matters to the Dependent is to get the drug into the body, via mouth, nose, or vein. He makes no effort to hide his addiction, no longer even cares what the rest of us are doing as long as we don't interfere with his drinking or drug use. If we move out of his life, he may even be relieved: he is alone at last, with the only thing that is capable of giving him what little pleasure there is left to feel.

Even at this point, in the latest stages of the disease, the Dependent can recover. But it may be too late to save the family. Once love is dead and apathy takes root, the family structure begins to crumble. But this is years away and much can be done *now,* when the family is still together, when love is still alive, when the good times outnumber the bad, and when hope and trust are strong enough to fuel the fight against the addiction.

The following questionnaire, adapted for the family from the book *Recovering: How to Get and Stay Sober,* by Ann Mueller, M.D., and Katherine Ketcham, is designed to help you recognize the early-, middle-, and late-stage symptoms of addiction and understand the progression of the disease from its early, benign stage to the increasing problems of the middle stage, and finally to the late stage, in which the damage is obvious and severe.

Answer the questions as truthfully as possible. Some of the questions actually ask several questions; if you answer "yes" to any one, count your answer as a "yes." If your answer is "sometimes," put down a "yes." After you finish the questionnaire, turn to p. 30 to find out whether the disease exists in your family and, if so, how far it has progressed.

QUESTIONNAIRE

1. Does your loved one have any close relatives—grandparents, parents, siblings—who have had drinking or drug problems?

2. Does he or she consistently drink or use drugs more than her friends? Is he often the last one to leave the bar or party?

3. Does he (or she) enjoy drinking or drugs and look forward to occasions when he can use them? Does he have a reputation as a great "party person" or "the life of the party"?

4. Does it sometimes seem that he doesn't want to stop drinking or using drugs, even though everyone else has had enough?

5. Has he experienced any change in his patterns of drug use—using more or using more often, using drugs when alone, or switching to other, sometimes stronger drinks or drugs?

6. Has anyone close to him—his spouse, parents, children, friends—ever worried or complained about his drinking or drug use?

7. Does the thought of an occasion without alcohol or drugs—a church wedding and reception with a nonalcoholic punch, for example—make him anxious or perhaps even angry?

8. Has he ever expressed bewilderment at how slowly other people drink, or wondered why they stop using drugs so soon after starting? Does he ever buy drinks or drugs for his friends in an effort to keep the party going?

9. Does he tend to gulp down his first drinks or drugs and then, when he appears to feel the effects, consciously slow his pace to match others'?

10. When he's sober, does he sometimes regret things he's said or done when drinking or using drugs, apologizing to the people he loves and insisting that things will be different in the future?

11. Has he ever tried to stop drinking or using drugs for a period of time (a week, or perhaps a month) because he felt it would be good for him, or because he wanted to prove that he could do it?

12. Does he sometimes make promises about controlling or cutting down on his drug use and then break these promises within a few days or weeks?

13. Does he seem to feel guilty about drinking or using drugs, and yet when someone he loves or respects mentions his his or her concern, does he become hostile and defensive?

14. Is she able to use more now than she did a year ago? Five years ago? Does she tend to drink or take drugs much more?

15. Has he ever had a blackout, when he can't recall some or all of the events that occurred when he was drinking? Does he have more blackouts now than he did a year ago?*

16. Has he had any difficulties at work—regular sick days, difficulty in concentrating, complaints from co-workers or supervisors—that might be related to drinking or drugs?

17. Does he sometimes say that he's better off when he's drinking or using drugs than when he's sober? Do drugs, in fact, appear to get rid of his headaches, tensions, anxieties, and mood swings?

18. Does he tend to think that his problems are the result of tension and stress, or lack of understanding from his spouse, or unreasonable demands at work? Does he feel sorry for himself because no one seems to understand him? Does he turn to drugs for solace and comfort?

19. Does he appear to crave drugs, actually wanting a drink or drug so intensely that he is willing to risk a fight with his spouse or a reprimand from his boss?

20. Does he increasingly use more than he intended? Does he have trouble stopping once he's started? Does he ever drink or use drugs in the morning?

21. Do his hands sometimes shake uncontrollably the morning after he's been using? Does he feel physically wretched (nauseated, shaky, queasy) and/or psychologically upset (depressed, anxious, tense, moody, irritable, paranoid) when sober? Do drugs make him appear to feel better instantly?

22. Does he have any physical disorders or diseases that might be alcohol- or drug-related, such as lack of appetite; recurrent nausea, vomiting, or diarrhea; broken blood vessels around the nose and/or cheekbones; yellow, glassy eyes; gastritis; high blood pressure; pneumonia, heart palpitations, fatty liver, hepatitis, cirrhosis, D.T.'s,* seizures, or pancreatitis?

23. Has he ever been hospitalized for injuries, accidents, or traumas suffered while using drugs?

24. Does he ever express suicidal thoughts? Has he ever had hallucinations after drinking or using drugs? Does he ever have unreasonable fears (for example, does the doorbell or telephone ringing seem to make him anxious and fearful)?

25. Has he experienced any losses because of his drinking or drug use—loss of a job or financial security, divorce, alienated children or family, driver's license suspended because of drunken driving, et cetera?

26. Does he neglect eating, particularly during and just after using drugs? Does he neglect his body and personal appearance by not exercising regularly or not taking showers or baths?* Is his sex drive noticeably lessened? Does he refuse to go to a doctor for obvious medical problems?

27. Is he able to use less of the drug than he once could, and when he does use, does he tend to keep using until he passes out or becomes physically ill?

   *Blackouts are a very distinctive feature of alcoholism; they are not typically experienced by people addicted to other drugs.
   *D.T.s are also a distinctive feature of alcoholism.
   *Cocaine addicts will often show an incresed interest in personal appearance when they begin using the drug; when use becomes abuse and addiction, the addict will typically lose interest in everything but the drug.

INTERPRETING THE QUESTIONNAIRE

The disease of addiction can be divided into three general stages: early, middle, and late. The questionnaire you just completed includes symptoms from each of these stages. Your answers will help identify (a) if your loved one is addicted to alcohol and/or drugs and (b) what stage of the disease he is in.

Early-stage addiction. Questions 1 to 9 cover the early stage of the disease, when the addiction is "hidden"; the Dependent and his loved ones typically don't even suspect that he has a problem. Many of the symptoms associated with this early stage are also experienced by nondependent, social drinkers or druggers. For example, both early-stage Dependents and non-Dependents may answer "yes" to the question: "Does he enjoy drinking and look forward to drinking occasions?" But most non-Dependents would answer "no" to the majority of these questions.

If you answered "yes" to several of these questions, your loved one may be an early-stage Dependent—even if your answers to the rest of the questions are a truthful "no." A "yes" answer to five or more of these questions is typical of the early-stage disease.

Middle-stage addiction. Questions 10 to 18 cover the middle-stage symptoms of addiction. In the middle stage, the Dependent's problems become more obvious, even though the great majority of middle-stage Dependents look healthy and are generally in control of themselves and their lives. The disease has progressed significantly but not to the point where the Dependent is destitute and deathly ill—that will come later, if the drinking or drug use continues.

In the middle stage, the Dependent can still exert some control over her drug use, and chances are good that she will deny or rationalize her symptoms if she's confronted. Denials and rationalizations are actually symptoms of the middle-stage addiction, and they indicate that the Dependent knows, deep inside, that she's in trouble. However, because of her addiction, she can't function without the drug, at least not for very long.

The middle stage of addiction can last for years before leading into the later, more deadly stage. People addicted to alcohol may continue as middle-stage alcoholics for as long as ten to twenty years. However, the alcohol-only addict is an increasing rarity; most alcoholics are also addicted to prescription or illegal drugs. Using more than one drug invariably causes a speeded-up addiction process, shortening the middle stage of the disease significantly. For some addicts, the disease progresses so quickly that the early and middle stages are left out altogether, and the addict is in serious trouble almost from the very beginning of his drug use. Free-basing cocaine, for example, can lead to late-stage symptoms within a few months.

Late-stage addiction. Questions 19 to 27 deal with the final, deteriorative stage of addiction, when the Dependent will look, act, and talk like he is addicted to alcohol or drugs. The disease has progressed to the point where the Dependent is physically ill both when he's using and when he stops. Medical complications may seriously undermine the Dependent's physical health.

The late-stage addict can no longer deny that he has a problem controlling his drinking or drugging, but neither can he imagine life without it. Because he is physically unable to control his intake, he usually ends a spree incoherent or passed out. Withdrawal symptoms (psychological and/or physical) become severe and incapacitating. As he continues to drink or use drugs, he will become increasingly withdrawn, fearful, and uncommunicative. Paranoia, hallucinations, and severe tremors are common in the late stage.

Unless he receives effective treatment, the late-stage Dependent will die of medical complications caused by accelerated drinking or drug use or from accidents suffered while using. Death is the final symptom of the late-stage addiction.

SCORING THE QUESTIONNAIRE

Early stage		Middle stage		Late stage	
QUESTION	SCORE				
(1)	1	(10)	2	(19)	3
(2)	1	(11)	2	(20)	3
(3)	1	(12)	2	(21)	3
(4)	1	(13)	2	(22)	3
(5)	1	(14)	2	(23)	3
(6)	1	(15)	2	(24)	3
(7)	1	(16)	2	(25)	3
(8)	1	(17)	2	(26)	3
(9)	1	(18)	2	(27)	3

ACCUMULATED SCORE

Early stage: 5–8 points
Middle stage: 9–27 points
Late stage: 28 or more points

FIVE

What Is Addiction?

You now know a good deal about the early-, middle-, and late-stage symptoms of addiction, but the doubt—could he really be *addicted?*—may linger still. The early symptoms are so deceptive and seemingly harmless that a clear, obvious answer to this all-important question seems impossible. Your confusion is fueled by the fact that nothing stays the same. At one moment, you're sure that disaster is about to strike; a day or a week later, everything appears peaceful and serene.

It is precisely this inconsistency that has you bewildered and paralyzed. Yet, ironically, it is the very inconsistency of the Dependent's actions, thoughts, and feelings that provides a clue to whether the addiction is present. In the early and middle stages of the disease, you can be assured that the Dependent *will* behave in inconsistent, paradoxical ways. At one moment he will be gentle, attentive, affectionate, understanding, and caring; at another he will be coarse, unfeeling, rude, and obnoxious.

Addiction has a gradual, slow-burn impact on the great majority of its victims' lives. Because the changes in behavior, mood, and thought are so subtle and take place over such a long period of time, the family becomes accustomed to them, adjusting their own behavior and learning to accept the abnormal as normal. If addiction worked like most other diseases—if it affected its victims quickly and dramatically, caused measurable physical symptoms, or allowed its victims to remain lucid and clear-thinking—the family would be spared the agony of waiting, wondering, and wishing that the intermittent hellish days would simply go away.

But, as we've said, addiction doesn't play by the rules, so we have to learn exactly how it *does* play. What are the general "rules" of this disease? Are these general characteristics similar for every Dependent? How do the rules change as the Dependent moves from early to middle to late stage?

GENERAL PRINCIPLES

The general principles underlying the disease of addiction are *progression, tolerance, withdrawal,* and *loss of control.* As you read about each of these characteristics of addiction, you will notice that they are "fluid"—they change over time. Thus, in the beginning, the Dependent's tolerance is high; in the later stages of the disease, his tolerance will decrease dramatically. Withdrawal symptoms are mild in early-stage Dependents; they get worse as the disease goes on. Loss of control is typically not evident until the middle and late stages of the disease, when the body's cells become damaged by the toxic drugs.

If there's one thing you can be sure of in drug addiction, it's this: *Nothing stays the same.* And there's a corollary to that rule: *Nothing gets better, at least not for very long.*

Progression. In the beginning, the addiction can be tamed and brought under control without obvious effort. But as the disease continues its slow burn, it will gradually destroy willpower, create psychological and emotional anguish, and undermine physical health. Like cancer, addiction can conceal itself inside its victims for years without causing any noticeable symptoms. But just as cancerous tumors enlarge, so does the addiction; and as it grows, it becomes more and more demanding.

Addiction will always, inevitably, progress, causing increasingly severe problems. It may seem that the Dependent is not getting any worse, but if you know what to look for and if you watch closely, you will be able to see the relentless and persistent march of the addiction. The only way to stop this progression is to stop the drinking or drug use. Recovery depends on abstinence; there is no other way to put a halt to this disease.

Tolerance. In the early stages of addiction, the Dependent will typically restrict his drinking or drug use to "normal" amounts. Soon, however, he experiences a dramatic climb in his ability to "tolerate" large amounts of the drug. Ironically, his increased use does not, in the beginning, lead to decreased function: in fact, the early-stage Dependent is able to tolerate larger amounts of the drug than his nondependent friends while at the same time acting less affected by the drug.

Increased tolerance indicates changes in cell structure that allow the body to function normally even in the presence of large amounts of alcohol and/or other drugs. These changes, or adaptations in cell function, take place in two primary areas of the body: the brain and the liver.

In the brain, tolerance occurs when the cells adapt to the effects of the drug, requiring larger amounts to experience these effects. In the liver, the cells adapt and become extremely efficient at processing and eliminating (metabolizing) large amounts of the drug; this "metabolic tolerance" contributes to the addict's ability to use increasingly larger amounts of the drug and still function somewhat normally. A heroin addict, for example, may shoot up as many as twenty bags (individual doses) of heroin daily; most first-time users would die taking just one bag. Likewise, a middle-stage alcoholic can drink as much as a quart of whiskey a day, an amount sure to cause acute alcohol poisoning and possible death in a nonalcoholic.

The Dependent's tolerance will decrease over time as he

continues to use drugs or to drink. The same cells that adapt to the drugs gradually become damaged by the drug's toxic effects. In the late stages of addiction, the Dependent will use lesser amounts of the drug and yet become totally incapacitated, a symptom of decreased tolerance due to cellular damage.

The withdrawal syndrome. Withdrawal is the addiction's perverse way of maintaining control over its victims: when the Dependent doesn't drink or use drugs, or when he cuts down on his intake, he suffers. Although each addictive drug has its own particular set of miseries, common withdrawal symptoms include nausea, diarrhea, headaches, elevated blood pressure and pulse rate, tremors, sweating, anxiety, agitation, nervousness, paranoia, insomnia, depression, violent mood swings, hallucinations, and seizures.

The distress of withdrawal tells a vivid story about what has happened in the addict's brain: the cells have adapted to the point where they actually *need* the drug to function normally. If no drug or not enough of the drug is taken, the withdrawal syndrome grinds on its slow, excruciating course.

As the disease progresses into its middle and late stages, the suffering grows steadily more severe. The Dependent denies that he is sick, refuses help, hides his growing dependence, breaks his promises, lies, deceives, distorts, and misleads, all in the effort to protect his right to relieve his ever-increasing pain. As the pain gets worse, the lies and deceits become more desperate and the efforts of the family to intervene become more futile. Victims of alcohol or drug addiction become obsessed with their drug of choice because their bodies are obsessed with avoiding the pain of withdrawal. This obsession is often referred to as compulsion, an overwhelming need or drive to use the drug as a requirement for "normal" living.

Why does the Dependent keep on drinking or drugging when the consequences are so devastating? The avoidance of physical or psychological pain—not the pursuit of pleasure—is the major motivating factor for the middle- and late-stage Dependent's continued drinking or drugging. When the Dependent drinks or uses drugs, he feels immediately and incredibly better; the drug releases him from his nervousness, anxiety, shaking, queasiness, and depression. No other disease makes willing collaborators of its victims; in no other disease can victims find relief from pain in the very substance that is destroying them. The disease of addiction turns the body against itself: it becomes a willing agent in its own destruction.

Loss of control first becomes evident when the early- or middle-stage Dependent experiences an inability to stop using drugs or drinking once he has begun. This does not happen every time he uses, but episodes increase as the disease progresses. In later stages, the Dependent will begin to use drugs at socially inappropriate times, he will frequently use too much and become incapacitated, and eventually he will lose all control over the decision *not* to use. He has no choice but to use drugs because drugs are the only immediate, surefire "cure" for his mental and physical torment.

Loss of control occurs gradually and is related to decreasing tolerance, due to cellular damage and increasingly severe withdrawal symptoms. The Dependent's body needs the drugs and suffers horribly when he is sober. So he tries to take enough of the drug to make the agony go away. But his body is unable to efficiently process the large amounts needed, and he's caught in the horrendous, no-exit cycle of being sick without his drugs and sick with them.

WHO IS SUSCEPTIBLE?

While a great deal is known about the process and progression of the disease called addiction, controversy continues about why some people become addicted while others don't. "We are not even close to understanding what goes on in the brain of the addict," claims Dr. Floyd Bloom of the Salk Institute. Nevertheless, the age-old theories of psychological inadequacy and addictive personalities have been thoroughly discredited in recent years by numerous studies showing that addiction is, in fact, a process governed by internal, physiological rather than external, psychological events. The addict, it seems clear, is physically different from the nonaddict, even before he ever takes a drug or a drink.

While the precise nature of this built-in physical difference remains a mystery, researchers are offering compelling evidence that certain people are biochemically susceptible to addiction. For example, studies show that heredity—genes passed from parent to child—is a crucial element in determining susceptibility to alcoholism. Donald Goodwin's famous adoption studies, reported in his book *Is Alcoholism Hereditary?*, reveal that the children of alcoholics run a *four times higher than normal* risk of developing the disease—even if they are not raised by their alcoholic parents. Interestingly, children of nonalcoholics, raised by alcoholics, do not appear to be at greater risk. Taken together, these facts argue persuasively for nature over nurture.

Other researchers studying alcoholics and their offspring have attempted to determine the precise physiological mechanisms distinguishing addicts from nonaddicts.

- Dr. Charles Lieber, chief of the research program on liver disease and nutrition at Bronx Veterans Administration Hospital, discovered that acetaldehyde, a highly toxic breakdown product of alcohol, accumulates in greater amounts in alcoholics. Lieber theorizes that this unusual buildup of acetaldehyde is caused in part by enzyme abnormalities in the liver—abnormalities that exist *before* the alcoholic starts drinking heavily.

- Dr. Marc Schuckit, of the Department of Psychiatry, University of California, San Diego, School of Medicine, confirmed Lieber's findings and went on to report that in alcoholics, acetaldehyde is eliminated at one-half the rate of normal (i.e., nonalcoholic) metabolism. This inability to eliminate acetaldehyde at normal speed was evident in children of alcoholics who had never been exposed to alcohol or other drugs. Schuckit also discovered that people with a family history of alcoholism have a significantly *less* intense reaction to moderate doses of alcohol than people with no known family history of alcoholism. He suggests that this feeling of being less intoxicated or affected by alcohol may interfere with the alcoholic's ability to decide to stop drinking.

• Henri Begleiter and his colleagues at the Salk Institute have discovered a significant difference in P–3 brain wave patterns in children of alcoholics. The P–3 brain wave is related to memory and decision making, and the abnormal brain wave patterns indicate that children of alcoholics may experience memory deficits, an inability to experience pleasure, and a reduced capacity to adequately focus attention on their surroundings. Begleiter is presently studying the relationship between these neurophysiological deficits and a possible predisposition to alcoholism.

These groundbreaking findings are only a sampling of the research studies now being conducted into the genetic, biochemical, and neurophysiological bases of addiction. Information available at this time firmly establishes the theory that certain people are inherently susceptible to addiction to alcohol. And many researchers feel sure that what holds true for alcoholics also holds true for those addicted to other drugs; they have developed a new theory, called the addictive disease concept, to explain the remarkable similarities that occur in the addictive process, regardless of the specific drug used.

THE ADDICTIVE DISEASE CONCEPT

Addiction, according to the addictive disease concept, is a disease in and of itself: if you suffer from this disease and use an addictive drug with any regularity (even if you use it "responsibly"), you will eventually develop all the symptoms of addiction. If you do not have the disease, you can use addictive drugs and never become addicted to them.

The concept of addictive disease represents an abrupt about-face from traditional thinking about drug abuse. It used to be thought that anybody who used an addictive drug would eventually become addicted to it. The trick, everyone thought, was to develop a healthy respect for the drug, to learn to say "no" after a moderate amount, and to practice "responsible" habits regarding the drug. It was also believed that the addiction process varied significantly from one drug to the next.

But proponents of the addictive disease concept warn that for certain susceptible people, *any* drug use is dangerous and may eventually lead to addiction, and that the addiction process is fundamentally the same for all addictive drugs. For the susceptible individual, there is no such thing as a safe amount, and responsible attitudes toward drugs offer no protection against the body's inherent vulnerability to any drug's addictive effects. On the other hand, those not susceptible to addiction (the great majority of users) are protected because their bodies have a sort of built-in "wisdom" to use drugs moderately.

Researchers aren't claiming that people without the inherent susceptibility to addiction can use drugs indiscriminately. First of all, we have no safe or sure method of determining who will become addicted and who will not. Second, addictive drugs are simply too dangerous and their effects too unpredictable for use by even a nonsusceptible person. A recovering cocaine addict described the dangers of guesswork involved in taking drugs in a recent magazine article:* "We're all on a plane flying around over Kansas. We're going to give everyone a knapsack. Some contain parachutes and some do not. Now, who would like to jump out of the plane?"

Obviously, the concept of addictive disease is controversial. But those who work with addicts see so many similarities in

*Playboy, September 1984.

what they call the addictive process that they believe the conclusion is inescapable: some people are simply physically different regarding their reactions to drugs. This physical susceptibility, combined with the use of the drug, causes addiction and all the physical and psychological problems that go with it.

THE PROBLEM
OF MULTIPLE ADDICTIONS

When one drug is taken in combination with another drug—a practice so common that it's estimated that 70 to 80 percent of alcoholics, for example, are addicted to other drugs—the effects are unpredictable, explosive, and potentially life-threatening. John Belushi, Elvis Presley, Janis Joplin, Marilyn Monroe, Judy Garland . . . these are just a few, famous examples of the deadly dangers of combining drugs.

What happens in the addict's body when several drugs are used regularly over a period of time? *The normal drug reactions are changed* because the person taking the drugs is changed. The cells have adapted to the drug, making certain changes in their internal structure. These changes allow the cells to continue to function even in the presence of large and continuous amounts of the drug.

Cellular adaptation is the basic phenomenon underlying tolerance (see p. 36). But when more than one pharmacologically similar drug is taken, a phenomenon called *cross-tolerance* occurs: the body is almost instantly capable of withstanding the effects of the additional drugs. Thus, in order to experience the intended effects from the drugs, the Dependent must increase his dosage.

The dangers of cross-tolerance are real and frightening.

Toxic reactions. Although the Dependent may be able to function somewhat normally with one drug in his system, the addition of heavy doses of another drug can cause toxic reactions including coma, convulsions, respiratory failure, and death.

Overdoses are common when several drugs are combined because the Dependent is often intoxicated or unable to make rational decisions about how much to take; or he may be in pain from withdrawal and take additional amounts of one or more drugs in an effort to lessen his agony. In the later stages of addiction, the body's cells are damaged and unable to tolerate large doses of drugs. This loss of tolerance combined with increasingly severe withdrawal symptoms can lead to accidental overdoses or suicide attempts.

If your Dependent is taking several drugs at once, he will not only become tolerant to these drugs, he will quickly become *addicted* to them. Thus, an alcoholic who takes tranquilizers or sedatives for his nervousness or anxiety will soon develop an addiction to these prescription drugs. A cocaine addict who uses alcohol, sedatives, or heroin to ease the symptoms of the cocaine crash will become addicted to these drugs. An amphetamine addict who uses sedatives or sleeping pills to slow down will soon need both drugs to continue functioning. The serious effects of cross-addiction include:

Rapid progression. Addiction to more than one drug proceeds at a faster pace; this is one reason so many thirteen-, fourteen-, and fifteen-year-olds are now entering treatment: they're experimenting not just with alcohol but with a whole "garbage can" of drugs, including marijuana, cocaine, hallucinogens, depressants, and stimulants.

Intensified withdrawal. Withdrawal symptoms increase in intensity, and the process of withdrawal is generally longer and more unpredictable.

Craving. The drug "hunger" of polydrug addicts is typically fierce, prolonged, and often uncontrollable.

Relapse. After treatment or a self-imposed period of abstinence, relapse is much more common for polydrug addicts.

Just fifteen years ago, polydrug addiction was rare and most Dependents were alcoholics; today it is rare to find a Dependent who is addicted to only one drug. Fifteen years ago, most patients coming into treatment were between the ages of thirty-five and forty-five, and adolescent addicts were a rare breed; today, adolescents constitute 20 to 30 percent of the addicted population. And the drugs and drug combinations are changing all the time: crack, ecstasy, black-tar heroin, speedballs. . . .

At the same time, however, research efforts are intensifying, myths and misconceptions are dying, treatment methods are improving, and our understanding of addiction is growing. Our hope lies in learning everything we can about this disease; without accurate knowledge, we've lost the battle before we've even seen the enemy.

For a detailed, in-depth look at the specific properties and effects of individual drugs, please see the appendix, p. 211.

——

SIX

Learn to See the Addiction

In *The Exorcist*, the story is told of a young girl who is possessed by the devil. At times the girl acts like her normal self. But at other moments the fiend within shows itself, hideously transforming her looks, her speech, even her mannerisms. She is unaware of what is happening; she is simply a vehicle for the demon's need to express itself.

The possession described in *The Exorcist* was the fantasy of a writer's imagination. But no clearer image could have been created of the metamorphosis that takes place within the victims of drug addiction. The addiction is, in truth, a monstrous force capable of manipulating its victims' thoughts, feelings, and actions.

Hal, for example, was a good-looking, popular, self-possessed sixteen-year-old. Within one year, he had lost his confidence, his friends, and three part-time jobs. His grades plummeted from *B*s to *D*s, he lost thirty pounds, he stopped shaving and using deodorant, and he missed so many football practices that the coach kicked him off the team.

What happened in that one year to cause such drastic changes? Hal's addiction to alcohol and marijuana took over, changing his personality, subverting his goals, destroying his accomplishments, and throwing his family into a state of confusion and panic. Hal couldn't see those changes, and he wasn't responsible for them; he was the victim of an addiction so powerful that even if he understood it, he couldn't fight it by himself.

There will be times when you look at your Dependent and wonder, "Who *is* that?" At those times, he seems to be metamorphosing from a decent, sensitive person to a selfish, heartless brute right in front of your eyes. But then, just as suddenly, he's back again, the affectionate, good-hearted, generous person you've loved for all these years.

"What's happening?" you ask yourself. "Why is he changing? Is it stress? Midlife changes? Unhappiness? Boredom? Or is it *me?* Is it my fault? Will life ever get back to normal?"

In the beginning of the possession known as drug addiction, the force of the disease is weak and is able to exert only subtle, barely recognizable effects on its victim's behavior. But as the addiction progresses, it gains steadily in power and influence. The Dependent has less strength to fight the demon within him and, in fact, becomes less able to understand that a fight must be waged.

The Dependent, in truth, is *not* himself. He is being taken over, body and soul, by a force within him that he cannot recognize or understand. He is truly under the addiction's spell: he doesn't see that he needs help; he believes he is still in control; and he willingly takes the poison that feeds the addiction's insatiable appetite.

You have watched helplessly as your loved one tried desperately to cope with emotional and psychological stress. You thought his problems were the result of *outside* stresses, never even considering that the reason for the stress might lie within. You know the Dependent is drinking or using drugs, but you have always believed him when he told you that he was under a lot of emotional stress. In the beginning, how could you *not* believe, when not believing, you felt sure, would only add to his unhappiness? Not believing always seemed a clear and conscious betrayal of trust, a serious weakening of the bonds of love. You continued to believe, even as the evidence piled up, because you could not conceive that anything as monstrous as drug addiction could be threatening your life. In the meantime, you hoped desperately that the problems were temporary and that time would heal all wounds.

But drug addiction, as we have seen, is not the affliction of the depraved, the unloved, the degenerate, or the weak-willed, and time is not its enemy but its ally. Addiction has no prejudices, choosing its victims from the ranks of rich and poor, black and white, male and female, young and old, weak and strong alike. Families must learn this lesson well: addiction can and does strike at the "best" of people. And we must also learn that striking back at the addiction is not a betrayal of love or trust. In fact, love that accepts, protects, and adapts plays right into the hands of the addiction. Our love must, instead, be tough—tough love—if it is to stand a chance against the addiction.

All of us who love a Dependent must learn this new, tough way of loving. We must learn to "love *through* the illness." Loving through the illness means learning to see the person we love as separate from the person who is being taken over by the addiction. We have to learn to see our Dependent as truly *dependent* upon his addiction to drugs. He is incapable of rationally judging his behavior or understanding his predicament, and because of his blindness he is virtually powerless to wrest himself free of the prison being formed by his addiction.

We also have to stop thinking of the Dependent as capable of controlling his actions. "If he really wants things to turn around in his life, he'll stop drinking and drugging" is a belief that has ended in tragedy too many times. The Dependent wants to stop and at times is terrified of what is happening to him, but the addiction proves too cunning a foe, too powerful an enemy—he simply cannot win this battle by himself.

His tortured expressions of shame and remorse, the promises to change, the guilt, self-pity, and despair, the lies, evasions, and denials are all symptoms of his inability to fight the addiction within him. He wants desperately to drink or use drugs like everyone else. He tries, at various times, to quit.

He worries, on and off, about his preoccupation with drugs. He knows that his life is unraveling right before him. He's afraid. Yet he keeps on drinking. Why?

The addiction leaves him no choice. He literally needs to drink to feel normal. He feels wonderful when the drug is speeding into his bloodstream, rushing into his brain. The doubts, pains, and fears are suddenly, miraculously gone. Who could fight such an enemy? Who would choose pain and discomfort when pleasure and euphoria are so quickly attained?

Learning to see the Dependent as the prisoner he is means that you must become an expert at seeing *through* him and recognizing the subtle look, speech, and mannerisms of the addiction. Use your imagination and think of the addiction as alive. Think of that demon in *The Exorcist;* think of a beast hidden deep within the Dependent that is capable of manipulating his thoughts, feelings, and actions. Only in this way can you get the distance you will need in order to use your love to work against the addiction.

The disease of drug addiction affects all its victims in characteristic ways. If you know what to listen for, you can "hear" the addiction talking. If you know what to look for, you can "see" it in its victim's behavior, facial expressions, and mannerisms. By learning to recognize the enemy, you will be able to begin the process of separating both yourself and your Dependent from its relentless power.

SIGNS OF ADDICTION

Facial Signs:
EYES: watery, glazed, red-rimmed, joyless; pupils dilated
MOUTH: drawn tight, rigid, humorless
NOSE: red, swollen, sniffling, runny
NECK: muscles tight, distended
TEETH: clenched; constant grinding
JAW: muscles clenched tight
FACE: puffy, red, bloated; broken blood vessels
FACIAL EXPRESSIONS: bored, hostile, angry, humorless, joyless

Body Movements:
Hands clenched tight
Tremors (slight to obvious) in hands and facial muscles
Body tense and rigid
Body movements jerky, stiff, awkward
Legs jittery, constantly moving
Rubbing nose constantly

Behavior:
Short temper; sudden, angry outbursts
Anxiety, nervousness
Mood swings
Personality changes
Depression
Inability to express love, verbally or physically
Paranoia

Favorite Verbal Expressions:
"Get off my back."
"Why don't *you* take some of the responsibility for this family?"
"Who are *you* to judge *me?*"
"You don't love me, you can't hope to understand me, everybody's against me."
"You'd drink, too, if you had my problems."
"I can handle drugs, it's the stress of my life that I can't handle."
"This is all your fault; if you weren't always bitching and screaming at me, I'd be just fine."
"I'm sick of work, I'm sick of this town, and I'm sick of you."

Once you see and understand these signs as evidence of the addiction, you can begin to protect yourself from its hurtful manipulations. When the Dependent becomes angry or hostile and tries to blame you for his problem, you can say, "That's the addiction talking," and leave the room without feeling guilt, responsibility, or remorse. When your Dependent acts bored with you, when his entire body is tense and tight and ready for a fight, when he changes in front of your eyes to an insensitive, irresponsible caricature of himself—you can know that his addiction is causing the metamorphosis.

Your Dependent is still there inside—terrified, bewildered, paralyzed. The damage is not irreparable; he is not irretrievable. With knowledge, understanding, insight, and hard work, you *can* get him back.

SEVEN

━━━

The A to Z of Adolescent Drug Use

A recent suburban newspaper headline announced in big, bold letters: TEEN DIES TRYING TO BEAT BOREDOM.* The story described how a sixteen-year-old boy and his best friend "knocked down half a bottle of McNaughton's whiskey straight" and then, "sufficiently buzzed," decided to do something crazy. One of the teenagers climbed over the metal guardrail of a bridge and hung there, suspended forty feet above a cold, turbulent river. But after a few moments the boy's hands began to slip down the bars; he couldn't pull himself back up, and he plummeted to his death in the debris-clogged river.

This teenager didn't die of boredom; he died of alcohol poisoning. His alcohol-numbed brain didn't sense the danger, and the whiskey sapped his body of the strength needed to hang on. He may have been bored; he may also have been angry, hostile, rebellious. But boredom didn't kill him. Alcohol killed him.

"How could this have happened without warning?" parents and relatives wonder when their children are suddenly in big trouble with drugs. It seems that the drug problem appeared—

*Bellevue Journal-American, Bellevue, Washington, November 16, 1985.

massive, overwhelming, terrifying—out of thin air. But drug problems don't happen overnight. If we look back and think clearly, there were warning signs. There are *always* warning signs, if we know how to recognize them.

The early warning signs of adolescent addiction come on slowly, gradually; in the beginning, they can be seen in the adolescent's sullenness, boredom, refusal to communicate, behavior problems, and sinking grades. Unfortunately, and often tragically, these are the same symptoms (although greatly intensified) that are experienced by normal, nondrugging adolescents. Rebelliousness, temper tantrums, emotional ups and downs, hostility, defensiveness, and feelings of inferiority or ineptitude are shared by virtually every adolescent.

And so we don't make the right connections; instead, we assume that the adolescent is experiencing "typical adolescent problems," and we wait patiently for the problems to go away. But this misguided patience allows the addiction to progress unsuspected and undiscovered until the evidence is obvious and undeniable: the teenager overdoses, has a convulsion or psychotic episode, drops out of school, breaks the law, or in some other way shows he is in deep and serious trouble.

Many adolescent drug users express amazement at how deaf, dumb, and blind their parents are to the drug use going on right in their own homes. Teenager Michael Jackson expressed his own bewilderment in the foreword to his book *Doing Drugs*:

> Even when parents have some inkling of what's going on, they rarely know the real extent. They may know one of their children smokes pot—but few know about the Quaaludes and acid and speed.
>
> I'm not saying this to denigrate parents. I know that being a parent is a hard job. But as I look at the drug problem, I become more and more convinced that one thing that helps perpetuate it is parents' ignoring their kids' drug problem, or their mishandling of a problem that they perceive correctly. . . .
>
> Maybe it's just that parents don't want to admit something is wrong with one of their kids because that would force them to admit they had somehow failed.

Too often, an adolescent's drug problem is ignored or mishandled because the family members have come to blame themselves. The adolescent's problems are perceived not as a progressive, insidious, physical disease but as a statement of parental failure. The early symptoms of trouble are pushed away, excused, rationalized, and covered up because most of us have been taught that addiction is a disease of unhappy, psychologically maladjusted adults that takes years to develop. We just can't believe it could happen to a thirteen-, fourteen-, or fifteen-year-old.

But it can, and it does. Adolescents are an easy target for addiction. They use drugs to rebel against authority, to prove themselves, to fit in with their peers, to appear attractive to the opposite sex, to hide their fears, anxieties, and confusions. And they use drugs at an age when they are not able to make rational, mature decisions. The addiction is then able to use the adolescent's immaturity and rebelliousness as a shield, duping parents into thinking that their child is simply having a tough time with adolescence.

Teenagers are as misguided as their parents about the deadly potential of drug use. Rarely does the adolescent think of his drug use as a serious or potentially deadly undertaking. His very youthfulness convinces him of his invincibility; it simply doesn't occur to him that he might become addicted, overdose, or die from using drugs.

But even casual use can spell disaster for an adolescent. Drugs stop the emotional maturing process dead in its tracks: an adolescent on drugs loses interest in the outside world, reduces his interaction with others, particularly with nondrug users, and never learns the normal social skills. The long-term effects of addiction on an adolescent's self-concept and self-esteem can be disastrous.

Drugs also play havoc with the *physical* maturing process taking place during adolescence. This process is regulated by internal chemicals (hormones, enzymes, neurotransmitters, that are thrown into confusion by drug-supplied "outside" chemicals. An adolescent's body is an extremely vulnerable target for drug addiction because the rapid metabolism common in adolescence may lead to more rapid and more intense damage. For example, marijuana researchers working with rats have discovered more severe drug-induced damage in younger rats; their studies lead them to conclude that the brain cells of young human users could be similarly vulnerable to marijuana's damaging effects.

Generalizing from the brain cells of young rats to those of young humans may seem farfetched, but there is no question that adolescent addicts progress faster in the addictive process, sustain more long-term psychological and physical damage, and are more difficult to treat successfully. Whether these facts are due to the damaging effects of drugs on the emotional or the physical maturation process, or both, must be proved by future research. But the facts exist, and they argue compellingly for early diagnosis and treatment in adolescent drug addiction.

According to adolescent treatment experts, the drug causing the most damage to adolescents is the old standby, alcohol. In the last twenty years the average age when teenagers begin drinking has dropped from sixteen years old to thirteen. Drinking alcohol used to be a rite of passage into adulthood; it is now a rite of passage into adolescence. And, as a result, twelve-, thirteen-, and fourteen-year-olds are getting into big trouble with alcohol and other drugs. Kids as young as eleven years old are entering treatment with full-blown addictions.

How can parents learn to distinguish between the normal turmoil of adolescence and the early stages of addiction? Once again, look for *progression*. If your adolescent is addicted to drugs, you will be able to identify a progression from experimentation to more regular use to daily preoccupation with drugs and, finally, to dependency. The adolescent's problems won't ease off as he gets older and more mature but will instead become more serious and pronounced, creating tension at home, discipline problems at school, and serious disruptions in relationships with family members and friends. If you have evidence that your adolescent is using drugs, and if you can identify a downward spiral in your adolescent's behavior, emotional stability, and interpersonal relationships, you can be fairly certain that a drug problem exists.

If your adolescent is using drugs, you will need to know that threats, accusations, and raised voices won't work. Facts work. If you suspect a drug problem, learn how to be a good detective and get the facts nailed down. Your child's life depends on you.

Take a look around. Search your adolescent's room, looking for razor blades, mirrors, plastic bags containing marijuana seeds or leaves, unusual-looking pipes, pieces of screen, small glass vials, gram scales . . . all evidence of drug use, or even drug dealing.

Check things out. When your adolescent tells you he's going to a party or a friend's house, check it out—is he where he said he would be, at the time he said he would be there, and doing what he said he would be doing? If your adolescent has more money than he should have, check it out—where did he get the money? If he has less money, check it out—what happened to it? Check your valuables: Is there anything missing from your house? Cash? Jewelry? Sterling silver? Have there been any reported burglaries in your neighborhood or at school?

Talk. Talk to the adolescent's brothers and sisters, expressing your concern in a loving way; avoid the use of labels like "alcoholic" or "addict." You might begin by saying: "We're not interested in punishing Johnny, we want to help him. Are you concerned about him? Do you see things that are different lately? What do you think is happening?" Look, too, into what's happening at school. Talk to your adolescent's teachers, guidance counselor, school principal. Again, phrase your questions in a general way, mentioning that you are concerned about your child and wonder if they have noticed anything unusual.

Get in touch with an adolescent drug counselor. If you don't know of one and don't know whom to ask, look up "alcoholism information and treatment centers" in the Yellow Pages and call several of them to see if there is anyone on staff who specializes in adolescent substance abuse.

Get smarter. Take notes about what you're seeing and feeling. Keep a journal to help you stay focused on the problem. Read everything you can find on alcoholism and drug addiction— books, pamphlets, government handouts, magazine articles. Go to Al-Anon meetings; encourage other family members to go with you or to attend Alateen. (For more information about Al-Anon and Alateen, see chapter 20).

Keep your family together, if at all possible. Adolescent drug addiction, like adult addictions, is a family problem—it needs to be dealt with not by just one member of the family but by the family as a whole. However, the adolescent's addiction is particularly devious because the adolescent is doing double battle with the addiction and the normal chaos of trying to grow up and understand his place in the world. He will not understand what is happening to him, and he will perceive criticism as manifestly unfair and his critics as bitter enemies. The addiction will use his confusion and seek to sabotage all the relationships within the family, turning one member against the other, until the parents seek help through psychological or marital counseling and/or the siblings start acting out and causing problems themselves.

Adolescent intervention is ongoing and long-going, generally taking several weeks or months longer than intervention with adult users. The reasons:

- Adolescent addicts are extraordinarily deceptive. Again, the normal confusion of adolescence combined with the internal and external chaos created by the addiction will cause the adolescent addict to lie, cheat, and steal to protect his drug use. Adolescents will swear that they'll cut down and then continue to use as before; they will break down, cry, ask for forgiveness, and then walk away smirking at your gullibility; they'll turn one family member against another, accusing each of you of lying, exaggerating, spying, or not loving enough. The addiction will use every weapon within its arsenal to create tension and dissension within the family in order to take the focus off itself.

• Adolescents are, quite literally, dependent on you for financial and emotional support. You can't just kick the adolescent out of the house if he doesn't stop using—where will he go? How will he support himself? Fathers are particularly reluctant to carry through on threats or take any decisive action with their adolescent daughters, since the obvious alternative would be for the daughter to live with other drug users or dealers or become a prostitute in order to support her addiction.

The healthier you are as a family and as an individual, the more you know about the disease, and the more facts you have, the faster you can get your adolescent addict into treatment. (For more information on adolescent intervention, see chapter 18.) The following A to Z list of symptoms will help you in your efforts to pull your facts together and make an assessment of your child's drug problem. This list of symptoms is not intended to be all-inclusive; it is simply a guide to understanding the enormous impact of the addiction on your adolescent's behavior.

THE A TO Z OF ADOLESCENT DRUG ABUSE

Anger: Quick to become angry; temper tantrums; blow-ups over insignificant events.

Bloodshot eyes: Attempts to disguise with sunglasses; Visine or other eye drops frequently used.

Change in physical hygiene: Sloppy physical appearance, wearing same clothes day after day; cocaine addicts, on the other hand, often take showers two to three times a day, buy new, expensive clothes, and take great pains to appear well dressed and immaculate.

Defensive: Fiercely protects his right to use drugs, resists attempts to discuss his drug use, reacts with suspicion or hostility when confronted, and generally shields his drug use from "prying" eyes.

Emotional highs and lows: Emotions change rapidly and uncharacteristically: the Dependent doesn't seem the same person he used to be. He becomes oversensitive, irrational, unreasonable, despairing, jealous, tearful, afraid, and agitated.

Fear: As drug use continues and addiction progresses, fear changes from mild apprehension to anxiety, foreboding, despair, suspicion, dread, mortal terror, and panic.

Getting secretive: Refuses to confide personal problems or anxieties; phone calls and mail jealously guarded; meets friends away from the house; locks door to room.

Hardheaded: Willful, stubborn, headstrong, obstinate.

Inadequacy: Feelings of inferiority, ineptitude, incompetence, and inability, often unexpressed but evident in the adolescent user's increasing seclusion and refusal to join in activities or conversations.

Joylessness: Cheerful, playful, good-humored, or lively behavior is gradually replaced by constant complaining, weariness, and episodes of weeping, sadness, depression, and grief.

Keeping to himself: Becomes more and more reclusive; avoids human companionship.

Legal problems: Periodic entanglements with the police or legal system including driving citations, parties broken up by police, citations for possession of controlled substances, public nuisance arrests, et cetera.

Money problems: Always out of money, steals money from parents or friends, or has a lot of money but no job (indicating that he might be dealing drugs).

Nervousness: Highly sensitive, high-strung, and neurotic; easily agitated and annoyed; often apprehensive, tense, restless, and jittery.

Oblivious: Preoccupied, forgetful, unaware, and absorbed in his own thoughts, the adolescent user is in his own little world; he is uncaring, thoughtless, and unmindful of what everyone else in the house is doing or feeling.

Possessions sold or missing: Parents and siblings begin to notice money or valuable items such as clothes, jewelry, records, tools, or gifts suddenly missing; if confronted, the adolescent claims he knows nothing about the missing items or that they are lost, misplaced, or loaned out to friends.

Quirky behavior: Begins to adopt unusual and uncharacteristic behavior patterns; drops old friends for new, "unusual" friends; changes hairstyle, clothes, body movements, daily patterns.

Resentments: Old friendships are abandoned in fury or exasperation; the slightest criticism is met with defensiveness and hostility; grudges are held for weeks or months; long-term feelings of hatred, bitterness, antagonism, and annoyance appear and begin to take over.

Smell: Alcohol or marijuana can be smelled on breath or clothes; body odor apparent due to lack of interest in personal hygiene; mouthwashes, deodorants, or colognes used to hide the smell of alcohol or marijuana.

Temper tantrums: Appears always to be angry, is easily annoyed or upset, and is often difficult to reason with, restrain, or pacify.

Underachiever: Slow to learn; seems unconcerned with the future; gives up previous goals; passively sits and watches TV or listens to rock music; refuses to become involved in hobbies, sports, or outside activities; grades begin to drop.

Violent episodes: Enraged or inflamed actions and emotions alternate with periods of passivity and lethargy.

Weight changes: Rapid loss or gain in weight, accompanied by a lack of interest in food, and neglect of physical health or appearance.

Xenophobia: Fear or hatred of anything foreign or strange; suspicious or paranoid around strangers.

Yammering: Constant or persistent complaining, whining, or nagging.

Zany: Manic laughter or giggling; constant, meaningless chatter; incomprehensible ravings; foolish and unusual behavior patterns.

PART II

Understanding

In the first seven chapters, we asked you to look at your Dependent and the circumstances of your life in order to identify the ways in which you and your family have been affected by addiction. We discussed some basic information about the disease and offered specific methods of assessing your particular situation.

Now it is time to probe a little deeper into the ways in which this disease has impacted you and changed your life. The purpose of this section is to help you get ready for the actual intervention: to give you the understanding necessary to sort out your confused thoughts, steady your shaking knees, and slow down your pounding heart.

Throughout this section, we use numerous case histories to show how other people have dealt with the pain, the grief, the fear, the sadness, and the shame of this disease. These true stories (names and identifying characteristics have been changed) will help you to understand that your emotions are shared by thousands of others who are living with a Dependent. You are not alone. You are not responsible. And you are not powerless.

You have a choice: to move or to stand still, to act or to react, to lead or to follow. You have the power. You need only understand it and then learn how to use it.

Use these chapters to gain back your confidence, to become sturdy and strong, and to act from a position of power, based on knowledge and self-understanding. Take the time to reflect, to look deep, to understand yourself better, and to understand the pressures and problems the other people around you might be experiencing. Give yourself comfort, space, and time to breathe. If you are feeling scared, lonely, or unsure, slow down so that you can see clearly the choices available and make the right decisions at the right time.

It's your life. You have the right to choose how you want to live the rest of it.

EIGHT

—

Why?

Every family confronted with the fact of drug addiction will ask the same questions, and they all begin with *why: Why* me? *Why* my family? *Why* did it have to happen to us? *Why* didn't we see it sooner? *Why* couldn't we stop it?

But *why*, as you will come to see, is a dead-end question. Every time you find yourself asking a *why* question, say to yourself: "It doesn't matter why, it just is." If you find yourself looking back at the past and trying to find reasons for the addiction—perhaps he was lonely, you think; perhaps I didn't reach out to him enough; perhaps I should have been a better friend or a better listener—gently turn off the thoughts. Think instead of what you can do now, in the present, to solve your problems, to make life a little easier.

All of us who love a Dependent must learn to unhook ourselves from the past. We must unhook ourselves from searching for past answers to present problems; from trying to find someone or something to blame; from mentally flogging ourselves with guilt and shame. We are not responsible for this disease. Our past behavior did not cause it to happen. We may have made mistakes, but we did the best we could with the information we had at the time.

We can't change the past or the fact that the disease exists. But we can change the way we perceive the past and the way we live in the present. If we can give up the *why* questions, we can begin the process of giving up self-pity, guilt, shame, and fear. We can begin to move forward, instead of always looking over our shoulders at the past. We will be able to act instead of always just reacting. We will give up conflict in search of peace of mind.

The experiences of Chuck and Melissa Morrison help illustrate how initially pressing the *why* questions can be and how difficult they are to give up. For if there were an easy answer to that one question—*why?*—everything else would be easier to accept.

■

Chuck and Melissa Morrison had no idea what to expect when their son's high school principal called them in for a conference. Ted's grades had been gradually slipping over the last two years, but lots of students got by with Cs and a few Ds; they felt sure that his grades weren't the reason for this conference. Besides, Ted was such a nice kid, popular with his friends, active at church, a good athlete. . . . They hadn't spent much time with him lately, that was true, but he'd been off skiing or playing tennis or talking with his friends—and what could be wrong with that? Perhaps, they thought hopefully, he was receiving an award for something; yes, surely it had to be something like that.

They sat down in the principal's office, leaning forward in their chairs, their faces reflecting an anxious curiosity. The principal ran his hands through his thinning gray hair and gave them a weak smile.

"I'm afraid I have some news that will be tough for you to hear," he began. "I've just spent several hours with Brian Carson . . ."

The Morrisons looked at each other; Brian was Ted's best friend.

". . . and he has given me some rather unsettling information about Ted. Brian is worried about Ted's involvement with drugs."

"His what?" *Chuck Morrison's voice revealed his shock.*

"Brian tells me that Ted is dealing drugs," the principal continued. "Marijuana, cocaine, LSD—and that he's been using these drugs for years. Brian is worried because Ted is now heavily involved with cocaine."

"Mr. Scott, are you talking about our *son?" Chuck Morrison asked in bewilderment. "I think you've got the wrong kid."*

"I'm afraid not, Mr. Morrison."

"But how could this be? We live with Ted—he's our son—we would know if he'd been dealing or using drugs. This is impossible!"

"I've been talking to a drug and alcohol counselor whom we often call on for help and advice," the principal replied. "It's his experience that parents are often completely in the dark about their children's use or abuse of drugs; often, the parents are the last to know. He suggested that you search Ted's room for drugs and drug paraphernalia."

"We couldn't do that—we have a policy that Ted's room is his own and that we won't invade his privacy."

"I suggest that you break your policy this once. If what Brian says is true, you owe it to your son to find out the extent of his drug use."

The Morrisons drove home slowly. They didn't say much; they were numb with fear and anxiety. Outside Ted's room, they both took a deep breath and then hesitantly opened the door. It was just a boy's room, they thought with relief—an unmade bed, shades drawn, clothes strewn about. Just a typical teenager's room. Without speaking, they began to look around, opening drawers, looking under the bed, searching the closet.

Stuffed in the back of the closet, behind some shoes, Mr. Morrison found a large metal box; it was locked. Their hearts pounding, they cut open the lock with a pair of pruning scissors. Inside they found six Ziploc bags containing a green substance they recognized as marijuana; a little plastic bag of white powder; four empty containers of Visine; a scale; a tiny silver spoon;

several dozen pills of different colors and shapes; three small pipes; and a package of cigarette papers.

"Oh no. Please, God, no," Melissa whispered as she sat down on her son's rumpled bed. She began to slowly and methodically smooth the sheets with the palm of her hand.

"Why?" she finally asked. The word contained all their broken hopes and unspoken fears.

The next day the Morrisons met with the drug and alcohol counselor recommended by Ted's principal. "Why?" they asked him. "Why did this happen to Ted?" They desperately wanted to find answers to their questions, but the counselor shocked them with his calm, matter-of-fact reply:

"It doesn't matter why, Mr. and Mrs. Morrison. It just is."

"But of course it matters why!" Melissa Morrison answered. She wanted to add, "you insensitive idiot," but restrained herself. "How are we to understand what happened if we don't know why it happened? How are we to cope with this situation?"

"If your son was diagnosed as having cancer, would you spend your time wondering why? What possible good does the question do? Is there any peace of mind to be found in the question why?"

The Morrisons were silent.

"There are all sorts of reasons why kids like Ted start taking drugs," the counselor said. "Peer pressure, tension, stress, the desire to be 'in,' the need to challenge authority and establish independence . . . But none of these reasons explains why Ted became addicted." The counselor looked at the Morrisons and felt their misery. He loved his job, but at times like these he felt overwhelmed by the family's sadness and confusion.

"Drug addiction is a disease," he explained, taking care to speak slowly and calmly. "It's no one's fault. You aren't to blame. Your Dependent isn't to blame. You might as well ask why Ted has blue eyes, or why he's six feet tall, or why he's got big feet. These are facts. They have no explanation beyond the fact that it's just the way things are."

"You're trying to let us off the hook," Chuck Morrison interrupted. "You're trying to make this much too simple, too easy for us. Cancer just happens to people; drug addicts choose their misery."

"There's nothing easy about drug addiction, Mr. and Mrs. Morrison; and, as you will learn, drug addicts are innocent victims, too. But right now you have a long, hard road ahead, and I'm simply trying to steer you in the right direction, to get you to go forward instead of backward, to help you to ask the questions that do have answers instead of the questions that will drive you crazy because they have no clear-cut answers."

The counselor took a deep breath and leaned forward in his chair. "By asking why?," he explained, "you're trying to find someone or something to blame; the question focuses your attention on the past when you need to be concerned with the present. Asking why? only increases your feelings of powerlessness, of self-pity, and of being victims. You need to stop trying to control the past—which has already happened and over which you have no control—and put your energy where it matters, in the present."

The counselor stopped for a moment. The room seemed to vibrate with tension and fear. "I know how confusing and shocking this situation is," he said at last. "Does any of this make sense to you?"

"No," Mr. Morrison said, taking his wife's hand. "It makes no sense at all. But I think we're ready to listen."

■

Remember: It doesn't matter why. It just is.

NINE

Learning to Live in the Here and Now

As you think back about your life and the decisions you have made, you will be tempted to put moral judgments on your actions. "I should have done this instead of that," or, "Why did I put up with the addiction for so long?" or, "It was bad to leave him, I should have stuck it out," or, "It was wrong of me to yell and scream; I should have been able to be calm and decisive."

You are haunted by the mistakes you believe you made in the past—mistakes that you feel sure are responsible, at least in part, for the hell you and your family have been living through. You look at your children and think about the pain they have experienced, and you wonder, "If only I had done things differently, I could have spared them all those years of suffering." You look at your Dependent and you say to yourself, "If only I had understood what was really happening, I wouldn't have spent all those endless hours crying, begging, praying, and hoping that things would change." You look at yourself, and you mourn all the wasted years; years of youth, promise, and hope, now turned to ashes, dead things of the past. Your memories hurt. You ache for the pain and waste of it all.

Don't. The past is gone and cannot be changed. Rather than agonize over it, try to make "good" come of "bad." Those years, as painful as they were, were not wasted, since they brought you to the point where you are seeking understanding and reaching out for help. It's futile to wonder "what if" or to worry about "if only . . ." Things are simply the way they are. Try to remember that the events of the past have accomplished one crucial goal: they have brought you to the present, and you are now willing to look at the possibility of changing your life.

"Good," then, does come of "bad." Perhaps the suffering had to be done; perhaps all those angry words had to be said; perhaps the tears and fears and self-doubts had to be experienced before you could see that a change needed to be made. But none of these things matters, really, for the past is over and done, and no amount of worrying will change it.

Worry about "good" and "bad," however, often extends beyond thinking about the past to making judgments about your present self-worth. This is where the disease can trap and keep you, long after the Dependent has recovered from his addiction or made his exit from your life. You might think, for example:

"I was a *good* wife because I stuck it out all those years."
"It's *good* to protect and care for the people you love."
"It's *good* to forgive."
"It's *good* to be patient and understanding."
or, you might think:
"I'm a *bad* person because I spend all my time being resentful and angry at everyone else."
"It's *bad* to leave someone you love."
"It's *bad* to make judgments about other people's behavior."
"It's *bad* to get angry."

The "bad" thoughts cause self-doubt and increase guilt and fear. But the "good" thoughts are equally damaging. Trying to live up to a certain standard—to be good, kind, patient, understanding, forgiving—can tear you apart. After all, you're doing all the good work and you're not getting much good back. You're always reacting rather than acting, giving and never getting.

But, even worse for both you and the Dependent, these attempts to rise above your situation and take all the responsibility ultimately backfire. While you might feel better, temporarily, because you respond to a particular situation with kindness or forgiveness, and while other people make remarks about what a saint you are for putting up with such a rotten situation, the Dependent keeps right on drinking or drugging. Your good deeds make no impact whatsoever on the addiction.

And, of course, the ultimate damage to your self-esteem and self-confidence is horrendous. For your reactions have been based on a sense of false pride and an expectation of being a certain type of person. You are acting the way you think other people think you should act, a rather convoluted and precarious set of presumptions. And you are not being true or honest to your feelings. Once again, you lose and the addiction wins.

■

John's situation illustrates how devastating the "good" behaviors can be. John is a good son: loyal, devoted, caring, forgiving, uncomplaining. But John doesn't think about himself as "good" because he is convinced that he's the major cause of his father's drinking and drug problems. He can't remember when his father didn't yell at him for one thing or another—getting Bs instead of As, making too much noise with his friends, forgetting to mow the lawn or make his bed, listening to rock music, leaving the lights on all over the house, even getting too many cavities.

John believes, deep down, that his grades, his friends, his personal habits, the music he listens to, and even the condition of his teeth all contribute to his father's bad moods, bad temper, and bad drunks. He tries to get good grades, to lose weight, to bring home the "right" kind of friends—but nothing he does makes any difference.

And so, gradually, John begins to think of himself as useless, inconsequential, and unworthy. His shoulders slowly hunch over, his face breaks out, he can't approach girls to ask for a date, and he never, never talks about his real emotions with anybody. I'm worthless, *he thinks, over and over, and after a while even his anger is gone. He just takes in his father's abuse, absorbing it like a sponge, then drying up and waiting to take some more.*

Numb, anesthetized, unable to like himself, unable to make a move toward others or to reach out for help, John doesn't think there is much in life to care about. He believes life can be endured if you just put one foot in front of the other, keep your mouth shut, don't look around, don't fight, don't argue, and don't think about anything for very long.

I'm a bad person, *he thinks.* I'm responsible for my dad's problems. I'm worthless. If only I could be different somehow, maybe things would get better. *These aren't just idle thoughts— they have become part of John himself, a thick coat of emotional enamel that has been baked on by all the heat and horror of the years of living with a Dependent.*

There's no magic way to quickly and effectively remove that tough enamel coating; removal involves a long process of chipping away at the accumulated years of false beliefs and doomed hopes. John must learn that nothing he did or didn't do could have made any difference in the progression of his father's disease—if he did not exist at all, the disease would still be there. John must learn also that the disease has actually used his guilt and his grief to gain strength. By making him feel that he was responsible, that his behavior in some way provoked his father to take drugs, the addiction shifted the focus away from itself and onto John. "I'm bad, I do things that annoy Dad, so he drinks too much," John reasoned. The truth is that Dad drinks too much because he's addicted; John's behavior has nothing to do with it. But John is a handy and vulnerable scapegoat, and the addiction latches on to his soft underbelly of guilt and fear and doesn't let go.

John is a victim as surely as his father is, and his suffering is as deep and constant. He will need to work hard to understand his self-doubts, overcome them, and create a new self-image.

Shedding the ideas of "good" and "bad" and realizing that his father's drug addiction exists independent of anything he has said or done are a necessary beginning for John's progress toward healing and health.

■

Overcoming the doubts and fears that come from living with the disease of addiction takes time, understanding, and persistence. But they can be overcome; and they must be overcome if you are to escape the pain of the past and the fear of the future and begin to live in the here and now—the only place in time that makes any difference.

Living in the here and now also means letting go of fear and anticipation about the future. Worrying about what will happen next is as corrosive to your emotional health as guilt and regret about the past. The only way to have a positive impact on your future is to work on your present. The future will take care of itself if you devote yourself to improving your present.

Let the past and the future go; take each moment as it comes; give up labeling your life and give in to living it as best you can.

Things are neither good nor bad, they're just the way they are; and they will get better, with your help.

TEN

The Survival Roles

To survive life with the disease of addiction, you have had to adjust your personality, behavior, and feelings. The problem, in the beginning, was that you didn't know that the Dependent had a disease that would kill her if it was allowed to run its course. All you knew was that she was beginning to behave differently. The doubts came on slowly, and by then you were all mixed up because she was blaming you, too, for her problems: "You don't love me enough," she told you. "You don't understand me." Slowly the focus shifted even more. Suddenly it was your fault that she was drinking (or drugging) too much. Your worrying and constant pestering drove her to it. "You're not the man I married," she tells you. "What," she wonders out loud, "has happened to you?"

If all this came on suddenly, overnight, or over a period of a few weeks or months, you'd be able to see the craziness of it. Your thoughts would be fresh and clear, and there would be no doubt in your mind that something was very wrong and that the problem wasn't in you. But addiction typically grinds on for years before it is recognized, and during those years you become numb to its craziness and blind to its manipulations. You get crazy, too. Which is just fine with the addiction, because if you're crazy, you're not much of a threat. If you're taking the heat, the drinking or the drugging can continue pretty much uninterrupted.

Having made the decision to stay—what other choice is there? you think. How could you possibly leave her when she's in such turmoil? How could you live without her?—you had to learn how to survive. And the only way to survive living with a drug addiction is to adapt to its demands and become a little (and inevitably, a lot) crazy yourself.

Family members adapt their behaviors in characteristic ways. Sharon Wegscheider, in her book *Another Chance: Hope and Health for the Alcoholic Family,* has identified five basic roles that she believes are played out in one way or another in every family: the Enabler, the Hero, the Scapegoat, the Lost Child, and the Mascot. As she explains in her book, "In a small family there may be more than one role for each person; in a large family, there may be more than one person for a single role. But in all families all roles are played by someone, and everyone plays a role."

Many people understandably resist being labeled or shoved into a role, finding it difficult and demeaning to think of themselves as fitting into a specific mold shared by thousands of other people. But it's important to remember that this isn't the true "you" whom Wegscheider is describing, but the "adapted you," who, by choosing to live with the addiction, has had to make profound changes in the way you think, feel, and behave. Once you break free of the addiction, you can also break free of your role and begin to get back to who you really are. Being able to recognize yourself in these rigid survival roles is actually the beginning of the process of breaking the mold and freeing yourself from the addiction.

The following are brief summaries of the survival roles described in detail in chapters 5 to 10 of *Another Chance: Hope and Health for the Alcoholic Family* (see bibliography, p. 247). The reader is strongly encouraged to read *Another Chance* for its in-depth descriptions and fascinating insights.

The Enabler. This role is usually played by the Dependent's spouse or, if the Dependent is unmarried, the parents (one or both) or perhaps a roommate or lover. The Enabler is the chief protector, hiding the Dependent's mistakes, covering up, lying, and making excuses for his behavior. The Enabler acts out of a sincere sense of love and loyalty, is motivated by fear of the consequences of the Dependent's behavior ("If I don't lie for him, he'll lose his job," "If I don't take care of him, he'll die," et cetera), and believes that there is no choice but to continue covering up and taking responsibility. As the Enabler tries harder and harder to make things right and as things get worse and worse, she suffers from growing self-doubt, self-hatred, guilt, anger, and fear.

The Hero. In the typical family, the Hero is the oldest son or daughter. The Hero's role is determined by the fact that he is "locked into a system where the Dependent is overreacting to a chemical, the Enabler is overreacting to the Dependent, and both are either overreacting or underreacting to . . . their child, because of their other problems." The Hero feels a tremendous responsibility to make his family system work, and so he gives up his own needs and hides his own feelings, in an effort to make things right, to make them work, to heal the family's pain. But nothing he can do is ever enough. So he gradually becomes a perfectionist, striving always to do a little better and never taking any satisfaction in his achievements.

On the outside, the Hero appears to function well, but on the inside he's an emotional mess. His predominant emotion is anger: "Anger at having to strive so hard and be so good," Wegscheider writes, "anger at living in a family that needs so much and gives so little back; anger at parents who are so often critical and irritable when he is trying so hard; anger at himself for constantly discounting his own needs and selling out to other people's demands." Yet, being the "good" child that he is, he is deeply ashamed of this anger and buries it deep inside, where it nurtures and feeds on a growing sense of guilt and inadequacy.

The Scapegoat. Always the outsider and the outcast, always the inferior to the Hero, the Scapegoat withdraws from the family, acting out his frustrations at school or with his friends. The Scapegoat's behavior is actually the reverse of the Hero's: while the Hero is the overachiever, the Scapegoat is the underachiever; while the Hero is responsible, the Scapegoat is irresponsible; while the Hero works hard, the Scapegoat stops trying. The Scapegoat is often self-destructive, becoming involved with drugs, running with a "fast" crowd, being promiscuous, stealing, running away from home, et cetera. Since he has no measurable self-worth, these behaviors at least bring him some attention and even some importance. Scapegoats perceive the family as failing them, and they perceive themselves as having no effect or impact on the other members of the family. Intense anger, which masks the painful feelings of rejection, loneliness, and hurt, is expressed outwardly as hostility, rebellion, and belligerence.

The Lost Child. Like the Scapegoat, the Lost Child is an outsider, but instead of acting out, the Lost Child withdraws from the family chaos, becoming a loner, staying out of the way, and keeping to himself. He is, according to Wegscheider, "a stranger in his own family. . . . Because he is so often out of sight, he and his needs are also out of mind." Lost Children often grow up shy and introverted, finding it difficult to make friends or to reach out to others for companionship or support. The Lost Child, like the Scapegoat, suffers from a lack of self-worth; but instead of adopting the hurt, anger, and self-hatred of the Scapegoat, the Lost Child turns his pain even further inward, feeling increasingly lonely and worthless.

The Mascot. Often the youngest child in the family, the Mascot is protected and babied by the other family members. This child knows intuitively that something is dreadfully wrong with the family, yet he is constantly being told that everything is fine. The family tries to protect and coddle the Mascot because he is the youngest, the most helpless, or the most vulnerable. They deny the disease, cover up, screen what they say, and offer vague reassurances in an effort to shield him from the harsh realities of living with a Dependent.

As a result, the Mascot experiences deep anxiety and confusion—he doesn't know whether to believe his family or trust his own senses, and he wonders if he's going crazy. Showing off, clowning, joking around, acting "cute," and talking incessantly help to relieve the tension in the family and shift the focus away from those deep, dark, unspoken problems. Mascots experience a deep and overwhelming sense of fear, made all the worse because they can't identify exactly what it is that's frightening them. They run away from problems instead of confronting them, they are chronically immature, and they never learn how to deal adequately with the considerable stress in their lives.

The chains forming the rigid boundaries of these survival roles can be weakened and eventually broken by one simple realization: that there is a *choice*. Staying and adapting is a choice in and of itself; but it is not the only option. The family members have the choice, individually or collectively, to break free of their roles and learn to be true to themselves. But to do so requires three often difficult and time-consuming steps:

1. Recognize the Dependent's helplessness. Without outside help, the Dependent cannot overcome his disease. He acts the way he does, not because that's the way he is, but because the addiction is in control of his behavior. Willpower won't help him; strength of character can't save him. If you wait until the Dependent helps himself, you will be waiting until the addiction destroys him.

2. Acknowledge your present helplessness. You adopted your particular survival role in an effort to keep the family together at whatever cost. But you can't make the Dependent stop drinking or drugging by keeping your emotions tightly locked up or by accepting the blame for what has happened to the family. If you continue in your survival role, you are helpless to change your situation. The only hope lies in breaking free.

3. Accept the risks. If the family members and the Dependent are ever to recover, certain risks must be taken. The family must be willing to confront the Dependent with the facts of his disease, to stop covering up, and to accept as necessary the jolts and strains that such actions will bring about. Each family member must decide for himself if these are acceptable risks; no one can make the decision for anyone else.

Recognize, acknowledge, accept—these three steps form the heart of the intervention process. Recognizing your Dependent's helplessness involves being able to "see" the addiction and identify your Dependent as its prisoner. Acknowledging your present helplessness means putting yourself in the present, learning how to express your true feelings, and refusing to blame yourself for what the addiction has done to your life. And accepting the risks marks the stage when you are willing to move forward and embrace the challenges of recovery.

In the next chapter we will witness what happens when a family continues to operate within the survival roles. The dangers of continuing to "survive" become clear, and another choice appears: to stop merely surviving and to start taking an active role in changing the circumstances of your life.

ELEVEN

———

Peace at Any Price
Is War

Henry had worked out a perfect retirement for himself and his wife, Carol. He sold his home in Los Angeles and bought a twenty-acre farm in Montana, with fields of gently waving corn, mountains nearby for skiing, lakes and streams for fishing—it was, for Henry, a dream come true. His letters to friends back in L.A. were filled with superlatives about his new life and blanket denunciations of his former, hectic, traffic-jammed urban existence. "I wouldn't move back to that place, with those people, if you gave me ten million bucks," he crowed to his wife.

Carol seemed in perfect agreement. She never talked about her life in California, or her friends, or the part-time job that she had loved and had to give up. She never complained about the wind, the snow, or the ice on the road that kept them virtual prisoners in the house for five months of the year. She didn't ski; she didn't hunt; she didn't fish; but she didn't seem to mind the loneliness. She smiled when Henry smiled, she played cards when he wanted her to play. She placidly worked the garden and canned vegetables every year because he bought a Rototiller and decided they'd "live off the land." She left the house only on Sundays, when she went to church.

All seemed perfectly content until Christmas vacation, when

81

their three grown children arrived. The first day was generally peaceful; and often the second day slipped by without a major argument. But soon enough the tension was thick. Henry swore at the TV news anchorman, calling him a "liberal faggot"; his "liberal" sons and daughter had to bite their tongues. On a drive to the store, he shook his fist at a woman driver and then loudly denounced the entire female race as dumb and uncoordinated; his daughter immediately clenched her fists. A phone call from his ski partner canceling a planned trip to the mountains turned his face red with fury; he refused to talk to anyone for hours. He kicked his elder son's dog for barking in the house; his son seethed inwardly, feeling sick with the tension of keeping quiet while wanting to strike back at his father.

Around four in the afternoon, everyone began to think about cocktails. Alcohol made Henry happier and less agitated, at least for a little while. No one really cared that he drank his gin straight or that a gallon disappeared in less than a week. Everyone else drank, too, and the refrigerator was always crammed with beer and wine. For an hour or two, calm seemed to settle on the uneasy group. Dinner, however, was a frightful, silent event, with all the family members terrified of saying something that might upset Henry. Everyone ate as fast as they could and otherwise kept their mouths shut, anxious to avoid an argument at such close range.

At night Henry's children stayed up late, talking quietly in their rooms. They asked themselves why their mother "took it," how she lived with the man they all called a "tyrant." But the children had just as big an investment in keeping the peace. They stayed out of Henry's way; when the evening news came on, they left the room. Everyone walked around on tiptoe, holding their breath, afraid to make any noise, terrified that a comment would provoke an argument. At the end of the vacation, they all breathed an inward sigh of relief; they'd made it through one more Christmas, and the next one was a full year away.

Every member of Henry's family has agreed, at least subconsciously, to a silent and solemn pact to keep the peace at any price. What they don't understand, or can't articulate, is that the price of external peace is internal warfare. Each member of the family experiences waves of feeling helpless and powerless. Each feels overwhelmed with anger, frustration, resentment, and guilt. And each keeps his feelings to himself, because to talk about them is both too dangerous and too painful.

To protect themselves, the family members quickly slide back into their survival roles, learned from years of living with their father. The mother becomes the protector, trying to preserve the peace, reading books to the grandchildren to keep them quiet, smiling, staying calm, appearing not to notice the tension, steering the conversation into "safe" areas, and generally trying to put out all the little emotional fires before they threaten to consume whatever is left of the family. At the end of each day she is mentally and physically exhausted. She feels as if she's been on a wild treadmill, running like mad and getting nowhere. At the end of the week she is exhausted and more than ready for everyone to leave, even though her children and grandchildren are her greatest (and, in fact, her only) sources of joy. But she has made a choice: peace, rather than outright warfare, which could only, she thinks, make things worse.

The elder son, a successful business executive, slides back into feelings of inadequacy ("I can't do anything that pleases Dad,") and guilt ("I'm not doing enough; I should try harder; it's my fault"). In some deep place inside, he feels that he should be able to make everything right in his family—but no matter how hard he tries, no matter how much interest he shows in his father's new life or how many times he nods his head and says, "Yes, sure, anything you say," no matter how considerate, successful, and kind he is, his father stays the same. Every night during these yearly visits, he cries bitter tears and agonizes over the same old questions: "Why can't things be different? Why doesn't he give me the recognition I deserve? Why do I feel that no matter what I do, it won't be enough?"

The middle son suffers with choking feelings of anger and shame as it becomes apparent that nothing is different, that he is still the "loser," the outsider, the outcast. Any discussion with his father inevitably ends in anger, raised voices, and statements full of scorn and disdain, such as, "I never could talk to you." This son sits in the same chair day after day, smoking cigarettes and drinking beer; every few hours he goes to his room to snort, secretly, a line or two of cocaine. He seethes inwardly at his father's comments, but he never directly confronts him; instead, he takes his anger out on his wife and at one point blows up at his elder brother's wife for a comment that he felt put him down, "just like Dad always does." "She's just a snotty, rich bitch," he says to his wife after his outburst that night, his jaw still clenched in anger. His age-old resentments of his favored elder brother resurface, and he spends most of his energy trying to keep his seething emotions from boiling over.

The youngest child, the daughter, simply withdraws. Her one effort to establish some closeness with her father—a welcoming hug—was met with stiff resistance. And so she decides, as she always does, to stop trying. She stays in her room most of the time, her Sony Walkman turned up high, the loud music blasting all thoughts and emotions out of her mind. At meals she sits passively, answering in monosyllables when asked a question. As soon as the dishes are cleared, she retreats to her room. She feels an aching loneliness, but she suffers in silence with her sadness, confusion, and fear.

This family, like so many others, has chosen to live with the addiction and adjust their behavior to accommodate its demands. They don't actually see that they have made a choice—the choice, they think, has been made for them. The Dependent's behavior, it seems to them, has been set in stone; if they are to stay together as a family, they must adjust to that rigid, cementlike core of the family's existence.

Their choice—to keep the peace—means to suffer in silence, hoping that things will somehow change, stuffing emotions inside, where they won't cause any outward trouble, and looking outside the family for emotional needs to be met. The mother turns to her church; the elder son immerses himself in his work;

the younger son finds solace in drugs; the daughter hopes that silence or its reverse, loud music, will fill in her emotional holes.

But the cost of keeping the peace for this family—and, indeed, for all families—is exorbitant. Each family member suffers physically, mentally, emotionally, and spiritually. Each feels unloved, unworthy, frightened, confused, lonely, angry, and, in one way or another, abandoned. These feelings result in an inner turmoil that can never be expressed outwardly because of the unspoken commitment to "keep the peace."

As we become adept at hiding our emotions, we also become expert at denying that these emotions exist. No one in the family is allowed to say what he is really feeling; the feelings simply hurt too much when they are exposed to the open air. It's much safer, much less immediately painful, to shove the feelings back inside, ignore them, and attempt to deny their existence.

But the feelings leak out, in one way or another. Inner hurt is outwardly expressed as anger; feelings of helplessness are masked by efforts to control other people's behavior; guilt is expressed as attempts to put the blame on others; fear metamorphoses into aggressive behavior; confusion is expressed as frustration.

The internal warfare that takes place as the result of attempting to keep the peace is inevitably directed both inward and outward, at others—spouse, friends, children, co-workers, teachers, et cetera. The original innocent victims take on new innocent victims as the disease spreads its poison in ever-widening circles and eats away at love, trust, hope, and the courage to change.

—

TWELVE

Guilt Is Living in the Past

If there's one emotion that characterizes the thinking and feeling life of the family, it's *guilt*. The spouse feels guilty because she fears she hasn't been understanding enough, or she's nagged too much, or she should have done more to protect the children. The kids feel guilty because they think they've been too selfish, noisy, bothersome, or inconsiderate. Friends feel guilty because they didn't see the problem coming, or because they did see it and were afraid to say anything. Relatives feel guilty for being unable to offer any kind of help or advice that makes any difference.

Everyone surrounding the Dependent feels guilty, believing that, in one way or another, the problems in the family are their fault. Family members are filled with self-reproach, self-condemnation, and self-disgust. They grieve and mourn as they look back on the past, wishing they'd done things differently, mentally berating themselves for their errors and weaknesses, and wishing, hopelessly, that somehow life had worked out differently.

Guilt is like a magnet with a powerful, almost irresistible attraction for those who live with a Dependent, providing a release for emotions that are otherwise too painful to express.

Guilt allows self-pity, turning the accusations inward, where they at least provide some company, instead of outward, where they are met with hostility, anger, and bitter resentment. Guilt seems as if it might hold some promise of changing things, when nothing else works; at least if you feel guilty, you are able to punish someone for the torment in your life . . . even if that someone is you.

If we decide to accept guilt for things gone wrong, we set ourselves up as admirable people, martyrs of sorts who are willing to take the responsibility and suffer the consequences. While we might feel bad about something we did (or didn't do), we can at least comfort ourselves with feeling guilty about it. Or, if we decide that someone else should take the guilt, we can justify our feelings of anger and resentment, deflect the attention from our own actions, and slough off the responsibility onto someone else. Once guilt has been soaked up, everyone feels more at ease, as if just feeling bad will make things better.

The thing about guilt is that we have to open our arms to it. In order to feel it at all, we have to believe that we deserve to feel guilty or that by feeling guilty perhaps we can take the heat off someone else. And that's why those of us who live with Dependents are such easy targets for guilt: we can't pinpoint the cause of our suffering, so we assume that the fault must lie, at least in part, within ourselves. The frustration of having so many things go wrong and no one person to blame makes everyone who lives with an addict extremely vulnerable to carrying the load of guilt.

And the addiction is masterful at manipulating this most manipulative of emotions. Here's a typical case of addiction-inspired guilt:

■

It's 6:00 A.M. on a Monday morning and Dan, a forty-six-year-old, middle-stage alcoholic, has a whopping hangover. He slugs down a cup of coffee, feeling sick at the thought of breakfast, and eases himself into the car. Groaning softly, he rubs his head and

*tries to focus his eyes, dreading the rush hour traffic. Sure
enough, the highway is jammed with cars. Dan pounds his fist
on the wheel, clenches his teeth, and glares at the other drivers.*

*Inching along, he turns the radio on and the car is suddenly
blasted with rock music. Dan practically jumps out of his seat.
"Damn that kid," he swears out loud, thinking of his eighteen-
year-old son, who borrowed the car the night before. Taking his
eyes off the road and reaching for the radio dial, Dan doesn't
notice the brake lights on the car ahead of him. He smashes into
the back of the car, causing a chain reaction of fender-benders.*

*"I'll kill him!" Dan explodes. There's no doubt in Dan's mind
that his son is responsible for this accident. Throughout the long
ordeal of exchanging phone numbers with the other drivers, Dan
seethes with anger; he can't wait to get his hands on the kid.
When he arrives home, he yells at his wife to call his boss and, in
a fury, strides into his son's room. He pulls the sleeping boy out
of bed by the collar of his pajamas.* Good, *he thinks, seeing the
terror on his son's face,* I'll give you the scare of your life.

*"Do you know what you did to me?" Dan yells. His terrified
son shakes his head. "You almost killed me! You left the radio
on that damned rock station and when I went to change it, I
rammed the car ahead of me. The front of the car is a mess—
who do you think is going to pay for it?" Dan viciously shakes the
boy again. "That's the last time I let you drive the car; don't even
think about asking."*

*Dan lets go of his son's pajamas, visibly restraining himself
from striking the boy. Swearing, he walks into the kitchen. His
wife hesitantly puts her hand on his arm.*

*"Honey," she says softly, "don't you think you were a little
hard on him? I'm sure he didn't intentionally leave the radio
on."*

*Dan turns sharply toward her, his eyes narrowed. "Oh, now,
what's this? You're taking his side? I've got probably a thousand
dollars' worth of bills to pay, the insurance company will either
up my rates or drop me, my neck feels like I got whiplash, and
you're telling me to go easy on the kid?" Dan's voice rises in
anger. "I tell you, I've had it with this family—all you think*

about is yourselves! What about me? Who has to go to work at six A.M.? Who pays the bills? Do I ever get any recognition? Does anybody ever thank me for anything I do?"

"Sweetheart, I'm sorry," his wife says, trying to calm him down. "You've had an awful morning. Sit down, and I'll fix you some breakfast."

"I don't want any breakfast, I feel like hell. Did you call the office?"

"Yes, everything's all set. They're very concerned about you."

"At least someone is," Dan mumbles.

■

Dan's wife and son soak up the guilt like dry sponges. As absurd as Dan's charges are, his wife believes that she is partly responsible for his misery; she should have been more loving and understanding, she thinks, as she watches her husband collapse in misery at the breakfast table. Dan's son cries for hours in his bedroom; angry, ashamed, and afraid, he feels unjustly accused, yet he can't rid himself of the thought that he could have caused his father serious injury. For days, Dan's wife and son wallow in guilt, accepting the blame for the accident and wishing they could have changed the events of that awful morning.

If guilt is such a useless, self-destructive waste of time, why do Dan's wife and son put up with it? Because, as damaging as guilt is, it has its payoffs. By accepting the guilt, Dan's wife and son immerse themselves in the past, going over and over the events of the day and wishing that things had worked out differently. As miserable as this is for them, living in the past also allows them to avoid taking responsibility for the present. *How much worse things would be,* Dan's son thinks, *if I yelled back at him—he'd never forgive me, he probably would have hit me, and he'd refuse to talk to me for days, maybe weeks.*

His son is convinced that it is better to take the punishment, as unfair as it might seem, and hope that the whole thing will blow over in a few days. Dan's wife knows all too well what will happen if she attempts to throw some of the responsibility back on her husband—he'll explode, storm out, fume, and be miserable to live with for weeks. It's not worth it, she decides; better to absorb the blame and responsibility and hope everything will return to normal soon.

Dan's wife and son actually feel a sense of power, even hope, in taking responsibility for the events that led to the wrecked car. Maybe Dan will love them more for their willingness to take the guilt; maybe he will see how good they really are, how eager they are to please him, how desperately they want to help him through these periodic crises. They hope that if they take the blame this time, he'll be more reasonable next time. Perhaps he'll see how truly good and loving they are; perhaps things will get better after this.

■

Suppose, now, that Dan's wife were to say "no" to guilt; what would happen? Here's a likely scenario:

"The car wreck wasn't Johnny's fault, Dan," she says to her irate husband. "It's unfair of you to blame him for it."

"What are you saying?" Dan answers, suddenly furious. "Whose fault do you think it was?"

"I'm not pinning the blame on anyone."

"You think it was my fault, don't you?"

"I think you were driving the car, and it's unfair to blame the accident on Johnny; he wasn't driving."

"Oh, this is great," Dan says sarcastically. "This is just the support I need from my wife. You know, it's no wonder things are no good between us anymore. You have absolutely no understanding of my job, my life, the pressure I'm under. I'm surprised we've lasted this long." Dan heads for the door, shouting out his parting words: "But let me tell you, I'm not taking it anymore. Take his side if you want. I've had it with both of you!"

■

Dan's wife is now in the unenviable position of either backtracking and accepting the additional guilt that he has just thrown at her, or facing up to the reality of her situation. The first choice is the passive, easy one; all she has to do is sit back and take it. There is even the additional payoff that she can feel sorry for herself and proud of her ability to take the pain, spare her son any additional suffering, and continue on, just as before. This is a pathway she has followed many times; she is familiar with it and can reliably predict the outcome.

The second choice, however, is filled with danger. If she stands up to her husband, she risks the comfortable schedule of her life, the future of her marriage, and her financial stability. She fears that by openly rebelling, she might even lose her son's love and loyalty. After all, he needs his Dad; would he forgive her for forcing him out of the house? This second choice is filled with unknowns.

While accepting guilt is unquestionably the immediately easier course of action (or, more properly, inaction), the long-term consequences are disastrous. When family members accept responsibility for the Dependent's behavior, they are actually allowing the addiction room to expand and increase its power. They feed right into the Dependent's denial system and, in fact, end up denying the disease themselves.

As the addiction grows stronger, guilt causes the family members to grow weaker. It feeds their depression, justifies their anger, and destroys their self-esteem. Guilt also blocks the family's ability to experience love and forgiveness; as they become more thoroughly wrapped up in guilt, they become more resentful, fearful, and filled with dislike, even hatred, for this person who is making them suffer so relentlessly.

Guilt will eventually destroy love and the ability to forgive; all it takes is time. But once again, we have a choice. We can continue to live with guilt, *or* we can accept the need and the responsibility for changing the course of our lives. This latter choice takes work, requiring a course of action and the commitment and resolution to see that action through, no matter what the consequences. Getting rid of guilt means that we must examine ourselves, our values, motives, feelings, and needs. Getting rid of guilt involves taking responsibility for ourselves and learning how to help others take responsibility for their feelings and actions. Getting rid of guilt requires a commitment to live in the present and release ourselves from our bondage to the past.

But how do we do all these things? *Slowly,* with the inner assurance that this is the route to health, forgiveness, and happiness, and the understanding that the other way—holding on to guilt—will eventually destroy not only our relationship with our Dependent, but our ability to find happiness in any relationship. Guilt is not a life preserver; it is a deadly weight that will gradually drown us in self-pity and self-reproach.

Getting rid of guilt begins with the following steps:

1. Learn to practice forgiveness. To forgive means to let go of resentment, hatred, and the need to retaliate. Forgiveness is a release of all those poisonous emotions that make it impossible to like yourself and to love and trust others. Whom do we need to forgive? Ourselves, first and foremost. We need to stop holding ourselves responsible for events over which we had no control. We aren't responsible for this disease, and nothing we did or didn't do could have stopped it. We need to stop looking at the past and wishing things were different; the past is over and done with, and nothing can change it, not even massive doses of guilt.

We must also learn how to forgive others and to stop trying to control the people we love with accusations or confrontations calculated to make them feel guilty. Guilt only breeds more guilt and deeper levels of resentment, anger, and fear. We need to let go of our desire to right the injustices of the past by putting the blame on others. Nobody is to blame for the misery that permeates the family of the Dependent—nobody but that thing we've personified as a monster and a demon: the addiction.

2. Take responsibility for what you see, feel, and experience. If you are feeling sad (or mad, or angry, or depressed), don't accept the feeling as inevitable or as an integral part of who you are. Feelings come from the way we have learned to think about events; yet, most of us imagine that the events themselves cause the feelings. Thus, if the toast burns and we blow up in anger, it seems obvious that the burned toast caused the anger. But why should burned toast make us angry? Why should rain make us sad? Why should another person's grumpiness make us irritable?

Our feelings come from the way we *think* about an event, not from the event itself. If we can learn to challenge our irrational feelings ("Why should I get angry at the toast?") and create a new way of looking at the situation ("I'm in too much of a hurry this morning; maybe I should slow down"), then we can begin to take responsibility for our emotions.

We can, in fact, choose what we want to feel, because what we feel and perceive is a direct result of what we think. If we can change our thoughts, we can change our feelings.*

3. Help others to take responsibility for their own feelings and perceptions. Giving in to guilt might lead to the following short conversation between a mother and her child:

CHILD: Why did you stay with him all those years? Why did you always take his side?

PARENT: I made you miserable, didn't I? I should have been stronger; I should have done things differently.

End of conversation. The objective—to have someone take the blame—has been quickly achieved.

Getting rid of guilt, on the other hand, takes a little longer:

CHILD: Why did you stay with him all those years? Why did you always take his side?

---

*This is the basic message of Rational Emotive Therapy (RET). RET is used in many treatment programs to help Dependents and their families learn that they are in control of their emotions and feelings.

PARENT: You feel that I let you down; that things would be different if I'd only acted differently.

CHILD (sullen): Yeah. That's right.

PARENT: I did what I did, thinking it was the best way to handle the situation. I know more about the disease now than I did then; but still, you're talking about the past, which I can't do anything about.

CHILD: You're just going to write it all off? You're refusing to take any of the responsibility for what's happened to this family?

PARENT: I'm taking responsibility for myself and for my behavior right now. I can't, I won't, preoccupy myself with the past or with wishing that things were different. If you want to dwell on the past and try to pin the blame for your pain on me, there's not much I can do to dissuade you. That's your battle, not mine. I'm choosing to live in the here and now. I'd rather be involved in a battle where there's a chance to win than one in which I already know that I'll fail.

4. Learn to believe in progress, not perfection. Striving for perfection means that we have put a judgment on what is correct or ideal, and any other goal is then seen as somehow imperfect or incorrect. But people live their lives differently, and it is this difference within us and in the way we approach problems that makes the world such an interesting and exciting place. There is no right way to live our lives. Perfection, in fact, is an impossible standard by which to judge human behavior, and if that's all we will settle for, we'll have to live with a great deal of disappointment, guilt, and grief.

Progress, measured by small steps, not quantum leaps, is a much more human, more achievable goal that will bring continual and enduring fulfillment.

THIRTEEN

Can You Love Too Much?

When being in love means being in pain we are loving too much.
When most of our conversations with intimate friends are about
him, his problems, his thoughts, his feelings—and nearly all our
sentences begin with "he . . .", we are loving too much.

When we excuse his moodiness, bad temper, indifference, or
put-downs as problems due to an unhappy childhood and we try to
become his therapist, we are loving too much.

When we read a self-help book and underline all the passages
we think would help *him,* we are loving too much.

When we don't like many of his basic characteristics, values,
and behaviors, but we put up with them thinking that if we are
only attractive and loving enough he'll want to change for us, we
are loving too much.

When our relationship jeopardizes our emotional well-being and
perhaps even our physical health and safety, we are definitely
loving too much.*

How is it possible to love "too much"? Doesn't love mean total
preoccupation with another person? Isn't love a selfless, continuous giving, without expecting anything in return? Loving
well means overlooking moodiness, faults, flaws, and tempo-

*Women Who Love Too Much, by Robin Norwood.

rary problems—doesn't it? If we give ourselves totally to loving and supporting another person, isn't that the very best kind of love?

Not when it destroys *you*. Love, like all emotions, has its boundaries; when these boundaries are stretched too far, love ceases to be love and becomes instead obsession, pity, or even martyrdom. When caring for someone is relentlessly painful, surely that is not love. When devotion is inspired by pity, or a sense of duty, love has been demoted to second place. When living with someone means living in a state of perpetual fear and anger, where is love? When total preoccupation with another's needs and demands results in completely ignoring your own needs, love has ceased to be a joyful emotion. And when "love" is joyless and becomes an exhausting drain on energy, enthusiasm, and self-esteem, it can no longer be called love.

What, then, is love? Here's a partial list of some of the characteristics of this complex emotion:

- Partnership
- Friendship
- Mutual trust and respect
- Sharing of basic values, interests, and goals
- Joy in shared experiences
- Tolerance of individual differences
- Willingness to make compromises and expecting that your partner will do the same
- Serenity, security, and stability

As you read through this list, try to determine honestly which of these characteristics apply to your relationship with the Dependent. Remember that each of the above definitions is just a part of love; to be fully realized, love should include many of these parts.

Now let's look at what love is *not*. Love is not, simply:

- Predictability
- Putting someone else's happiness above your own

- Being dependent on another person
- Having another person dependent on you
- Willingness to suffer for another
- Fear of being alone
- The ability to "take it" and come back for more
- Preoccupation with someone else's needs or desires
- Feeling responsible for another person's happiness

While people who love each other may experience any or even several of these aspects of loving "too much," the difference between constructive and destructive love can easily be measured by looking at both lists and honestly assessing which best describes your relationship.

One thing is certain: in time, the addiction will destroy all the healthy and constructive aspects of love, leaving you with a number of distorted emotions that will slowly erode your self-confidence, your self-esteem, and, worst of all, your ability to take a realistic look at the quality of your life. Guilt is one of the first emotions associated with the erosion of love; resentment, confusion, and anger inevitably follow.

Fear, however, is the root cause of loving too much. As Norwood puts it, "fear of being alone, fear of being unlovable and unworthy, fear of being ignored, abandoned or destroyed." That's a lot of fear to contend with, and fear is not a healthy atmosphere in which love can thrive. In fact, fear eats away at the constructive aspects of love, leaving only the destructive, obsessive needs and emotions that are often mistaken for love but are, in fact, seriously deformed mutations.

What exactly do we mean by "fear" and where does it come from? Fear is a feeling of agitation, uneasiness, and dread, caused by the awareness (conscious or subconscious) that trouble or danger exists or lies ahead. These feelings, as we all know, are constant companions for anyone living with an addicted person. Trouble, in fact, is ever present once the addiction is well established, and dangers—to the family unit, financial security, friendships, mental and physical health—loom real and large. As the addiction grows stronger, so do the fears; and as the fears multiply, love withers.

Love cannot continue to exist in an atmosphere that is full of fear, for fear destroys trust, respect, sharing, honesty, tolerance, and freedom—all the emotions and conditions necessary to nurture love. But fear is more than a destroyer; it is also a creator of emotions—anger, neediness, resentment, guilt, and worry—that will eventually sound the death knell of love.

Anger, for example, is a direct response to fear; the two emotions are actually interchangeable. It's much easier to be mad than to be afraid, for fear makes you vulnerable, and anger is a way of lashing out against that vulnerability and denying it. Likewise with resentment, guilt, worry, and neediness—all of these emotions have their roots in fear, the source of their power and intensity.

Fear expresses itself in any number of statements that are all too familiar to chemically addicted family members; each of these statements represents an attempt to deny or cover up the underlying fear:

- "I'm sure that if I just try hard enough, I can make it all work." (*Fear translation:* "I'm afraid I'll fail; I'm afraid if I do fail, I'll lose him; if I fail, what do I have left?")
- "I can't leave him; he needs me." (*Fear translation:* "I'm afraid to leave; I'm afraid of not being needed.")
- "I can't stand to see him hurt or in pain." (*Fear translation:* "I'm afraid something awful will happen to him if I'm not here to help; and then how would I deal with the guilt?")
- "He's just having some temporary problems; he'll get better soon." (*Fear translation:* "I'm afraid to even think about the fact that he might be an alcoholic or drug addict; I'm afraid of the shame and stigma associated with those labels.")
- "He loves me, he just doesn't know how to show it." (*Fear translation:* "I'm afraid he doesn't love me.")
- "I can't put all the blame on him—I have to take some of the responsibility for what's happened." (*Fear translation:*

"I'm afraid I caused many of these problems, but I'm even more afraid that the problems are out of my control; I'm afraid of losing control.")

- "His happiness is more important to me than my own." (*Fear translation:* "I'm afraid to even think about my happiness because I'm so unhappy, and I'm terrified of being alone.")
- "I can't imagine life without him; what would I do? Where would I go?" (*Fear translation:* "I'm afraid of change; I'm afraid to risk what I've got, as bad as it is, for the unknown.")
- "I can take it, I can still stand it—it's not that bad." (*Fear translation:* "I'm afraid to admit how bad it is; I'm afraid to admit that I might, in fact, be powerless to stop it.")

Once we can identify the fear in these statements, we can also begin to see the ways in which love has been transfigured and damaged. Contained within each of these statements is the belief that love is measured by the degree of suffering experienced: the more we are willing to suffer, the greater, we think, is our love. And so we take the blame, accept the responsibility, and assume control of the situation, hoping all the while that if we can only love him enough, the possibility exists that we can change him and put an end to our pain and fear.

We deny ourselves, sacrifice our needs and feelings, ignore our emotional starvation in an effort to love him so much that somehow the sheer, desperate intensity of that love will make a difference. His happiness becomes more important to us than our own; being needed, in fact, is the sum total of our emotional fabric, the driving force of our thoughts and behavior.

But this is not love; this is self-destruction. Continuous suffering is not a natural part of love but a symptom that love is rotting at its core. The depth of love is not measured by the pain it causes us but by the joy it allows us to feel and express; if there is no joy, there is no love.

If we give away ourselves, we also give away our ability to accept and give love. If love flows only one way, it is flowing from a stagnant stream.

FOURTEEN

How Long Do You Hang On?

"Katie! *Don't* nag! All of us are what we have to be and everyone lives the kind of life it's in him to live. You've got a good man, Katie."

"But he drinks."

"And he always will until he dies. There it is. He drinks. You must take that along with the rest."

"What rest? You mean the not working, the staying out all night, the bums he has for friends?"

"You married him. There was something about him that caught your heart. Hang on to that and forget the rest."

—From *A Tree Grows in Brooklyn,* by Betty Smith

"**H**ang on to that and forget the rest." How many times have you told yourself exactly that? Hang on to the love, the affection, the memories, the security, those precious times when everything seems right again, and forget the rest—the worrying, the anger, the fear, and the pain. But how long do you hang on? And how do you continue to forget when "the rest" begins to seem like all there is?

There will come a time when hanging on becomes too much like hanging yourself. *When the pain of the known is greater than the fear of the unknown*—you will feel the need to act. When you realize, finally, that nothing you do is going to make a difference, that he will continue to use drugs whether you're there to witness it or not, then you've hit a sort of bottom. You've been tumbling for a long time, but your hope that somehow, someday, things would change has kept you afloat. You've been clinging to the last remaining shreds of hope because without hope all seems lost. Fear overwhelms you when you think about what lies below—suspended, you're at least temporarily safe. If you come crashing down, who knows what will happen? Will you survive? What will life be like "down there"?

It is not the pain that immobilizes those of us who love a Dependent, it's the fear. We've dealt with the pain for a long time, and we're convinced that we can continue to live with the pain—but our fear has us paralyzed. Given a choice between pain and fear, we'll choose pain every time—until we come to the understanding that in the long run, the pain is more deadly than the fear.

But what is it, exactly, that we fear? Our most encompassing fear is of *the unknown*—that vast universe of "what ifs?" that circles round and round in our heads whenever we even think about making a move: "What if he dies? What if I leave and nothing changes? What if I leave and everything gets worse?"

We fear change—changing ourselves, changing our lives, changing our routines—because change would catapult those unknowns from our heads into our living rooms. Change is unbearably risky, and we will fight it for a long time. Only when our pain is greater than our fear will it seem that change might, in fact, be worth the risk.

We fear moral disapproval. What will our relatives and friends think if we turn against our spouse? What will our minister or priest think? What will the neighbors, the boss, the teachers, the policeman, and the mailman think?

We fear our own conscience. How could we live with ourselves if we leave him and he gets worse or maybe even dies? How could we turn our back on him when we promised, all those years ago, to love, honor, and obey in sickness and in health, until death do us part? How could we betray his trust, his love, his need?

We fear concrete things, too. There's the mortgage to think about, and all the other bills that need to be paid. How could we possibly make it on our own? How would we provide for the children? What kind of a life would they have, separated from their father or mother? Even if we have no children, we doubt our ability to provide for ourselves. It may have been years since we worked, or maybe we've never held a job outside the home. What would we do? Who would hire us—the aging, wrinkled, worried spouses of alcoholics or drug addicts? What would we possibly have to offer anyone? We can't even keep our own family together; it takes an extraordinary effort to make it from breakfast to dinner; even answering the phone tires us. Who would ever consider taking on such classic cases of incompetence?

We fear his reactions. He would hate us. If we leave him, it would kill any remaining emotions left inside him, turning him against us for life. At least now he is dependent on us, and thankful for our care—he *needs* us! If we leave him, he'll never forgive us. How could we live with the knowledge of that hatred and the absolute death of all remaining emotions?

We fear the loss of identity that would come with a separation. Now we're wife, mother, housekeeper, organizer; we arrange all the details of life in our home, we stick to a schedule, everything has its place—what would we do, who would we be, if we gave up just the little bit of control that we have left? We'd have no home, no marriage, no self—we'd be absolutely alone, surrounded by people who don't know us and couldn't care less about us. We have no confidence in our ability to make friends or become successfully involved in new relationships—look at the mess of our relationships now! How could we possibly delude ourselves into thinking that things would be better with anyone else?

Loneliness is a terrible fear. We're lonely now, no way around that, but we're not *alone*. We have tasks to do, people to watch out for, events to control. It's our house, as full of pain as it is, and we can at least find comfort in its familiarity. How would we feel in an apartment somewhere, with four naked, staring walls and not even any good memories lurking in the corners? How could we go to bed at night, alone, with no one to care if we woke up in the morning? How could we endure a place that was silent all day, a reminder of the utter emptiness of our lives?

And if we give him up, what then? What if we never find anyone else? What if we get stuck with someone even worse? At least we know his faults, we know how to maneuver around him and how to control him. He's not *that* bad, after all; certainly he could be a lot worse. Besides, a lot of this is our fault—if we just love him enough, things might change. If we just keep trying, at least things might not get any worse.

As bad as life is, we feel sure that it is better with him than without him. And so we stay, the fears, uncertainties, and insecurities keeping us locked inside the pain of our lives. But at some point the pain will become too much to bear: the sheer force and power of it will push our fears away, at least for a moment, leaving a clear space in which to think, plan, and begin to move. We will see the choice, then: to stay and suffocate slowly from the pain, or to begin the journey toward recovery.

The clouds of fear will roll in again, temporarily dulling the pain and obscuring the choice; but the pain will hold steady and gradually increase, and, as it does, our fears will begin to seem less ominous and overwhelming.

The choice between pain and fear seems a bleak one. But if we can look directly at our fears, they lose their power to overwhelm us. We can learn to seek them out, accept them, and try to understand their origins; in these ways, we make them concrete and identifiable. And we can be comforted by the fact that everyone who lives with a Dependent suffers with the same general fears. Slowly, then, we can begin to move into our fears and, by approaching them, dispel them.

One step—that's all it takes to begin the process of changing our lives. One step away from the pain.

FIFTEEN

Moving Away from the Edge

Cindy *tiptoed into her eighteen-month-old daughter's room, stood over the crib, and watched her child as she slept.* This is the only peaceful place in the house, *Cindy thought. She sat down in the rocking chair in the dim light and rocked slowly, trying to calm herself.* "Take a deep breath," *she told herself,* "that's it, breathe deep."

The tears began to roll down her cheeks. It felt good to cry this way, she thought; alone, softly, no racking sobs, no screaming fights, just good old warm tears. Her tears actually comforted her, for if she could still cry, she knew she was at least feeling something. There had been times in the past when she felt that she was beyond feeling, and that had frightened her more than all the accumulated years of crying and screaming and wanting to die from the pain.

Joe was having an affair, she knew that now. Her suspicions had been confirmed in the oddest way, really: he had made love to her that morning, for the first time in months, and he had held her so gently, with so much unspoken guilt, that she knew the truth. For weeks he had been staying late at work, sometimes returning home after midnight; loan applications pouring in, he'd explained. One night she had called at ten o'clock and his secretary had answered. Joe had always talked about Sheila's great legs. Other nights she had called and the phone rang on and on.

I should hate him, *she thought,* but I don't. I should leave him; but I can't. Not yet. *Her daughter, Erica, was the major reason; and she was pregnant again, almost four months. Joe didn't know yet; she would have to tell him soon. He would be thrilled, for he'd always wanted a large family.*

I'll leave when the baby is Erica's age, *Cindy thought. She wondered where she would look for a job. At least she could always count on secretarial work. The local college offered day care for students' children; she would have to call and find out the rates.*

"Poor Joe," Cindy whispered to herself. She knew how awful it would be for him without Erica. She took a deep breath and let the tears flow again. She repeated to herself something she had heard at Al-Anon the night before: "You didn't cause it, you can't control it, and you can't cure it."

I've given him seven years of my life, *she thought,* and nothing I did or didn't do made a difference. He has a disease; he acts the way he does because he's sick. He needs help, but I need help, too. It's time for me now.

Erica was stirring in her crib. Cindy picked up her daughter and held her tight. "And time for you," she whispered.

Cindy is moving; not in dramatic, giant leaps but in little tiny baby steps, she is drifting away from the edge. She is able to move, finally, because of her growing awareness that her husband is addicted to alcohol and prescription drugs. For years she believed that he used drugs because he was under stress or overworked, or unhappy with his boss, his family, his life. She accepted the blame for his depressions and mood swings, passively agreeing with him when he told her that her worrying and nagging only made everything worse. "Just be patient," he used to say. "Things will get better. I just need to get a good job and an understanding boss. When we get all the bills paid off and can afford our own house, life will be easier." But the good job, the understanding boss, the paid bills, and the new house didn't change anything. The drinking and drugging steadily progressed, and Joe became ever more depressed and emotionally distant.

It took a long time—seven years—for Cindy to stop blaming Joe's behavior on the circumstances of their life and to begin to make the connection that the drugs, in fact, caused the problems. He didn't use drugs because he was depressed, she knew now; he was depressed because he was addicted. He didn't use drugs because he lost his job; he lost his job because of drugs. Their arguments didn't drive him to alcohol and marijuana; he would actually provoke an argument in order to have an excuse to get high.

Cindy realized how simple it all was when you just switched the facts around. When he yelled at her now, she didn't yell back or burst into tears. She told herself, "That's the disease talking," and left the room. She refused to call in sick for him anymore; he would have to accept that responsibility himself. Slowly, she detached herself from her husband, letting go of each of the tiny, invisible strings that had wrapped her up in his disease and made her incapable of acting on her own.

It would be some time before she could sever all the connections; but in the meantime, she was able to cope, emotionally, with her husband's behavior, make plans for the future, learn about the disease, and find support for herself through Al-Anon. From the outside it might seem that nothing had changed; but from Cindy's perspective, everything had changed. She was making progress. She was beginning to believe in herself again.

As Cindy's case illustrates, the process of recovery need not be dramatic. For most people, in fact, it begins with a vague awareness that something is not quite right. That awareness is the germination of the realization that something, in fact, is very wrong. Slowly, the connection is made that whatever is wrong is due, at least in part, to the drinking or the drugging.

Once the seed of this idea is planted and begins to take root, the process of recovery has begun—even though it may take months or perhaps years for any obvious, outward change to become apparent.

Awareness, then, is only the beginning of a long process that may or may not lead to action intended to get help for the Dependent. For awareness involves two insights, each with its own set of solutions. First, the insight that people who are addicted to drugs are completely at the mercy of their addiction, with the addiction actually controlling the Dependent's thoughts, feelings, and behavior; second, that people who live with an alcoholic or drug addict are gradually overwhelmed by the addiction's power and lose their ability to think, feel, or behave in "normal," rational ways.

The second insight actually determines the course of action necessary to overcome the addiction. Because of the addiction's effect on us, we cannot hope to help the Dependent until we get help for ourselves. Only by meeting our own needs first can we become healthy and strong enough to begin to pull our Dependent toward health and recovery.

Awareness is only the beginning of the process that will lead us to recovery. After awareness comes the search for knowledge and understanding: what causes this disease, why it happens to some people and not others, how it impacts the Dependent's behavior, and how it affects the family.

With knowledge comes responsibility: once we know about the disease, we must accept responsibility for that knowledge. This does not mean that we must act immediately; but we must be willing to accept the consequences of *not* acting. For many people, not acting may be the most appropriate action. The important point is that the decision to act or not to act is based on knowledge of the disease instead of misconception and ignorance.

Cindy, for example, made a concrete decision, based on knowledge of the disease and her particular circumstances, *not* to act until her new baby was born. Having weighed the options, understood the facts, and accepted the consequences,

Cindy decided it would be best for her and her children to stay with her drug-addicted husband for a few more years. Her decision not to act was, in fact, an action, because it was based on an analysis and evaluation of her specific situation, *with an understanding and knowledge of the disease.*

With the search for knowledge comes the need for support. No matter how much you know about this disease, it will continue to drive you crazy if you don't actively seek the support of family and friends and, through Al-Anon and other support groups, the wisdom and solace of time spent with others who are suffering with the same problems. You will need to find allies whom you can turn to when you become confused, angry, resentful, or afraid. And you will need the support of others who will reaffirm what you are doing and, by their own experience, confirm that there is indeed a light at the end of the tunnel. It doesn't matter how long it takes you to get there, as long as you keep your eyes focused on the light, your feet pointed forward, and your back turned to the pain and darkness of the past. If you go forward, each small step can be counted as a victory.

At times the process may seem agonizingly slow; at those times, try to keep in mind that even the slightest of movements, the tiniest of steps, is infinitely better than paralysis. As long as there is movement away from the edge, there is progress. And as long as there is progress, there is hope.

■

PART III

Overcoming

When you know it in your head, when your insides are tense, and when your heart is ready to break—only then will you be ready to stop living on the edge. Only when knowledge, fear, and love come together in a sort of chemical interaction and explosion will you reach a state of "wisdom": a deep and profound understanding that to continue as you have been is not only futile but dangerous and that your only hope lies in moving in a different direction.

What has brought you to that understanding?

- *Awareness* that you are not alone, that other families have known the same kind of despair.
- *Assurance* that you, like so many others, can confront your pain and survive it.
- *Understanding* that addiction is a true disease—of the body, first and foremost, but also of the mind and spirit.
- *Courage* to face the unknown without covering your eyes or hiding your heart.
- *Acceptance* of the fact that you have to learn to let go before you can grab on.
- *Faith* in the process of recovery and *patience* to work through it step by step.
- *Trust* that taking risks is infinitely better than doing nothing and losing everything you have.

Of these, trust is most important of all. You must trust yourself, trust the people you have turned to for help, and trust the process of growth and change that we call intervention. As your trust builds, you'll feel steadier and the conviction will grow inside you that this is the right course; that you are willing to accept the risks because this is the right direction for your life.

Finally, you must be willing to accept the fact that your life will never be the same again.

And that is good. You are moving forward now, rather than standing still and watching helplessly as your life crumbles around you. You are not helpless. You have a choice. The challenges you will experience in your recovery hold the ultimate promise of life and the resurrection of love. They are challenges that you will embrace willingly because they offer hope, and joy, and the promise of a new life.

When you are ready . . .

SIXTEEN

Finding a Counselor

For some lucky families, an intervention can occur spontaneously, take place in a period of several minutes, and end with the Dependent's firm commitment to get help. Before you decide to go ahead with a "formal" intervention, try a "soft" intervention on your own. Prepare yourself first by reading this book and other recommended books in the reading list (see p. 243). Search out your treatment options so that you know what is available, what you can afford, and what your insurance covers. Write down the facts that you have observed related to your Dependent's drinking or drug taking and practice expressing your concern in a loving, noncombative way.

When you feel ready, and when your Dependent is sober, ask her to give you a few minutes of her time. Try to talk calmly and coherently.

"Kathy, I love you, and I really care about what's happening to you. I have a problem. My problem is that I'm worried sick about your drug use." Then keep quiet—that's the hard part. You're going to be answered with denial, silence, or a willingness to listen. If you get denial or silence, you can say, "You need to know that whatever you decide to do, I'm going to get help." That's it. Don't fight, don't argue, don't say another word.

115

If your Dependent is willing to listen—if she says, for example, "What do you think I should do?"—tell her that you want her to get help. Then give her the name and phone number of a counselor or treatment center you have selected. You might even say, "Let's go to treatment; let's just get in the car and go."

The "soft" intervention gives the Dependent a chance to seek help. If she chooses not to get help, she knows that *you* are concerned and that you are going to get help for yourself. Then, when you conduct the formal intervention, you have all your bases covered. You can explain that you've tried before and it didn't work, and that's why you felt the need to get together with a professional counselor and with others who are concerned.

If you have tried such an intervention and it didn't work . . .

If you can't imagine finding the courage to face her . . .

If other members of your family disagree about the need for intervention . . .

If you are too angry, afraid, confused, hurt, or overwhelmed . . .

. . . you will want to get professional help. A professional counselor can help you in a number of ways. He or she will:

- Make sure the family *as a whole* is being treated, and that each family member receives individual help for individual problems and specific answers to specific questions.
- Bring family members together, healing divisions and allowing the family to focus on the common goal of defeating the addiction.
- Identify the family members who need additional help or counseling and refer them to appropriate individuals or agencies.
- Help family members learn how to separate the Dependent from the disease by "seeing through" the addiction.
- Handle difficult, delicate, or highly emotional situations with objectivity and calm detachment.

- Keep the process from veering off into individual squabbles.
- Maintain control in a highly emotional and volatile environment.

CHOOSING A COUNSELOR

At this writing no established network of private intervention counselors exists, and the intervention services offered at different treatment centers vary in both quality and quantity. Your best first bet is to talk to your friends at Al-Anon or personal friends or acquaintances who have been through treatment or have been involved in an intervention themselves. Another option is to call or write A.A. directly (local phone numbers are listed in the Yellow Pages under "alcoholism information and treatment centers") and explain that you're looking for a counselor skilled in intervention. The National Council on Alcoholism (NCA) and state and community alcohol and drug agencies will also recommend individual intervention counselors. Counselors from Families in Crisis (6101 Green Valley Drive, Bloomington, Minnesota 55437, (612) 893–1883) will conduct out-of-state interventions; the fee is high (over $2,000 plus air fare), and the preparation and actual intervention are conducted quickly, in an average period of six to eight hours. Families in Crisis will also refer you to a counselor in your area.

You may also want to contact the human resource department (formerly the personnel department) of your Dependent's company or your own company and ask if they offer an Employee Assistance Program (EAP) as a benefit. All contacts with EAPs are strictly confidential. (For more information on EAPs, see p. 156). Companies are becoming more progressive in their alcoholism and drug addiction benefits and some will cover several visits to a counselor.

Treatment centers are another resource, and many offer excellent counseling and intervention services. Nevertheless, we would like to offer a warning. Treatment center intervention counselors are hired by the treatment center, their job involves marketing that particular center, and their success is gauged at least in part by how many patients they bring into treatment. The danger here is that you will feel pressured to act quickly (particularly if the counseling services are offered for free) and that, having used the treatment center's counseling staff, your Dependent will be expected to enter that particular treatment center.

If you intend to use the intervention services offered by a particular center, be sure (1) that you investigate the treatment philosophy and understand the type and quality of care your Dependent will receive there (see pp. 154–156 for more information about choosing a treatment center); (2) that *your* health, as a family member, is considered a vital part of the intervention process; (3) that you have a good working relationship with the intervention counselor; (4) that you not feel rushed into actions you're not ready for; and (5) that "success" be determined not just by whether the Dependent enters treatment but also by the family's progress in recovery.

You should also check into the training and experience of the treatment center's intervention counselors. Virtually every treatment center will claim that they have intervention counselors on staff. If you ask to speak to an intervention counselor, a likely answer will be, "All our counselors do interventions." But not every treatment center has counselors specifically trained and experienced in intervention techniques. Make sure you find a professional.

WHAT TO LOOK FOR IN A COUNSELOR

You will need to find a counselor you can *trust*. Does he make you feel comfortable, or do you feel anxious and self-conscious when you talk with him? Does he truly listen to you and your concerns, or does he seem to have a hidden agenda that he wants you to follow? Do you feel you can open up with him? Do you feel calm, settled, and relaxed when you talk with him? Does he acknowledge your pain and give you credit for surviving as long as you have, or do you feel that he is judgmental and unsympathetic? Does he make you feel you are okay just the way you are, or do you feel he wants to change you? Is he patient or pushy, secure or insecure, demanding or accepting? Is he able to relate to your life? Is he able to accept critical comments from you or another family member without becoming defensive, hurt, or angry? Do you feel that, at every point in the process, you are the one who is making the decisions—that you always have a choice—or do you feel that he takes over and leads you where he wants you to go?

Annoying personal habits may come between you, making it impossible for you to trust or open up completely. Perhaps he smokes cigarettes, and you are irritated by cigarette smoke; or you smoke, and he doesn't permit it in his office. Perhaps he wears jeans and has a beard, and you are disturbed by his "unprofessional" look. Or perhaps he wears a three-piece suit and seems to you uptight and too businesslike.

The way he handles his business may also make a difference to you. Is he up front about how much he charges and when he expects payment? Is he willing to work with you if you can't afford to pay the entire fee at once?

No one else can determine who is the right counselor for you. If you do not feel comfortable with a counselor—if you cannot open up and trust him—do not hesitate to ask for a referral to another counselor. Some free-lance counselors do not charge for the initial consultation and may even suggest that the family contact one or two other counselors so that they can choose exactly whom they want to work with.

SOME QUESTIONS TO ASK

Once you locate a counselor or treatment center offering intervention services, you will want to be prepared with some questions designed to help you learn more about the counselor's experience, training, and personal approach to the disease. Here are some sample questions you might ask in your first conversation with a counselor:

- "Are you experienced in working with both alcoholics and other drug addicts?"
- "Would you mind telling me about your training and experience in intervention?"
- "How many interventions have you conducted or been involved in?"
- "What is the purpose, as you see it, of intervention?"

The intervention counselor should be knowledgeable about all aspects of alcohol and drug addiction, familiar with the addictive disease concept discussed in chapter 5, specifically trained in intervention techniques, and experienced in applying these techniques and working with families. Experience is an absolute prerequisite to selecting a counselor; after working with families, the counselor will have a firm understanding of the process, sensitivity to the fact that every family is different, and the confidence and clearheadedness needed to deal with the unexpected. And remember, *your* health and enlightenment must always be considered a major goal of both the intervention and the recovery process.

WHAT AN INTERVENTION COUNSELOR SHOULD BE

A guide. When most people call an intervention counselor, they look for answers, not more questions. They are eager to hand over their "problem" to a professional who can "fix" it and make everybody well again. Your counselor should firmly but gently advise you that she is your guide in the intervention process, helping you to move forward instead of backward and to solidify as a group instead of disintegrating into warring factions. *You* must assume both the control and the responsibility for the intervention if it is to be successful.

You and other family members are the leaders in the intervention process and will make the crucial decisions about treatment and recovery. If the counselor takes over for you and makes all the decisions about the future of your life, if she allows you to lean against her as your only support, then she is setting you up for a hard fall when she exits from your life. You are the only person who can take the responsibility for the rest of your life; don't give that precious responsibility away or allow someone to take it over, even temporarily.

An educator. The counselor should be knowledgeable about every aspect of addiction, and she should be a good teacher, able to explain to you clearly and coherently the facts about the disease and the intervention process. When she does not know the precise answer to a question, she should be willing to acknowledge that fact and refer you to a specific book, individual, or agency for an appropriate answer.

An evaluator. By listening, watching, and asking the right questions, the intervention counselor is able to evaluate the specific needs of the family members. It is her job to determine whether someone in the family needs immediate care for a problem (for example, incest or child abuse) or whether the person is capable of dealing with the problem while the intervention process continues. She will also evaluate the family as a whole, to make sure that they are agreed about the need for intervention.

The family must be made aware that intervention is an emotionally charged process that can bring into sharp focus a number of previously hidden problems and hostilities. Unexpected emotions may seem overwhelming to the family members as they focus for the first time in years on their own feelings, needs, and desires. They may experience genuine grief over the past and deep anger at what the addiction has done to them. Facing these problems and working to resolve them can be both awkward and painful, and the intervention counselor should always acknowledge the family's need to become emotionally prepared to deal with both the unexpected and the unfamiliar.

A referral center. Your counselor should continually encourage you to build up and maintain an outside support system. She should not, in other words, be the only contact or source of information you have within the alcoholism/drug addiction community. One of the intervention counselor's most important roles is to refer you and your family to appropriate sources of help, including Al-Anon and/or other support groups (see p. 249), psychologists, social workers, lawyers, and so on. She should have a detailed list of resources and be willing and able to refer you to other agencies and professionals in your community.

An ally. The intervention counselor is the family's ally and should stay on the family's side of the fence; if, at any point in the intervention process, the Dependent asks for help or counseling, the family's counselor can recommend someone else. It's too easy for the counselor to become a pawn in this high-stakes chess game, with the Dependent claiming that he was told one thing by the counselor, and the family claiming that they were told something else. By staying closely allied with the family, the counselor avoids the problems of being manipulated by one side against the other.

A professional. The counselor should always maintain a professional position and attitude. If any one member of the family seeks to sabotage the intervention, it will almost always be on the personal side; a counselor who allows herself to become emotionally involved with one or more of the family members loses the objectivity and detachment that are so essential to her role.

TIMING

Finally, a word about timing. For most families, three to four meetings held over a period of one to two months are all that is necessary to prepare for an intervention. Unless a family is completely and bitterly divided or one member of the family has severe problems that require immediate attention, there is rarely a need to continue the counseling or preparation for more than a month or two. If additional counseling is necessary, it can usually take place *after* the Dependent is in treatment.

However, if you're not ready, you're not ready, and it would do more harm than good to be pushed into acting. Unless there is an immediate crisis, your particular family situation must be the determining factor in how fast or how slowly the intervention proceeds. Every family is different, and your counselor should always maintain a healthy respect for your family's unique problems and ways of approaching them.

━━

SEVENTEEN

Coming Together

UNITED WE STAND; DIVIDED WE FALL

The intervention counselor's most crucial and pressing task is to bring the family and friends together into a cohesive group that is able to agree about the problem and the need to do something about it. Each member of the intervention "team" must be able to set aside his own problems and hesitations and join with the others in a united front. No one member of the team can be allowed to bully or browbeat the others; no one member can be permitted to sit in silent disagreement or disapproval.

Helping the family to come together is often the intervention counselor's greatest challenge. For families who have lived with an addiction are not typically healthy and whole; they have become isolated in their own pain and fear, they are not accustomed to working together to solve problems, and they find it extremely difficult to open up and talk about their feelings.

They may also bitterly resent the person who asked them to come to the meeting, the counselor, and the whole idea of intervention. It often happens that one family member (usually the initiator of the intervention) has "hit bottom" and decided that life cannot go on as it has. This person makes the initial contact with the intervention counselor and arranges for the first meeting. Other members of the family may be dragged, kicking and screaming, to that meeting; others may be suspicious of the counselor, fearful that the intervention will make things even worse, or just plain scared to death of the whole process.

Many people feel that intervention is a betrayal and an invasion of privacy. Still others fear the process because they don't think it will work ("She'll just drink until she dies, and nothing will stop her"), they see it as a threat to their own alcohol or drug use ("What if the counselor tells me that I have a problem?"), or perhaps they fear the consequences of their actions ("What if Dad cuts me out of the will?" "Will Mom ever forgive me for going behind her back like this?").

If one family member attempts to push all the rest into actions that they fear or don't believe in, the entire process can break down before it begins. Even if everyone agrees that something needs to be done, they may feel that intervention is too drastic and deceptive a solution. And sometimes the family members have no emotional connection left and thus no interest in whether the Dependent continues to drink; they just don't care anymore.

THE FIRST MEETING

Your first meeting with the intervention counselor will probably take place at his office or, if he is connected with a treatment center, at one of the center's offices. No one ever walks into this first meeting calm and collected, and the counselor's first task will be to help you relax. He may discuss the weather, or your car, or ask what you do for recreation. He is not trying to pry or to avoid the issue at hand, but to make you feel comfortable with him. He knows that if he pushes too hard, too fast, the fear and tension can overwhelm the group and destroy the trust that is so essential to the work ahead.

After five or ten minutes, when he feels that you're ready to talk about the problem, he might say to the group, "Eloise called me last week because she is worried about Randy's drinking and marijuana use. She has asked all of you to attend this meeting in an effort to find out if you are concerned, too. Would you be willing to tell me about your personal experiences with Randy's drug use and perhaps talk a bit about your concerns?"

What happens at this point tells the counselor a great deal about the cohesiveness of the group and how much work needs to be done to pull the people together. Everyone might begin talking at once, followed by giggles and nervous laughter. Or one member of the family may begin to cry, in relief, in fear, or in dread. Someone might lose his temper and lash out at someone else, or everyone may simply sit in silence, hands clasped, staring at their feet.

One method of breaking the tension is to ask the family members to complete the following short questionnaire. In addition to giving each family member some quiet time to focus on the addiction and its impact on their personal lives, the completed questionnaires give the counselor crucial insights into the family's agreement or disagreement about the problem, and even the quality of the relationships between family members.

FAMILY QUESTIONNAIRE

Answer "yes" or "no" to the following questions; on a separate sheet explain in a paragraph or more your reasons for answering yes.

1. Are drugs making your home life unhappy?

2. Does your loved one lose time from work due to drinking or drugging?

3. Does he or she use drugs because of "shyness" or fear of being around other people?

4. Does he or she express the need to drink or use drugs to build confidence?

5. Are drugs affecting his reputation?

6. Does he express remorse after drinking or drugging?

7. Does he have financial problems related to drug use?

8. Is he careless about the family's welfare when using drugs?

9. Has he dropped or changed friends, turning to people who seem more interested in drug taking and/or activities that involve drugs?

10. Has his ambition decreased as the drug use increased?

11. Has his efficiency decreased since he started using drugs?

12. Does he rationalize taking drugs at a certain time every day?

13. Does he ever drink or take drugs in the morning?

14. Does drinking or drug use cause sleep problems?

15. Has drinking or drug use jeopardized his job?

16. Does he drink or use drugs alone?

17. Does he justify drinking to escape problems?

18. Has he experienced loss of memory due to taking drugs?

19. Has he ever been treated by a doctor for drug-related problems such as ulcers, hepatitis, fatty liver, cirrhosis, pancreatitis, heart problems, seizures, et cetera?

20. Has he ever been hospitalized due to drinking or drug problems?

21. Has he had legal or police problems due to taking drugs?

The Dependent's spouse is often the person who knows the most about the drinking or drug problem; the spouse may also be responsible for hiding many details of the drug use from the rest of the family, in an attempt to protect them. When the spouse discusses her answers to the questionnaire, other family members may look utterly perplexed. "Mom, you never told me that!" someone might say. Or, "How could you have kept that a secret!" In discussing the questions and answers, it often becomes apparent to everyone that the problem is bigger than they thought, and that the addiction has isolated them from one another.

Another way to get people talking is for the counselor to say, "Tell me what Christmas [or Thanksgiving] is like at your house." Chances are good that the family members will answer with groans, moans, tears, or sad smiles. For people who live with someone who is chemically dependent, Christmas or another traditional family holiday is often the worst day of the year, the epitome of unmet expectations and crushing disappointments. Sharing the misery of past "celebrations" can help family members to see the devastating impact the addiction has had on their lives.

THE DATA BASE

Once the family members begin to open up and share their personal insights and experiences, the counselor can establish a "data base." He will want to look at the specific concerns each person has regarding the Dependent's drinking or drug use. And he will try to help the family members see how these concerns fit into a total picture. The next step is to determine if this "picture" bears any resemblance to the disease of addiction.

At this point, the counselor will need to talk about what addiction is, how it progresses, and why certain people become addicted, helping you to identify how far the disease has progressed in your Dependent, what particular drugs are being used and their specific effects on behavior, and the unique problems you, as a group and as individuals, might face in attempting to confront the addiction.

If your Dependent is addicted to cocaine, for example, you will need to know that cocaine addicts are often extremely paranoid and capable of becoming physically violent; the family needs to take precautions for their own safety. Polydrug addicts experience severe and unpredictable withdrawals and persistent craving for drugs for months and even years after treatment; the family needs to be prepared for this in the recovery period. Adolescents are often extremely hostile, defensive, and devious, and so the family needs to be particularly diligent in pulling together the facts for the intervention.

A basic problem confronting the counselor is the general misinformation and misconceptions surrounding alcoholism and drug addiction. The family needs to be able to agree on the Dependent's specific problems, but they also need to come to a common understanding about what, exactly, addiction is. So many of us are misinformed about the nature of alcoholism and drug addiction that it may take some time before an agreement can be reached.

For example, an adult son or daughter might say, "Dad is just a mean, rotten person. He's always been a loser, and if he didn't drink, he'd still be a loser. I think we should just let him drink himself to death, since that's clearly what he wants to do."

Or the Dependent's brother might say, "There's no way we can help Martha; she's got to want to help herself."

Or an adolescent might say, "Who are *you* to talk about Mom's drinking, Dad? You keep up with her drink for drink!"

Or a child might say, "I don't want to hurt Mommy."

Only by educating the family about the disease of addiction and the process of intervention can the counselor overcome the inherent misconceptions contained within each of the above statements. Rather than spending hours of time (and hundreds of dollars) educating you himself, he will ask each family member to do some work at home before the next meeting. This "homework" may consist of the following:

Reading. A real eye-opener for most families is *Under the Influence: A Guide to the Myths and Realities of Alcoholism*, by Milam and Ketcham; many counselors consider this book "must" reading and will not schedule additional sessions until every member of the intervention team has read it. *Recovering: How to Get and Stay Sober*, by Mueller and Ketcham, gives the family practical information about diagnosis, treatment, and the process of recovery. For other helpful books, see the reading list, p. 243.

Keep a journal. In the days or weeks before the next meeting, the counselor may ask each family member to keep a daily journal, writing down specific events or situations that can be tied to a drinking or drug problem. The actual event should be recorded in detail, and the observer's *feelings* should also be included. The purpose of this daily journal is (1) to show how the Dependent's behavior is directly affected by his addiction; (2) to show *patterns* developing over time (i.e., he drinks almost a quart every day; he gets belligerent around 4:00 P.M., right before cocktail time; he can't get to sleep without a pill; his hands shake when he drinks his morning coffee, et cetera); and (3) to connect the observer's own feelings (anger, sadness, guilt, fear) to the Dependent's addictive behavior.

Attend Al-Anon and Alateen meetings. Many counselors insist that each family member attend Al-Anon or Alateen meetings as a prerequisite to continued counseling. See p. 249 for addresses and phone numbers of Al-Anon, Alateen, A.A., Adult Children of Alcoholics, and other support groups. For specific information about the purpose and goals of Al-Anon and what you will experience there, see chapter 20.

TALKING THINGS OUT

As you learn more about the disease and its impact on you, your family, and your friends, it's extremely important that you feel free to express your feelings and emotions; it's equally important that these feelings be regarded as both valid and legitimate. It's the counselor's job to allow each member of the group to feel that he has a right to express his opinion and that his opinion is important, even if it is at odds with the majority opinion.

Unifying the family members doesn't come about from a dictatorial stance by the counselor, insisting that there is only one way to approach the problem, but instead from the sharing of concerns, feelings, and experiences of each member of the group, and the eventual coming to an agreement about how to proceed, based on these shared experiences. In the beginning, there may be wild disagreement; anger, fear, and distrust may be the predominant emotions. It is the counselor's job to allow these feelings to be expressed and then to help the family members focus on the addiction and understand how the addiction has pulled them apart. It is not always possible to make a fractured family whole again, but it rarely happens that the family members can't at least agree to come together to help the Dependent.

If the counselor feels that someone is holding back, he might ask, "Does anyone have any doubts about whether Randy has a problem?" At this point, the reluctant and skeptical are likely to speak up:

"I don't think it's so bad."

"I don't think we need this formal intervention stuff; we can handle it on our own."

"This whole setup is deceptive and unfair."

If one member of the group expresses fears that the intervention process is demeaning or too much like "ganging up" on the Dependent, the counselor might then ask if the family has another suggestion for combating the addiction—can Randy's problem be confronted, in other words, without this formal intervention? It sometimes happens that the family has never even approached the Dependent and suggested the need for treatment; they just always assumed he would refuse. A first step, in such a case, might be to direct one of the family members to share with the Dependent the concerns of the group and to ask, point-blank, if he would consider going into treatment. Sometimes this "mini" or "soft" intervention is all it takes, and continuing to plan for a formal intervention is unnecessary.

ALL'S FAIR IN
LOVE AND ADDICTION

In most cases a certain amount of deception is necessary. To help the family understand this, the counselor might ask the group to imagine what would happen if they simply said to the Dependent, "Mom, a group of us would like to talk to you about your drinking. May we come over Friday morning to discuss our concerns with you?" Each family member should ask himself if Mom would agree to this arrangement: Would she be there when you arrived? Would she listen?

For 99 percent of us, the answer is "no." Of course she wouldn't be there. Asking this question is often enough to make the family understand why they need to be secretive about the intervention.

Remember, you are acting out of love for your Dependent, your family, and yourself. You are being devious because the addiction is devious. You are having to wage this fight according to the ground rules established by the addiction. It's not the way you would choose to fight, but if you want to win, you'll have to turn the tables on the addiction, disarming it through surprise and deception, before it once again turns the tables on you.

OVERCOMING DENIAL

One of the most common problems dividing families is *denial*. Everyone who lives with a Dependent also lives with some measure of denial: denial that the disease exists, denial that it is getting worse, denial that it is bad enough to get worked up about.

DENIAL

The family's denial expresses itself in any number of statements:

"It isn't that bad."

"It's just social use."

"There's a lot of stress in his life."

"It's only marijuana, at least it's not the heavy stuff."

"He doesn't drink every day."

"Lots of people take a day off from work once in a while."

"If I take good care of him, he'll see how good our life really is and maybe he won't drink as much or as often."

"If I lose weight, if I learn more about football, if I agree to play the card games he likes . . ."

"He isn't as bad as my dad was."

"At least he sleeps with me."

"At least when he hits me, he doesn't draw blood."

"He only yells at the kids, he never hits them."

"He has psychological problems, that's why he withdraws into himself."

"This is just a stage he's going through."

"When he gets the right job and when the right opportunities open up, he'll be okay."

"It's just a matter of working it out for a few months, maybe a few more years. . . ."

Why are those of us who are closest to the problem also the most adamant in refusing to see or acknowledge it? Because we live, day in and day out, with the "other" side of the addiction: the loving, sensitive, passionate person who apologizes for his behavior, expresses genuine grief and guilt, begs forgiveness, and makes sincere promises to change. It's the *inconsistency* of this disease that has bewildered and paralyzed us—one day we can see the problem clearly, the next day the clouds of confusion and indecision roll in, and we're back to hoping, praying, and waiting for things to change.

Fear is the other leg holding up denial: fear of the words *alcoholic* and *drug addict* and everything they imply about the character of the victim; fear of being viewed as sick, debilitated, or "abnormal" just because we live with an alcoholic or drug addict; fear of what the neighbors will say, what the boss will do, what the insurance company will pay for, what the future will bring. . . .

These fears must be acknowledged and confronted during the counseling sessions. Often the fears can be dispelled simply by bringing them out into the open and discovering that everyone else has them, too. When everyone in the family is able to agree about the nature of the disease, its causes, symptoms, and the need for treatment, fear will be replaced by a calm determination to fight the common enemy: the addiction.

WHERE THERE'S SMOKE ...

As a ground rule, your counselor might insist that you take a look at your own drinking and drug use and make an agreement to abstain until the actual intervention. The counselor needs your full support in order to break through to the Dependent. If the family can say to the Dependent, "Your life is more important to us than anything else, and we have decided to stop our own drinking and drug taking so that we can understand what it will be like for you," then they have given the Dependent a powerful statement of support and encouragement. Actions speak louder than words.

By asking you to choose abstinence for several weeks, the counselor is not trying to pounce on you or make you the focus of the intervention; he is your ally, not your enemy. His purpose is twofold: to provide an obvious statement of support from the intervention team, and to defuse a situation in which the Dependent could use someone else's drug use to rationalize his own.

For example, during the actual intervention, the Dependent might say, "How dare you call *me* a drunk, Frank! I've seen you passed out cold; I've carried you home from parties. Don't tell me I've got a problem!"

Frank is prepared for such an assault and answers, quietly and honestly, "I am willing to take a look at my drinking, John. But today I am here to say that I am concerned about you and that I care too much about you to keep quiet."

Agreeing to a period of abstinence can be extremely difficult for some people. Addiction is a genetic disease—it runs in families. If one parent is an alcoholic, for example, there's a better than 50 percent chance the children will be; if two parents are alcoholic, the risk rises as high as 80 percent. And research shows that children of alcoholics tend to marry alcoholics. Thus, it frequently happens that one or more of the intervenors—the Dependent's brother, sister, parents, grandparents, children, cousin, aunt, or uncle—also have a drinking or drug problem.

By focusing on the Dependent and *his* problem, however, the intervention counselor will let the other family members know that she is not on a witch hunt; she is simply trying to make the clearest, strongest statement to the Dependent. Once they know that they are not on the hot seat, the other family members are often willing to take an honest, in-depth look at their own drinking and/or drug habits. At that point, a domino effect sometimes occurs, with one or more of the family members or friends making the decision to stop drinking altogether or even to enter treatment along with the Dependent. Happiness and good health can be contagious.

PEOPLE IN PAIN

The intervention process is a time for healing and recovery, and most of the people involved will slowly grow stronger, happier, and more self-confident.

But for some people the pain goes too deep and the wounds cannot spontaneously heal themselves. It is the counselor's job to identify those who need extra support or counseling and to make sure they get it. Often, these are the people who are extremely angry, belligerent, and violently argumentative; but they can also be the quiet, submissive members of the group who appear to be just fine.

The needs of these family members must not be ignored or overlooked in the emotional turmoil of conducting an intervention or in the family's haste to get the Dependent into treatment. Often an individual's serious problems with grief, anger, or fear can be eased through therapy with a psychologist or psychiatrist or regular attendance at one of the many support groups available. Your counselor can refer you to specific individuals or groups in your area.

In certain cases the needs of the family *must* be attended to before the intervention can proceed. These would include battered spouses, children, or grandparents; children with severe behavior problems, potential suicides, or nervous breakdowns. It may happen that an individual will have to drop out of the intervention in order to concentrate on his or her own health. He can then write a letter of support, like the one below, written from a father to his daughter, to be read at the actual intervention.

Dear Maggie:

I wanted more than anything to be with you today, but it did not work out that way. I want you to know how very much I love you and how concerned I have been over the years. You are so beautiful, inside and out. I know this intervention may seem harsh, but we have tried to get you help in the past and we didn't know how to do it. I talked to you about your drinking when you came to visit us last March. But you were hostile and angry. I didn't know how to tell you that we had seen you drinking from the bottle several times in the morning when you were out on the patio with your large purse. Now we know how to love you. Today, I want you to carefully consider what we are doing. We are asking you to give life a chance; to get the help you need. We are asking you to choose to get well. Please, give it a try. I love you so much.

Love, Dad

An intervention, as we've emphasized before, can have many successes. If even one family member is helped to escape from the cycle of pain and fear, the intervention can be called a success.

THE CRUCIAL LINK: LOVE

Drawing the family together, helping them to understand the disease of addiction and its impact on both the Dependent and themselves, and working with them to become a united, harmonious team are crucial first steps toward a successful intervention. But the most critical aspect of these preliminary steps is impossible to orchestrate. For whether the intervention succeeds is dependent on one quality that either exists or does not exist: *love*. The family's love gives them the emotional power to break through to the Dependent and pull him back to reality and into recovery. But love, as we've described throughout this book, becomes transfigured after years of living with the addiction; eventually, it can be destroyed altogether.

Anger, fear, shame, distrust, guilt, and grief are all symptoms of the breakdown of love. A family in pain—and all chemically addicted families are in pain—must be helped to understand where these feelings come from and how they affect their behavior so that they can get back to the love they feel for the Dependent and then *use* that love as the primary motivator in the intervention. If, instead, the family approaches the Dependent with anger and resentment as their primary emotions, the intervention will most likely fail.

The right motives for undertaking an intervention are love, caring, and concern; the wrong motives are guilt, anger, and resentment. The right motive is expressed in this statement: "I love him too much to allow this to go on any longer." The wrong motive would be expressed as: "I'm so angry at him that I refuse to take it anymore."

An intervention undertaken with the wish to inflict treatment as a sort of punishment or with the family's anger and grief used as a sort of club to beat the Dependent into submission will fail on two levels: the family will be left with their anger and grief unresolved, and the Dependent will either beat a hasty retreat, flatly refusing treatment, or agree to treatment reluctantly and without the essential emotional support of his family.

"Coming together" takes time, patience, persistence, and, most important of all, trust. You must come to trust your counselor's guidance, experience, and knowledge; you must learn to trust the other members of the group with your feelings and vulnerabilities; you must trust yourself and your ability to stand up to the painful process of self-awareness and self-growth; and you must trust the process, believing that the outcome is worth the effort you will expend to achieve it.

Without trust, you will not be able to accept the risks that come with this extraordinary and courageous effort to change your life. The risks are there, but your trust will make them acceptable and, eventually, surmountable.

EIGHTEEN

Brian

"**W**hat's going on with Brian?" Ruth was smoking a cigarette; as she raised it to her mouth, her hand trembled.

"What do you mean?" her daughter asked, keeping her eyes on the Formica pattern of the kitchen table.

Ruth watched Sarah, her always honest and outspoken oldest child, and knew she was hiding something. She wanted another drag on her cigarette but she didn't know how her shaking hand would make the long journey from the ashtray.

"Sarah, you know what I mean. Why won't you look at me?"

"I'll look at you," Sarah said, fixing her mother with a direct gaze. "See? No problem!"

"This isn't funny, Sarah."

Sarah's eyes fell again to the squiggles on the tabletop. If I look at them this way, *she thought,* they look like funny little birds; but if I turn my head, they don't look like anything at all.

"Have you noticed how much weight he's lost?" Ruth asked, trying to keep her voice calm.

"Yeah," Sarah answered.

"What do you think of his new friends?"

"I think they're jerks, that's what I think," Sarah said.

"Why?"

"Mom," Sarah's voice was a plaintive wail, "why don't you just leave this alone?"

Ruth felt as if she could hardly breathe. "Help me, Sarah," she said. "Please help me."

Sarah looked at her mother and saw the wrinkles around her eyes, the soft double chin, the graying hair . . . she was getting old, Sarah realized. She took a deep breath. "Brian has been a real creep the last six months," she said. "I can't stand to be around him. He's really a degenerate."

"What do you mean, a degenerate?"

"He's a jerk, Mom; he's a dumb, stupid kid."

"Tell me why, Sarah."

"No, Mom," Sarah said, her voice rising in anger. "You tell me why. Tell me why you think he doesn't go to youth group at the church anymore. Tell me why you think he's got these new, slick friends. Tell me why you think he dropped off the swimming team. Tell me why he comes home late at night, every night, and why he has so much trouble getting up in the morning. You tell me!" Sarah slammed her fist against the table.

"Sarah!" Ruth stared at her daughter in horror.

"Can't you see, Mom? Can't you figure it out?"

A bizarre image came to Ruth's mind: one morning several months ago she had walked into the kitchen to find a mouse trying to scramble up the side of a coffee can used for bacon drippings. The mouse was covered with grease and kept sliding back into the congealing fat. Ruth remembered the sound of its tiny feet trying to get a grip on the metal sides of the coffee can. She had pitied the poor creature; now, feeling the same desperation, she pitied herself.

"He said he dropped out of youth group because he was bored and he didn't have anything in common with the kids," she said finally.

"He was kicked out, Mom. The group leader told him to leave and not come back."

"Why?"

"Because he was arguing with everyone and jumping up and down like a yo-yo—he can't sit still, Mom, have you noticed that? Because he swore at one of the kids. Because he's a jerk."

"I don't believe it," Ruth said.

"Believe it, Mom," Sarah said in a voice without inflection. "Believe it."

"Why would he do these things?"

Sarah took another deep breath. "Drugs," she said softly.

"Drugs?" Ruth repeated.

"He's taking a lot of drugs. I think they're making him crazy."

Ruth felt the blood throbbing in her eardrums. Very slowly she said, "What kind of drugs?"

"I don't know, Mom. Ask him."

"I'm asking you, Sarah." Ruth reached across the table and took her daughter's hand. With a great deal of effort, she gave it a squeeze.

"Okay, Mom, you asked for it," Sarah said gently. "Alcohol, marijuana, cocaine, 'ludes, acid . . ."

"What are 'ludes?" Ruth said.

"Quaaludes. They're downers."

"Oh," Ruth said.

"You name it, Mom, he's taken it." Sarah looked at her mother's face and began to cry. "I'm sorry, Mom; I wish it weren't true. But he's in trouble. He's changed. Something's gone wrong."

"Yes," Ruth whispered.

Two days later Ruth found herself sitting in her living room with Len, her husband; Sarah; Bill, her ex-husband; Jan, his wife; and Tim, an intervention specialist recommended by her minister. Tim seemed a nice man, Ruth thought, watching him chat with her daughter. She hoped he wouldn't be upset with her for overreacting and playing the protective mother. She had always tried to protect Brian, ever since he was two years old and the doctor diagnosed a congenital heart defect. Everyone always told her she was too protective. Well, this time I've really done it, she thought to herself. If Brian knew about this meeting, he'd never speak to me again. She suddenly felt overwhelmed at what she *had done. How could she betray him this way? What had gotten into her? Why had she taken Sarah's word as gospel?* Sarah has always been the "good" girl, *Ruth thought.* She's a worrywart just like me.

"Ruth, would you like to explain why you felt it was important to bring us all together?" Tim said.

Ruth cleared her throat. "Well, I guess I'm feeling that maybe I overreacted," Ruth began, feeling the need to apologize to everyone for wasting their time. Sarah gave her a disgusted look, and Ruth lowered her eyes to the floor. "But, well, I guess Brian is different these days, and I'm a little concerned about him. Sarah and I had a talk the other day about Brian, and we both feel he's changed in the last six months. He's always been a likable kid, sweet-tempered, happy-go-lucky. Everyone always told us how polite he was, didn't they, Bill?" she asked her ex-husband. Bill nodded. "And he went to church every Sunday and sang in the choir. He's a good boy. He's never been a terrific student, but his teachers like him and always make a point to tell us how hard he tries."

Ruth felt herself choke up; Len, her husband, took her hand. "Brian's homeroom teacher called me a few weeks ago and told me that he's failing English and geometry. He said he will have to take summer school classes before he can graduate."

"Why didn't you tell me about this?" Bill said, his face suddenly red with anger.

"I'm sorry, Bill. I should have called you. I've been worried sick, and I just didn't know what to do."

"Go on, Ruth," Tim said.

"Well, a few months ago Brian dropped out of youth group. He told me it was because he had nothing in common with the people in the group. But Sarah told me a different story, and so I called the youth group leader. He said Brian was impossible to control. He said he argued with the other kids or laughed at things they said, or just sat there sullenly and swore under his breath. The leader told him to change his attitude or leave, and Brian left and never came back.

"Several days ago Sarah told me about a party she went

to where Brian was using cocaine. We knew he was using marijuana because a year ago when I was putting his underwear away, I found a Baggie and some cigarettes."

"Joints, Mother," Sarah interrupted.

"Oh," Ruth said, feeling suddenly like a very old woman. "Okay. I found some joints in his drawer. And we knew he was using alcohol and sometimes getting drunk—remember the party last year when we found him passed out at the top of the stairs? Sarah told us he was draining everyone's glass. Back then, we thought it was sort of funny."

"At my graduation party he drank all night long," Sarah said. "I went to bed at two A.M. and he was still drinking. I couldn't believe how much he could drink and still stand up."

"Don't forget to mention that citation he got last summer," Len said. "When the police caught him in the park with the beer. 'Minor in possession' or something like that."

"I never heard about that either," Bill said. "What's the matter with you, Ruth? Why didn't you tell me these things before everything blew up?"

"Everything's been quietly blowing up for months," Len said softly. "The kid is really getting on my nerves; haven't you noticed anything, Bill?"

"Kid stuff, for chrissakes. I mean, he's a mixed-up adolescent. That doesn't mean he's a junkie. Does it?" Bill turned to the counselor. "He's a good kid, he's just gotten in with the wrong crowd. Honestly, this whole thing is ridiculous. I can't believe we're here, talking about Brian like he's some sort of juvenile delinquent."

"Bill," his wife, Jan, said softly. "You've seen a change in Brian, too. We both have. When Brian was staying with us a few months ago, you told him he had to pay for his car's yearly registration fee and license tags. Brian has a job, and we felt he should start to take some responsibility. Well, Brian hit the roof. He screamed at both of us, he even hit his hand against the wall so hard that it knocked the mirror off and shattered it. Bill and I were furious. That's why Brian moved back in with you, Ruth."

"You told me it was because he wanted to be closer to his job at the pizza parlor."

"No," Bill said; he looked miserable. "It was because I couldn't stand to have him around anymore. I was afraid I'd hit him if he acted up like that again."

Everyone in the room was silent; they were all looking at the rug.

Finally Len spoke up. "Have you had any late night phone calls?" he asked Bill.

Bill groaned. "Oh yeah. You too?"

"They're really strange," Len said. "Most of the time it's his boss calling at two or three in the morning. The message is always the same—'Tell Brian he has something of mine that he needs to return.' But other people call, too—people we've never heard of."

"What the hell is going on here?" Bill stood up and confronted the counselor. "What's the matter with my son?"

"What do you think the problem might be, Bill?"

"You're the so-called expert." Bill's voice was rising to a scream. "You tell me!"

"But you've lived with him, Bill, you know what's 'normal' for him and what's not," Tim said gently. "I think you may have a pretty good idea what's wrong with Brian."

Bill looked at Ruth and then sat down on the couch. Tears filled his eyes; he ignored them. "Where did we go wrong?" he cried.

Two weeks later they met again. As the counselor had suggested, they'd all read some books and attended several Al-Anon meetings. Ruth had called the school principal and Brian's guidance counselor to say that she was concerned about her son and wondered if they had noticed anything unusual in his behavior. Both of them were worried about Brian's performance at school and what the counselor termed his "personality disintegration."

Ruth laughed when she described her conversation with the guidance counselor. "He went on and on about this psychological test they give all the students. The test showed that Brian is 'an *introverted thinker/perceiver.' Now you tell me, what in heaven's name is that? I mentioned drugs and the poor man acted as if I'd threatened him with a lawsuit. He insisted that Brian's problems were typical of adolescence; he told me that lots of the kids are experimenting with drugs. He said we were being too tough on Brian, that we weren't giving him the freedom to make his own decisions and to learn from his mistakes. He also said that if Brian is using drugs, then that's a symptom that something else is wrong in his life . . . and he implied that it was my worrying and snooping around that was pushing Brian away and making him act out.*

"You know, I wanted to believe him." Ruth smiled sadly. "I wanted to take that burden onto myself. I wanted so much to believe that drugs weren't a part of all this. And I had almost convinced myself that this was all a mistake. I was going to come in today and tell you that we had blown it out of proportion, that Brian really was okay, he was just working too hard, sleeping too little, playing too much.

"But then yesterday morning something terrible happened. Brian woke up in awful shape. His hands were shaking, his eyes were bright red, he was irritable and snappy. When he was about to leave the house, he said he needed a check for his license tags. I told him we wouldn't pay for the tags, that it was his car and he would have to take the responsibility. Well, he simply flipped out." Ruth's voice quavered. "He looked like a madman. He started screaming at me. He said we always make things hard on him. He said he was going to leave town and might not come back. He clenched his fists and actually bared his teeth at me. I backed up into the kitchen table; I couldn't talk or scream or anything. I just stood there, horrified, with my arms raised to protect myself."

Ruth began to cry. "Do you know what my son did? My baby boy, the sweet, gentle kid I raised and loved and protected all these years? He threw a chair at me. He just lifted it up and threw it at me. Then he turned around and left the house."

"Ruth!" Len cried. "Why didn't you tell me?"

"I was afraid you'd kill him," Ruth said quietly.

"I might have," Len admitted.

"We've got to do something," Ruth said. *"And soon. He's planning this trip to California and I have a feeling that he's not going to come back. We have to do something before he just moves out of our lives."*

"Hold on a minute," Bill said, holding up his hand as if he were directing traffic. *"Let's not rush into something we might be sorry for later. Why don't I try to talk to him, talk some sense into him. I'm his father; he'll listen to me."*

"Bill, I think that if anybody could talk to him right now, it would be you," Tim said. *"But I think that it's time we do it as a group. Brian has a lot of power when it's one on one; if everyone pulls together to talk to him, he'll get the same message from all of you. Then he won't be able to manipulate you or try to pit one against the other. You'll be a united group, with one sole purpose: to help Brian get well. And if he does decide to leave, you'll have the support of everyone in the room, knowing you've worked together and done the best you could."*

"I see your point," Bill said, trying to be diplomatic. *"But I don't see how it would hurt for me to talk to him just once more. . . ."*

Jan took her husband's hand. *"Bill, I think we need to do this together. I think we've run out of time."*

Bill put his head in his hands. His voice was tormented. *"I just don't know that we're doing the right thing."*

"Daddy," Sarah said. *"I think we'd better do it. I'm going to move out if things continue the way they have been. I can't be around Brian, and I can't be around Mom and Len the way they've been lately."*

Ruth looked shocked. *"Honey, what are you talking about? You've never said anything about this before!"*

"Brian has always been the favorite!" Sarah suddenly screamed at her mother. *"You never care about my feelings! I just come and go and it's always Brian this and Brian that. . . ."*

"That's not fair, Sarah! I love you just as much as Brian!

We've always shown you that we love you—haven't we, Bill? How could you say these things?"

"Sarah!" Bill called out to his daughter. Once again, his eyes filled with tears.

Tim gently interrupted. "It's really important that you understand that you're all out of balance because of Brian. He's had a tremendous amount of power, hasn't he? He's divided two houses; he has all of you thinking about him all the time. That's how the addiction survives—it sets people up against one another. Now it's time for us to gang up against the addiction. It's time for us to break its power."

It's nine A.M. on a Saturday. Ruth knocks on Brian's door. When he doesn't answer, she walks into his room.

"I need to talk to you," she says, gently shaking the crumpled figure on the bed.

"Oh, Mom," Brian groans. "Give me a break."

"I need you to come downstairs now, Brian."

"I gotta sleep, Mom. Stop bugging me."

"Now, Brian."

Grumbling, Brian puts on his bathrobe and walks down the stairs, his mother behind him. When he sees everyone gathered in the living room, he backs up, his hands raised above his head. "No way," he says emphatically. "No way." Behind him, Ruth gently pushes her son back into the room.

"Brian, I'm Tim Farrington. I'm a counselor," Tim says. "Your family has come to me because they are very concerned about you. Would you be willing to give them ten minutes of your time?"

"Look, what is this, anyway?" Brian says, glaring at his sister. "Did you cook this up, Sarah?"

"Brian, I think you know that your family is very concerned about you," Tim says. "They love you very much."

"Yeah, sure. I know, I know."

"They need to let you know how concerned and worried they are. Please, listen to them for just a few minutes."

Brian sits down in an empty chair. His teeth are clenched, his arms still extended outward as if to keep everyone at a safe distance. His feet tap the floor, a constant, nervous dance.

"Look, I'm fine, I can handle my life by myself," he says. "How come you're always on my back, anyway?"

"Ruth," Tim says, "would you like to go first?"

"Yes," Ruth answers, looking directly at her son. "Brian, I love you. And I'm very worried that if you leave on this trip to California, I won't see you again. And I couldn't live with that."

Ruth looks down at the written statement she has prepared and begins to read. "When you moved back in with us a few months ago, I was happy to see that you had new friends and were taking care of yourself, even to the point of taking three or four showers a day. But I gradually began to see you go from being talkative and fun to being moody and withdrawn. At times you've been hostile, even mean. You were never like that before, and I began to wonder if maybe you had a problem with drugs. I started reading about it, and things began to add up. Two months ago, I found some folded pieces of paper in your room—they were little squares cut out of the Time *magazines. I didn't think anything of it, but now I know that they're used for packaging cocaine. Then I noticed that the extra screening we keep in the garage for our screen doors and windows had holes cut out of it. I asked you about it, and you said you didn't know anything, to stop bugging you. Screens, I've discovered, are used in free-base pipes. You've been getting late night phone calls from all sorts of people and then you leave the house. In the mornings you sleep so hard that sometimes I can't wake you up. And you suddenly lost all that weight.*

"I know now that it's cocaine that is causing all these changes in you. I want you to get help before something really terrible happens. I love you, Brian. Please get some help. Please."

"Brian, are you willing to get help?" Tim asks.

"Look, man, I don't have a problem, I don't need any help," Brian says, glaring at Tim. "I can handle this on my own. Who the hell are you anyway? I'm going to California with my friends, dammit! Look, I don't have a problem, okay?" Brian's clenched *fist bangs the arm of his chair.* "Would you guys please get off my case?"

"Brian, I don't think you realize how much your family loves you," *Tim says.* "I want you to know that the last few times we've met, your father has broken down and cried. Bill, would you share your concerns with Brian?"

Bill looks at the written statement he is holding; the paper begins to shake. He puts his hand over his eyes and silently begins to sob, his shoulders shaking. "Brian," *he says in a strangled voice.* "Brian, we're going to lose you."

Brian stares at his father; he's never seen him cry before. Dad's always been the strong one, *Brian is thinking.* What's he doing crying? *Something seems to crumble inside Brian; he feels all soft and loose inside, and he begins to cry. His legs continue to jump up and down, as if they are controlled by hidden strings.*

"Come on, honey," *Ruth says.* "You've got to do this."

"Please, Brian. Please," *Bill cries.*

"Okay!" *Brian says, his voice strangled.* "Okay, okay, okay." *He folds his hands over his face and in a tiny voice repeats,* "Okay, okay, okay . . ."

Ruth puts her arms around her son. Bill walks over and gently strokes Brian's hair.

"What kind of help are you talking about?" *Brian asks, his head still buried in his hands.*

"In-patient treatment," *Tim answers.*

"How long is this treatment?"

"We're talking six weeks," *Tim says.*

Brian's head jerks up as he looks at Tim with astonishment. "But that's my whole summer!" *he cries.*

"It's a chance to break free of this, Brian," *Tim says.*

"What about my job? I'll lose my job!"

"I'll take care of it, Brian," *Bill says.* "I'll call the manager and negotiate a leave of absence."

"What about my trip to California?"

"You'll have to postpone that," *Ruth says.*

"Summer school?"

"They're willing to get the work to you," Ruth says. "You can do your studies at the treatment center. They're pulling for you, Brian."

"People at school know about this, too?"

"Yes," his mother replies.

Brian opens his mouth to say something, then closes it.

"This is a beginning, not an ending, Brian," Tim says. "It takes a lot of courage to get well."

"It's a beginning for all of us, Brian," Ruth says. "We've all been just as sick and crazy as if we'd been using drugs, too. We'll get well together."

Brian is quiet. He looks at his clenched hands. He's thinking about his deals; his clients; his trip to California and the ounce of cocaine that's waiting for him there. He's thinking about the grams he promised his friends and how angry his boss is going to be when he loses his cocaine connection. He won't hire me back, Brian thinks. Hell, he'll drop me like a hot potato!

As Brian gets dressed and packs a suitcase, he thinks about the two grams taped under his car's dashboard. He wonders how he can manage to get a snort or two before they haul him away.

Maybe I can go back to doing lines, he thinks as he gets in the car. I was getting ready to cut back on the free-basing anyway. Maybe they won't find the gram in my shaving kit.

The car turns onto the highway. Maybe they'll see that I don't have a problem and let me out early. Maybe I can get out on good behavior or something and still make the trip to California.

No problem, he thinks, settling back in his seat. I'll be out in a few days. He smiles to himself, and as his jittery legs keep time, he continues to repeat to himself, No problem. No problem. No problem . . .

NINETEEN

Dealing with the Real World

What problems are you likely to encounter as you move through the intervention process? What kind of plans will you need to make in order to have everything work smoothly? In this chapter we will discuss the most common problem areas for families and offer some suggestions for resolving them.

COSTS

A major concern for most families is "How are we going to pay for counseling and treatment?" Treatment for chemical dependency is covered by most employee insurance programs, but if you and your spouse are not working or do not have insurance, money can become a very real and pressing problem.

The average intervention involves three to four sessions with the intervention counselor; while rates vary, you can count on an average total fee of $200 to $300. If the intervention counselor charges for phone calls, phone time, travel time, and other incidentals, your costs will be higher.

If you meet with a private intervention counselor and believe that you can't afford her services, she will refer you to a private, in-patient treatment center where the counseling sessions are either free or are included in the total treatment fee and thus covered by insurance. If you do not have insurance, the counselor will discuss the options available to you: outpatient treatment, available through state or local alcoholism and drug centers on a sliding fee scale; state or county detoxification centers, also on a sliding fee scale; and regular attendance at Alcoholics Anonymous meetings. If the Dependent decides to try A.A. without any other kind of treatment, the family should get his agreement to a "90-90" plan—ninety meetings in ninety days.

Another option for families to consider is to split the cost of counseling and treatment among themselves. In-patient treatment can range from $2,000 to $12,000 for a twenty-eight-day stay. If ten people agree to split a total treatment fee of $4,000, the cost to each person would be $400. This is a workable alternative for many families.

When you are working out the financial details of treatment and recovery, remember the long-term savings. Supporting an alcohol or drug addiction is extraordinarily expensive. In addition to the cost of the drug itself (which, when you're addicted, can be a hefty daily amount), you've got medical bills, legal bills, loss of income due to losing a job, et cetera. In the long run, the family will save a lot of money. Don't be afraid to borrow from friends or family, dig into savings, or take out a loan if you do not have the insurance or available cash to pay for treatment.

People with terminal diseases would give up everything they owned if they could somehow buy back their good health. Your Dependent's disease isn't terminal, yet . . . you can buy back his good health. And your health is involved here, too. By getting help for yourself and your Dependent, you're investing in the quality of the rest of your life. Nobody can put a price on that.

TIME

When is the best time to do an intervention, and how long should it take? As soon as possible and as quickly as possible—but not before you are fully prepared and emotionally committed. Some experts insist that you put everything else aside and push through the intervention process as quickly as possible in order to get help for your loved one. The reasoning is that something drastic might happen to the Dependent during the time the family is planning the intervention; as the planning and preparing continue, chances of a crisis occurring increase.

These are realistic concerns, but always keep in mind that *your* recovery is a priority in this process. If you need additional counseling to work out your pain, grief, and fear, and if you need it *now*, before the actual intervention, do not allow yourself to be pushed faster than you can safely go. You will want to trust your counselor's advice here. If she suggests that the intervention wait while you or one of your family members gets help for a problem, please, do as she says. She is concerned about you and your Dependent, and she has the objectivity, expertise, training, and intuition to know when your needs are a priority. Trust her to guide you in the right direction.

Your counselor will also help you to design an emergency plan, in case a crisis does occur while you are in counseling.

WHAT TO DO IN A CRISIS

Emergencies happen to alcoholics and drug addicts all the time, and you will need to have a plan in motion in case it happens to your loved one. Your Dependent might fall down the stairs drunk and break his leg; his doctor may hospitalize him for cirrhosis; he may be seriously injured in a car collision; he may threaten suicide or homicide; or he might wake up one morning, feeling horrible, and calmly say, "I've had it. I need help."

If such an event occurs, your counselor will encourage you to get all the treatment details worked out so that you can take the Dependent directly to treatment. Some intervention counselors pay a monthly fee to a twenty-four-hour crisis line to give their clients continual access to emergency help.

PREGNANCY

When a pregnant woman drinks or takes drugs, her fetus ingests them, too; the difference is that the fetus has even fewer defenses against the drugs' toxic effects. Large doses of alcohol taken during pregnancy are known to cause a condition called *fetal alcohol syndrome,* which can include such devastating symptoms as mental retardation; central nervous system disabilities; learning disabilities; irritability; speech problems; hyperactivity; facial malformations (small head, flattened nose, narrowed eyes, short receding chin); organ malfunctions; kidney, urinary, heart, and muscle abnormalities.

If the Dependent is pregnant and drinking and/or drugging, get immediate help; her baby's life is in serious danger.

MAKING PLANS FOR TREATMENT*

Decisions about treatment should be made right in the beginning of the intervention process. During the first meeting, your counselor will describe the various treatment options available and recommend several nearby facilities. She should leave the final choice of a facility to you, since you are the one who has to live with the consequences of that choice.

Research the various options, ask specific questions about

---

*For detailed information on the different types of treatment available for chemical dependencies and how to select a specific treatment center, see chapters 7 to 14 of *Recovering: How to Get and Stay Sober.* (Mueller and Ketcham).

the treatment center's staff and philosophy of treatment, visit different centers to get a "feel" for each program and place, look into the costs and make your plans for financing; and then make sure a bed is available for your Dependent on the day you expect to conduct the actual intervention.

QUESTIONS TO ASK
IN-PATIENT TREATMENT PROVIDERS

Take notes. Time, date called, name of person you talked to.

Have all insurance information ready. You will need the insurance company name, plan number, individual policy number, name of company worked for, name of person the policy covers, social security number, birthdate, address, et cetera.

1. How long (days, weeks) is the program? Is it longer for drugs other than alcohol? How much longer?

2. What is the total cost of the program and are there any additional charges?

3. How much does your insurance plan cover and what would be the balance owed? What financial arrangements can be made for that balance (or for the whole amount, if you are not insured)?

4. After checking the insurance coverage, what percentage of the balance due must be paid in advance or when the patient is admitted?

5. Is there a waiting list? Are there only certain times during the day that a patient can be admitted? Are patients admitted on weekends?

6. What does the family program involve and is there an extra charge for this program?

7. How many beds are there in the treatment center, and how do the ages break down? (Some programs have a higher percentage of either young people or older people, and matching ages can be an important consideration.)

8. Does the center have a medical staff? (If the treatment center is located in a hospital, it will have a medical staff.) Are detoxification services available? If not, what plans are made for detox?

9. Does the program emphasize the importance of A.A. and require attendance at meetings both while in treatment and after discharge?

10. How often is the family able to visit?

11. Is there a follow-up for patients and family? If the person is from out of town, what arrangements are made for that? How long is the aftercare program for the patient? And how long is aftercare for the family?

As you consider your options, be sure that you select a treatment center that:

- Emphasizes the physical nature of addiction.
- Involves the family in the treatment program and emphasizes the need for the whole family to recover.
- Follows A.A.'s Twelve Steps and makes A.A. attendance a mandatory part of the program.
- Offers detoxification and medical care if your Dependent is late-middle stage or late stage, polydrug addicted, suffers from complicating diseases such as cirrhosis, heart disease, or diabetes, or has had convulsions, hallucinations, or D.T.s in the past.

CONTACTING THE EMPLOYER

Your counselor will be able to advise you about the wisdom of contacting your Dependent's employer. If the company offers an EAP (Employee Assistance Program), you're in luck. All

EAPs maintain strict confidentiality, their personnel are specifically trained in chemical dependency issues, and they are typically eager to help. The EAP can initiate a medical leave—again, in full confidence—help you with the insurance details, and even provide referrals to individual counselors and/or treatment centers.

If the company does not have an EAP, call the human resources department or the personnel department and ask (anonymously) what the company's policy is regarding alcoholism and chemical dependency and, specifically, what kinds of coverage they offer. Or you can call the insurance company directly and ask the same questions.

In certain cases it may not be a good idea to contact the employer. If your Dependent drinks regularly with his boss; if a promotion is in the works; if you know that the company has summarily fired other employees who had a drinking or drug problem . . . then secrecy may be a good idea. Whether you decide to talk openly with the employer or keep the intervention a secret, your counselor will warn you to never use labels such as "alcoholic" or "drug addict" in connection with job performance. Civil liberties issues may be involved here, and people have sued their companies for defamation of character due to being publicly labeled an "alcoholic" or "addict."

You will want to talk, instead, about problems at work and concerns about specific work-related or job-performance issues. Again, trust your counselor to help you work out the details and the precise terminology.

TELLING FAMILY AND FRIENDS

During the process of the intervention, it may be a good idea to keep the lid on. Secrecy is often important to the goal of getting the Dependent into treatment; while interventions can and do work if the Dependent finds out about the family's plans beforehand, they also lose much of their shock value. When the Dependent walks into a room, completely unaware, his defenses are down and he is extremely vulnerable. Often the intervention needs this vulnerability in order to break through the Dependent's defenses and denial.

If you feel that your friends or family members who are not involved with the intervention might disapprove of or disagree with your actions, don't tell them what you are doing. Don't set yourself up for arguments, squabbles, or well-intentioned attempts to talk you out of the intervention. Many people are misinformed and think that interventions are a cruel deception, a mental beating-up session, or a confrontation between bitter enemies. You do not want to put your energy, at this point, into changing the minds of the ignorant or misinformed. That can come later, when you and your Dependent are well into recovery.

CONTACTING YOUR PHYSICIAN

Physicians are sometimes Enablers: they allow the underlying disease to continue while treating the symptoms of depression, insomnia, nervousness, anxiety, stress, ulcers, liver and heart disease, et cetera. In the past, medical schools put less emphasis on alcoholism than on various tropical diseases, and medical students' experience consisted of observing late-stage, skid-row alcoholics in detoxification or mental health wards. This is changing, but many of the physicians practicing today have had little or no education about chemical dependency or training in how to diagnose and treat these patients.

Physicians, like many of the rest of us, are often misinformed about the disease of addiction and its victims. If you have ever approached your family physician before about your Dependent's drinking or drug problems and he responded by saying, "He should cut down," or, "Let's keep an eye on that," or, "Perhaps a tranquilizer will help his anxiety," or, "I'll refer him to a psychiatrist for evaluation," you will want to find a more enlightened physician.

The intervention counselor is in continual contact with physicians who understand alcoholism and drug addiction, are skilled at diagnosis, and have been trained to recognize the symptoms of the family disease; ask for a referral if you feel you need one.

The family also will need to be prepared if the Dependent claims that his doctor knows all about his drug habits and has told him he's in fine physical shape. In such a case it is often a good idea to have the counselor respond with a statement like, "Dr. Anderson is a fine doctor, but it's my guess that he doesn't know all the details about your drinking." If the Dependent continues to argue, the counselor should gently ask him to listen and give his family a chance to express their love and concern.

WHAT ABOUT THE CHILDREN?

Deciding whether to include the children in the intervention depends to a great extent on the individual child's emotional stability. In general, it isn't a good idea to include children under eight or nine years old. Infants are unpredictable and noisy; their cries can seriously disrupt the momentum of the intervention. Toddlers can be difficult to handle or control, and four-, five-, six-, and seven-year-olds often do not have the emotional maturity to handle the "what ifs" inherent in the intervention process. For example, a six-year-old can be devastated by the mere suggestion that Daddy might have to leave the house if he refuses to get help; he cannot intellectually grasp the need for such a dire consequence.

Eight-, nine-, and ten-year-old children have been included in interventions and handled the emotions beautifully. But again, it all depends on the individual child and the family's relationships and interaction with the child. Once a child reaches the age of ten or eleven, however, he should be included *if he wants to be*. Older children have been firsthand witnesses to the ravages of the addiction; they should be allowed to be firsthand witnesses and participants in the healing process. Many families are concerned about exposing the child to the sordid details of the drinking or drugging; many feel that they've been able to protect the children and keep them from seeing the worst of what has gone on. But silence filled with fear, anger, and sadness is sometimes worse than outright warfare. And the older child, although he may not be able to verbalize his feelings, has nonetheless been feeling a great deal.

Intervention may mark the first time the family has been honest, open, and outspoken about their feelings. The children deserve to be included in this process of growth and recovery. They need to know that conflict can be healthy and normal and loving. They need to hear the love and concern expressed as an antidote to all the poisonous exchanges of the past.

Whether the child speaks at the intervention should be left up to him. He should know that if, at any point in the process, he wants to back out or stay silent, he has the right to do so. In the actual intervention, the counselor can say to him, "Jimmy, would you like to say anything to your mommy?" And Jimmy can choose to be silent or say something simple and unprepared like, "I love you, Mom, and I want you to get help."

Simple messages straight from the heart can break down seemingly impregnable barriers. And expressing those heart-felt messages can begin the healing process for the child.

WHAT ABOUT OUR MINISTER?

Alcoholics and drug addicts have traditionally been treated by the clergy as sinners. If your minister, priest, or rabbi attempts to lecture you about the sins of drunkenness, the glories of moderation, or the saintliness of staying with your spouse no matter how desperate the situation, you should understand that he doesn't know enough about the disease to help you.

An enlightened minister can guide you to A.A., counseling, and treatment, and give you comfort, solace, and support in your recovery; an unenlightened minister can wrap you up in thick layers of guilt and righteousness and paralyze you with conflicting emotions. You are lucky to be one of the educated;

find support where you can and do not be afraid to extricate yourself from those situations and individuals who would put a dead weight on your spirit out of their own ignorance.

HERE WE GO AGAIN

Your Dependent has gone through treatment before and has relapsed. What do you do now? You need to know, first, that all is not lost; and second, that treatment techniques have come a long way in the last ten years. The specific treatment that the Dependent received may in fact be part of his problem. If your Dependent was "treated" by a psychiatrist who spent years trying to discover the deep, dark reasons for his addictive behavior; if, over the years, his physician has given him sedatives, tranquilizers, painkillers, or mood elevators; if he survives on coffee, candy, and fast foods; if he has always seemed worse off sober than drunk . . . then his treatment was seriously lacking.

Relapse is always a possibility with a chronic disease such as addiction, even after years of good health and sobriety. The Dependent must be helped to understand the physical nature of his disease and the need for ongoing, continual support through Alcoholics Anonymous and healthy lifestyle habits such as following a good, nutritious diet, exercising regularly, and learning how to rest and relax. He may need to unlearn some of the misinformation he learned in his first treatment. And if he has been drinking or drugging heavily, you should firmly recommend that he agree to in-patient treatment.

FAILURE

Everyone involved in an intervention worries about failure. What if the whole thing falls apart, and people start yelling and screaming at each other, pointing fingers of blame, swearing they'll never forgive each other—what then?

The process of intervention is designed to avoid just that scenario. With adequate preparation and the guidance of a skilled and experienced counselor, you cannot fail. For what, really, is failure? Failure can only be defined as doing nothing and allowing the disease to continue to swallow up everything you value and everyone you love. If you do something, even if it does not result in a storybook ending, you are taking the initiative and pulling away from the power of the addiction. That, in and of itself, is a success.

Intervention is not an ending but a beginning. It is a process of healing rather than hurting, of coming together rather than dividing and isolating. It is not an expression of hate but a declaration of love. By helping you to step into the light rather than hide out in darkness, an intervention will dispel ignorance and confusion and put an end to guilt and shame.

For at the heart of intervention is awareness. Once you become involved in the process of intervention, you also become *aware* of the real facts of your life. You become aware of the help available to you. You become aware of the steps you need to take away from the past and into a healthy present.

There is no turning back from this awareness. *Now you know.* You know you have a choice. You know that you have power. And you hold in your own hands the responsibility for the rest of your life.

Knowledge is a wondrous thing. Once you have it, you can't lose it, deny it, or pretend it doesn't exist; it can only grow and expand, clearing away at long last the clouds of confusion and fear, guilt, and grief.

- Knowledge promotes understanding.
- Understanding promotes healing.
- Healing promotes health.
- Health promotes happiness.
- Happiness promotes joy in living.

Within such a structure, failure has no meaning.

TWENTY

The Al-Anon Connection

You have undoubtedly had moments in your life when you felt overwhelmed with a sensation of peace, serenity, or joy. If you were able to isolate the moment and look at it, as if it were crystallized and could fit in the palm of your hand, you would be able to say, "This is happiness. For this moment, I'm happy."

For many of us, Al-Anon provides those isolated moments of peace, serenity, and joy that we can call forth later, when life is not so placid and undisturbed. Al-Anon is more than the lessons we learn there, the experiences we have there, or even the people we meet there. All of these combine to create a feeling, intangible and indescribable, of hope, joy, and peace of mind.

THE STRUCTURE

Al-Anon is a self-help group with one basic message: "Take care of yourself." Al-Anon, like A.A., is a spiritual program with practical consequences. By listening to what others have to say about their lives, you gain a sense of fellowship and belonging. By sharing your own experiences, you renounce your isolation and loneliness. And by looking inside, to the very center of your being, you will come to know yourself and to know what is essential to your happiness. You will learn about trust, honesty, humility, forgiveness, courage, and love. You will learn how to "try on" these spiritual values and become comfortable with them, strengthening the inner core—the heart—of who you are.

In Alcoholics Anonymous, Al-Anon, and Alateen, the Twelve Steps provide a basic structure; these steps are used as guides to help you develop and grow as a human being.

THE TWELVE STEPS OF A.A.

1. We admitted we were powerless over alcohol—that our lives had become unmanageable.

2. We came to believe that a Power greater than ourselves could restore us to sanity.

3. We made a decision to turn our will and our lives over to the care of God as we understood Him.

4. We made a searching and fearless moral inventory of ourselves.

5. We admitted to God, to ourselves, and to another human being, the exact nature of our wrongs.

6. We were entirely ready to have God remove all these defects of character.

7. We humbly asked Him to remove our shortcomings.

8. We made a list of all persons we had harmed, and became willing to make amends to them all.

9. We made direct amends to such people wherever possible, except when to do so would injure others.

10. We continued to take personal inventory and, when we were wrong, promptly admitted it.

11. We sought through prayer and meditation to improve our conscious contact with God as we understood Him, praying only for knowledge of His will for us and the power to carry that out.

12. Having had a spiritual awakening as the result of these steps, we tried to carry this message to alcoholics, and to practice these principles in all our affairs.

What do you have to do at Al-Anon? Nothing. You do not have to talk or "testify" about your life—you can go to a hundred meetings and never say a word. There are no requirements about how many meetings you must attend. You can go to one meeting a month or three meetings a day. You don't have to become a "member" of a certain group; in fact, many people try out different groups in order to meet new people and gain new perspectives.

The meetings take place in church halls, hospital conference rooms, community alcohol centers, and store basements. Some of the rooms are beautifully decorated; others are dark and dingy. Some meetings are huge, with fifty people or more seated in row after row of chairs; others are small, with ten to twelve people seated in a circle. Some meetings are formal, with one or two speakers addressing the group; others follow no set pattern, and people simply talk or listen, as they choose. Some meetings are open only to smokers or to nonsmokers; some are open only to men or to women.

If you are traveling to a different city, call the Al-Anon number listed in the phone book and ask for information. No one will care that you're a stranger in town. In Al-Anon there is no such thing as a stranger, for everyone who has lived with a Dependent is a kindred spirit.

As a newcomer to Al-Anon, you might expect a group of unsmiling, tight-lipped people who, in angry and bitter words, describe the pain of their lives. Nothing could be further from the truth. If there is one common denominator to all meetings, it is laughter. In Al-Anon, your anger, bitterness, and despair will melt away, and you will find yourself leaning forward in your chair, listening to stories so much like your own that your jaw will drop in astonishment. You will laugh, you will cry, and you will feel that you have found a home.

Many people wonder how long you have to go to Al-Anon. The answer is that you go for as long as you want to go. For most of us, that's forever. But the decision is yours—no one will call you, recruit you, or pressure you in any way. You are responsible for your life; Al-Anon celebrates your responsibility.

LETTING GO

The following true story illustrates the concept of "letting go," the philosophical foundation of Al-Anon.

■

Lorraine looked around at her grown children and felt a cold chill chase through her body. They looked like strangers, she thought; worse, they talked like strangers.

"You have to get help for Dad," her children were saying. "He's going to die if we keep covering up for him."

"What do you expect me to do?" she asked, trying to keep her voice calm. Inside, she was shaking violently; it was as if her body temperature had lowered twenty degrees.

"Get help for yourself."

"Stop calling the office and making excuses when he's too sick from a hangover."

"Leave him," her oldest son said coldly.

Lorraine recoiled as if he'd struck her. "Leave him?" she cried. "How could I leave him now? How can you dare to ask me to desert a sinking ship?"

Silence mixed uneasily with the tension in the room. Then one of her children started to laugh; it sounded as if she were choking. "Mother," she said finally, "do you realize what you just said?"

Lorraine first looked confused, then her face froze in horror. He is a sinking ship! *she thought.* And I'm ready to go down with him—I'm ready to die with him, knowing there's no hope, never having lived my life! *Her face crumpled, and she began to sob.* "What a mess I've made of my life," *she cried.* "What can I do? Who can help me?"

■

Lorraine had been taught by her parents, teachers, friends, and ministers that you give everything you've got for the people you love and when there's nothing left to give, you give that, too. Don't give up; stick with it through thick and thin; life isn't always easy or fair; don't expect every day to be a joyride; remember the wedding vows "in sickness and in health till death do us part"—these were the tried and true lessons of her life. She hadn't realized that by blindly following these general rules, she had stopped thinking, long ago, of her own needs. Thinking about yourself is selfish, she'd been taught; any satisfaction you can find in this life must come through sacrificing your needs for the needs of others.

In the intense emotional encounter with her children, Lorraine suddenly realized that she had a lot of unlearning to do and a lot of new learning to take its place. She was too confused to do it by herself; she needed help, and she went to Al-Anon. "Al-Anon saved my life," she said six years later.

What did Lorraine learn through Al-Anon? What did Al-Anon do for her that she could not have done for herself? The single most important thing that attending Al-Anon meetings accomplished for Lorraine was to pull her out of the emotional and social isolation that had developed from years of living with the disease of addiction. At Al-Anon meetings, Lorraine watched and listened to others who had had many of the same experiences she had been through; she learned to trust people again and to become emotionally involved with others; she felt a structure growing in her life, based on new feelings of self-respect, friendship, and confidence. Eventually, she learned to laugh and cry again and to help others with her own experiences and acquired strengths.

Lorraine learned that only by "letting go" of her alcoholic husband could she hope to save herself; but it took years and hundreds of Al-Anon meetings for her to understand the multitude of lessons within the one experience of "letting go." In learning how to let go, she had to learn how to detach herself from the person she loved and needed most in the world; how to deal with her guilt and grief; how to forgive him and forgive herself; how to stop trying to control the people and events in her life; how to let the past slip away and the future follow its own course; how to recognize certain emotions—fear, anger, guilt, resentment, shame—as harmful and counterproductive; and, finally, how to focus on her own needs and desires.

A COMMITMENT TO A WAY OF LIFE

Letting go is more than a single action or even a series of actions: it is a commitment to a way of life, and it requires a fundamental turnaround in the way most people approach life situations. Imagine yourself in a grocery store, pressed for time (your husband is waiting for you to pick him up at work), harried (the kids are sitting in the cart and threatening to dump the salt), and irritable (the lady behind you just ran over your foot with her cart). You're in the express checkout lane, with the large red sign that says "Eight items or less." But the man in front of you has fourteen items in his cart—you counted them twice, feeling the anger begin to boil inside. Should you say something to him?

You shift angrily from one foot to another, mumbling to yourself about inconsiderate, thoughtless people. You slap your three-year-old's hand when she reaches for a magazine; you give the checkout person a dirty look; the muscles in your back and neck bunch up. When you're finally through the line, you rush out the door, bump your child's head trying to get her into the car seat, bang the car door against the shopping cart, chipping the paint, and speed out of the parking lot, kids screaming, heart racing, to face a series of red lights, more frustration, more bunched muscles, and the beginning of a whopping headache.

Learning how to let go can begin with something as simple and commonplace as this experience in the grocery store. Instead of allowing yourself to get caught up in the whirlwind cycle of anger and frustration, try practicing the philosophy of letting go. When you begin to feel angry, stop the emotion by asking yourself (1) what good it would do you and (2) what purpose it would achieve. "So big deal," you say to yourself, "I'll be three minutes longer in the store . . . what's three minutes?" You smile at your children and they smile back. The woman behind you (the one who ran over your foot) smiles at you, too. You pick up a magazine and find an interesting article. You look outside at the sun shining and think about planting your garden. The man in front of you with his fourteen items doesn't matter at all, and you're through the line before you know it.

Learning how to let go often begins with these little annoyances in life; with much practice, the lessons can be generalized to the bigger problems that must be confronted in everyone's life. Every Christmas for the last ten years you've visited your husband's family for several days; these visits are always, without fail, unhappy, tense, and stressful. This year, you let go by saying "no." Your family, you explain, has decided to stay home and begin your own holiday traditions. Your mother-in-law acts surprised and hurt; you understand her emotions but trust her to work them out herself. You deal with your guilt and anxiety by knowing that you are finally beginning to meet your own needs rather than trying (and inevitably failing miserably) to meet everyone else's.

Suppose your cocaine-addicted husband tells you he spent the rent money on an all-night poker game; he asks you to make up some excuse to mollify the landlord. You've done this before and you've always felt angry, frustrated, and ashamed.

This time you say "no" to your husband, explaining gently but firmly that it's his responsibility to approach the landlord since he spent the money. When he rants and raves, accusing you of not loving him, you let go of your guilt and fear by telling him that your love won't pay the rent. You love him enough, you tell him, to stop making excuses for him. If he loses the rent money, it's his responsibility to approach the landlord.

At five o'clock one evening, your wife comes downstairs, drunk, and in a loud voice tells you that she won't go to the Fosters' dinner party because she can't stand all those snobby, pretentious people. You gently cut her off, saying, "Fine, stay here; you'll be okay by yourself." She stares at you with great fury and then says, "You're not going without me, are you?" Calmly, refusing to be drawn into an argument, you answer that the dinner party is important to you and that you're going because you want to go. You're not trying to teach her a lesson or to "get even" with her; you simply feel that your life has to continue on a normal track, regardless of what she does with her life.

Letting go is making the decision to act in your own interests, to think about your own needs, regardless of what your Dependent decides to do or what impact your actions may have on him. In order to meet your needs, you will undoubtedly upset and anger the Dependent and, possibly, other people in your family. Al-Anon provides the support system you will need to make the tough decisions and not give in yet again to guilt and fear. Al-Anon helps you to take responsibility for yourself and for the direction of your life and to let go of the feeling that you are responsible for what other people do with their lives.

But the only way to understand the teachings and experience of Al-Anon is to attend meetings—not just one or two, but several dozen. Read the books and articles available at meetings, talk openly, listen to what others have to say, and, when you're ready, share your own experiences. If you feel uncomfortable in a certain group, try another; even small towns offer two or three different meetings each week. After a few months, take some time to think about what you've learned and experienced at Al-Anon. How have you grown and changed? In what ways has your life changed? Do you feel more confident? Do you feel less confused and alone?

Only you can decide how to approach and work through your problems. No one can or should tell you what to do. But don't attempt to go it alone. It's not that you can't make it without Al-Anon or outside support systems; but your struggle will be more strenuous. You can learn all the important lessons without attending one Al-Anon meeting; but you will have to work harder, for a longer time. You can tough it out by yourself, without the help, support, shared wisdom, and understanding of others suffering with the same problem—but the price of being alone is too often confusion, fear, and devastating crises of self-confidence.

You have been alone too long, and it has not been a happy or productive loneliness. Accept the help that is available to you, and your pain and confusion will gradually lessen as your confidence and self-respect increase. That's a promise.

TWENTY-ONE

My Dad

"**D**ad, let me tell you first what I remember of how it used to be. I remember how handsome you were—you had thick dark hair, deep brown eyes (no red in them, then), strong arms. I remember you the best in the summer. You would come in from the golf course and see me at the pool—and yell, for everyone to hear, "Hullo, Kitten!" As if there were no one else there. You would walk to me and throw your arms around me, and laugh. Everyone would watch us and smile. You were so healthy, so alive! And you loved me so much.

I remember when you told me that Dusty, our cat, had been hit by a car. You took me to Hanson's Restaurant, and you held my hand when I cried. I never wanted to leave there because you held on to me so tight. It was just the two of us, no one else, and we weren't in a hurry to go anywhere. It was summer and we were in shorts and T-shirts, and as sad as I was about Dusty, I knew I would always have you.

Kim took a deep breath and stared out the window. The leaves were falling off the trees; summer seemed a long time ago. The summer she was describing was only eight years ago, but it seemed as if it were part of a dream. Tomorrow was her sixteenth birthday.

172

"Oh, Daddy," she said to herself. "Where are you? Where have you gone?" She sighed and, setting her jaw tight, continued to write:

"I watched you on the couch the other night. The bottle was empty, and you were snoring, your mouth wide open and your tongue hanging out to the side. You were drooling. I made myself look at your face because I needed to fix it in my mind that this is what alcohol and drugs have done to you. I must always remember that the drugs are my enemies. I hate the drugs. I love you, still."

Kim frowned and reread what she had written. Maybe I shouldn't put that in about hating the drugs, *she thought.* Maybe the word *still* isn't quite right; after all, I'll always love him; how could I stop loving him? *Kim shrugged and decided that she would ask her counselor about the right words to use.*

She had been seeing Sharon, a counselor who specializes in family problems, for three months, and this letter to her father was one of the exercises her counselor had suggested. "Get your feelings down on paper, Kim," Sharon had said to her. "Document those specific instances when you've been concerned about your father's drinking and drug taking. This will help you to understand the extent of the problem; once you understand your father's illness, you will be better able to help him."

Kim didn't think there was much they could do for her dad, particularly since no one else in the family would even talk about his drinking. Her older brother was in college and never came home anymore; he just seemed to have disappeared three years ago. Once a year, at Christmas, he would call and talk for ten minutes. Her mother acted as if nothing were wrong, picking up after her father, putting him to bed, calling the doctor for more prescriptions, buying the bottles for him because he was usually too sick or too drunk to go out himself. Her mother even poured him drinks at night when he was too unsteady to pour his own.

"Why?" Kim had asked her once. "Why are you helping him to die?"

"Sweetheart," her mother said, stroking Kim's hair, "try to

understand that Daddy is sick, and he's even sicker when he doesn't drink. He had a seizure two years ago when he tried to quit and then he was in the hospital for almost two weeks." She noted the hostile expression on her daughter's face. "You wouldn't understand, Kim," she said in a strange voice.

But Kim did understand: her mother was helping her father to kill himself. She sometimes hated her mother, hated her so much she felt sick inside; and then she hated herself for being so cruel and spiteful. Three months ago, Kim had tried to commit suicide by taking twenty-eight—she had counted them—of her father's sleeping pills. After a week in the hospital, her doctor had asked Sharon to see her. Now they met three times a week.

Kim read again what she had written and then, concentrating hard, tried to remember what her father had looked like, lying drunk on the couch. "Be detailed," Sharon had told her. "Present the facts as you understand them. And be sure to put your feelings in there, too—your anger, your sadness, your embarrassment . . . put it all down."

On a new sheet of paper, Kim wrote:

> *"I looked at your gray hair. It used to be so shiny black. I saw the stubble on your face; when I would kiss you, all those years ago, your face was always so smooth and clean. You always smelled to me like the woods behind our house after a rainfall—clean and fresh and sparkling. But now your face is red and blotchy, your nose almost purple and covered with little red veins, your skin saggy and loose. In that face, I can't find any part of the person I remember. I don't know who you are."*

Kim's mind flipped back again to those years that seemed so long ago, before her whole life was consumed with thinking and worrying about her father.

> *"I'm remembering back again, Daddy. I'm remembering the first time I saw you drunk. I was in grade school. I had a friend spend the night, and you embarrassed me so much. I thought I was going to die of shame. Nothing you said*

*made any sense at all. After that, I didn't have friends
spend the night unless I knew you and Mom were going to
be out.*

*Then in junior high you insisted on driving John Saybrook
and me to the movies. You had a beer can wedged between
your legs, and you were weaving in and out of the lanes. I
was so frightened I asked you to slow down and pull over.
You yelled at me to shut up. After you dropped us off, I was
so afraid that you were going to get in an accident. I
worried about you all through the movie.*

*That was about the time my friends started asking, "Is
your Dad okay?" I remember thinking what a funny word
"okay" was. What did it mean? I knew you weren't okay,
but I didn't know what you were. That's about the time I
started to put up a huge wall between you and me, for
protection. I needed to protect myself from you—and you
had always been my protector!*

*I think I grew up awfully fast. I remember how afraid I
was that you would have a seizure or start staring blankly
out at space, unable to move or speak or even smoke your
cigarette. This is the most horrible thing I've ever seen. You
look so vulnerable and scary when your face is all contorted.
I always have to look away to keep myself from crying.*

*You always said I was mean to you in the morning when
you would say, "Good morning, Kim, it's time to get up."
It was because I was punishing you for getting drunk the
night before.*

*I have never felt as much pain, shame, and anger as I
do when I see you drunk. I constantly worry about you.
You are always sick and weak. I just know one day soon
that you will be dead and I will have never really known
you, never have given you all the love I wanted to but
couldn't. Because I know that your damn, precious bottle is
more important to you than I am."*

Kim's pen was rushing across the paper. Now that her feelings
had come unlocked, she couldn't write fast enough.

"Daddy, I'm afraid the house will burn down with you and me and Mom in it. There have been so many times when you have been drinking and unknowingly dropped your cigarette on the floor. About three months ago you were passed out on the couch from drinking beer most of the day. I walked into the room and there was your cigarette on the floor next to you, burning up the carpet. You were asleep. I don't know what would have happened if I hadn't seen it in time.

We were at the summer house about two years ago. You had been drinking nonstop since we got there. We were working outside, painting the house, and you talked non-sense to everyone walking by. I was very embarrassed, and I felt angry and frustrated with you. Then the next day you passed out in bed in the middle of the afternoon because you had been drinking since morning. Toward dinnertime you suddenly came roaring out of the house, screaming and swearing at me. Within talking distance there was a party of about twenty people eating dinner. You then pushed me inside the house and kept screaming and yelling at me. I felt very scared of you and embarrassed and ashamed of what those people saw and heard. I didn't want to go down to the beach or see any neighbors after that.

There was another time about four or five years ago during the summer when Mom was out of the house, and you had been drinking all day. You told Bill and me to clean up the house for Mom. I started to clean one thing and you asked me why I was doing that and told me to do something else. Then you asked me why I was doing what you had just asked me to do, and again you asked me to do something else. This went on and on, and finally I told you I was going to finish vacuuming before I did anything else. You started screaming at me and came toward me as if you would hit me. I was terrified of you, for the first time in my life. After that, I had nightmares of you killing me. I have them still.

When you have been drinking, you often become upset

with me and sometimes you beat me with your belt. Mom never says anything about this; maybe she doesn't know, because you only do it when she isn't home. But sometimes I have black and blue marks and small welts on my body, and I have to tell people at school that I fell off my bike or down the stairs or something. I'm afraid to come home, and I have a sick feeling in my stomach every day walking home from school. You don't beat me much anymore; you're too drunk to even notice I'm there.

There were times in the past when you'd been drinking and my friends came to pick me up to go somewhere. You would answer the door and tell them to come in and sit down to talk to you. You'd slur your words and ask them the same questions over and over again. You made them very nervous, and I would be so embarrassed. They didn't want to come to my house after that, or to even call me. Have you noticed, Daddy, that I don't have any friends anymore?

When you have been drinking, you become very hostile toward me. Last Friday, I came home from school, and I could smell the alcohol in the air. You didn't have anything nice to say to me. You were speaking slowly, and your eyes were bloodshot. You started arguing with me right away, and when I wasn't willing to argue back, you started coming after me. I didn't do anything! You started grabbing me and hurting me, and I sat there and took it until you started shaking me and I got scared. I ran outside. I was crying. Some of my friends saw me and stopped and asked me what was wrong. I couldn't tell them. What would I have said? That my dad yelled at me and shook me and scared me to death? I was afraid I would break down and cry if I tried to explain. I felt like a fool in front of them and just wanted them to go away and leave me alone.

Daddy, these things happen only when you're drinking, never when you're sober. You're never happy when you've been drinking. And when you drink, you put yourself in danger. I've seen you when you've been drinking and playing with the cat. The cat is scratching you and digging his claws into you (he's scared of you, too!). He'll claw you until you start to bleed, but you still hang on to him. I don't think you even feel the claw marks.

I don't bring my friends over anymore. I don't sleep well at night because I'm afraid we'll all burn to death from one of your cigarettes. Two or three times a night I get up to look at you. I bought three smoke alarms and installed them myself; I check them every day. I don't smile or laugh anymore, I don't do anything but worry and think about what I can do to make things better.

I understand, now, that the drinking isn't my fault. I used to think it was because I was a bad kid, or I made too much noise, or I'd somehow disappointed you and Mom. But really, I have nothing to do with it. It's something in you, a disease, and it's making you say and do these awful things.

You need help, Daddy. I'm so afraid you're going to die. Please don't die. Please choose me and Mom over that bottle."

Suddenly, without thinking, Kim threw her pen against the wall. Then she began to sob. She laid her cheek against the piles of paper and cried until there were no tears left. "I can't take it anymore," she moaned. "I just can't stand it anymore."

But in the middle of the pain there was a part of her that felt strong and strangely elated. It's out of me, *Kim thought, looking with something like triumph at the tear-stained pages.* I didn't know all this was inside me. Now it's outside me. I can give these pages to Sharon, and she can help me. She'll understand.

For the first time in years, Kim felt some hope; if she could put all that pain down on paper, then it seemed to her that there must be something that could be done with it. Gently, she stacked the pages of her life together. "It's a beginning," she said, repeating to herself what Sharon had said at their last meeting.

"I'm on my way," she added softly.

■

TWENTY-TWO

Who, When, Where, How, and What If?

Who should be included in the intervention? Who should not take part? When should it take place? Where? How should the whole event be planned and orchestrated? What if the Dependent tells you all to go to hell?

Who. Every family has its own unique dynamics, so there is no readily applied formula that can be used to determine who should be present during the counseling sessions and actual intervention. Every Dependent is surrounded by a group of people who are meaningful to him, in one way or another; in selecting the intervention team, the primary criterion should be to include people who care, who have witnessed the problem firsthand, and who have some clout, either emotional, psychological, or possibly financial, with the Dependent.

The Dependent's family (spouse, children, grandchildren, parents, siblings, and, when appropriate, in-laws) is the most important group because they have lived with the disease, know it intimately, and have the emotional power to cut through to the Dependent. Furthermore, while the Dependent can stand up and tell a friend or business associate to get the hell out of his life, it is much more difficult (if not impossible) to do so with a family member.

But not every family member is an appropriate or even helpful addition. In one family, for example, the daughter-in-law was the first to call a counselor and bring the group together; but during the counseling sessions she expressed bitter resentment of her father-in-law, becoming emotionally distraught whenever she talked about him and blaming other members of the family for "putting up with his shenanigans." She had initiated the intervention because of the pain she witnessed in her husband, but she did not have the love for her father-in-law that would allow her to put her resentment and anger into perspective and approach the Dependent with caring and concern. The group as a whole decided that she should be present at the intervention but that she not actively participate by talking or sharing her concerns.

People outside the family—friends, employers, co-workers, minister or priest, neighbors—can be powerful additions to the intervention team. These "outsiders" add a new and deeper dimension to the intervention, signifying that the Dependent's problems have been noticed by those who see him for only a few hours a day.

Once again, deciding whom to include in the intervention depends on your situation. If the Dependent is no longer employed and spends most of his time at home or drinking with his buddies, it may be difficult to find an outsider who would have any meaningful impact on him. Sometimes a complete stranger who has intimate knowledge and experience with the disease, such as an A.A. member or a staff member at the treatment center you have selected, can make a powerful impact on the Dependent. Just call A.A. (it's in the phone book) or the treatment center and ask if someone would be willing to help you with an intervention. Once again, these are decisions that must be carefully discussed with your intervention counselor, taking into account the dynamics of your family, the Dependent's personal situation, and how far the disease has progressed.

In terms of size, the intervention team should be neither too small (which might indicate to the Dependent a lack of power, interest, or cohesiveness) nor too large (which might confuse, anger, or overwhelm the Dependent). A group of four to eight people seems to work well, but the *quality* of caring and concern, not the *quantity* of people present, is the most crucial element in determining who should be part of the group. A successful intervention can be conducted with the presence of just one or two people who care a great deal about the Dependent, understand the disease, and have been adequately prepared for the event.

When. Determining when the formal intervention should take place depends on all sorts of complicated arrangements and decisions. If the Dependent works, when can he take a four-to-five-week medical leave? In order to answer this question, the family would need to find out how much vacation or sick leave the Dependent has, what his workload is at the time, when his employer feels he can spare him without major trauma to the business, et cetera. A lawyer, for example, might refuse to go into treatment because he has an important trial date; in such a case, it may be wiser for the family to sit tight for several weeks or even several months until the trial is wrapped up and the lawyer has no ready-made excuse to argue against treatment.

Determining "when" will also depend on the schedules of everyone taking part in the intervention. If the family members are scattered throughout the country, schedules must be coordinated, travel plans arranged, hotel reservations made, and so on. If family members work, arrangements must be made beforehand to take the day off. Baby-sitters will need to be lined up.

The family will also need to brainstorm about whether certain family events might complicate treatment arrangements: a child's graduation from high school or college; an important birthday or anniversary party; a planned vacation; an annual family event such as a Fourth of July picnic, Christmas party, or reunion.

Another crucial consideration is whether the treatment center you have selected has an opening at the time you've scheduled the intervention. In many private treatment centers, space is not a problem, but public facilities such as Veterans Administration hospitals or public assistance hospitals often have a waiting list of several weeks or even several months for in-patient alcoholism treatment.

In one hastily planned, ill-conceived intervention, the family neglected to check at the local VA hospital to see if there was room; only after the intervention took place did they call to discover that the Dependent would have to wait thirty days before a bed was available. In the chaos that followed, the Dependent's wife asked if each family member would be willing to contribute several hundred dollars for private treatment. The family members refused, saying that they doubted treatment would work anyway, and they weren't going to throw away any more money on someone who clearly didn't give a damn about anything. The Dependent quickly became defensive and hostile, leaving the house in fury and heading for the nearest tavern, while his wife broke down in tears and everyone began to blame everyone else for the failure.

Financial considerations are an important part of determining when the intervention takes place. Can the bills be paid if the Dependent is out of work for a month? If insurance does not cover the full cost, or if the family has no insurance, how will they pay for treatment? Can they get a bank loan? Will the family members agree to band together and come up with the necessary cash? When can such arrangements be made?

All these questions must be thoroughly researched and discussed within the group long before the date for the intervention is set. If the Dependent finds any holes whatsoever in the plan, if he detects any weakness within the group, he will use that weakness to argue against treatment and possibly tear the process, and potentially the family, apart.

Where. The intervention should not, if possible, take place in the Dependent's home or office. On his own turf, with his possessions gathered around him, the Dependent has a great deal of power. He can refuse to let the family in, kick them out once he understands what they're up to ("How dare you come into *my* house and say these things to me!"), or escape by locking himself in the bedroom, sneaking out to the garage and driving away, or just walking to the liquor cabinet and fixing a drink. Legally, the Dependent has a right to order everyone out of his own house; if it comes to that, there's not much the counselor or the family can do.

Whenever possible, the intervention should be conducted in a neutral place—the intervention counselor's office, an employer's office, or perhaps a relative or friend's home. Distractions and interruptions such as phone calls, crying babies, or traffic noise must be kept to an absolute minimum. Restaurants, bars, country clubs, and lounges are obviously inappropriate because of the noise, confusion, presence of strangers, and frequent interruptions.

Determining where the intervention takes place is often emotionally difficult for the family because at this point they will have to confront the deception inherent in the intervention process. In order to get the Dependent to agree to come at all, they will have to deceive him about the purpose of the event; and this deception is often seen as cheating and a betrayal of love and trust. Again, the intervention counselor must help the family to understand their emotions, acknowledge their fears and anxieties, and, if possible, come up with alternative solutions. Would the Dependent agree to a meeting if he knew his drinking or drug use would be discussed? Has he ever been approached about treatment? In the past, has he been willing to look at his addictive behavior and admit that he might need help?

Most families have made countless attempts to approach the disease "honestly" and have gotten nowhere. Once they look back at the past and are able to acknowledge that all their former efforts to help have done nothing to change the addiction and in fact have only worsened the situation, they will understand why deception is sometimes necessary. It's crucial that the family always keep in mind that any deception that is used is necessary because of the nature of the addiction itself: in order to free the Dependent, they must first break through the steel wall that the addiction has erected around the Dependent. The only way to do that is to catch the addiction when its guard is down.

How. One of the family's first questions will be, "How are we going to get him to the intervention?" This question involves both general and specific concerns. How, the family wonders, will they get the Dependent to agree to a scheduled event when he has been so unpredictable and unreliable in the past? And how, exactly, do they get him there? Who will call him and make the arrangements? Should they count on him to show up by himself or should someone be assigned to pick him up?

The family will need to brainstorm about all the possible alternatives, taking into account the Dependent's schedule (When does he go to work? When does he play racquetball? What time does he eat lunch?); family favorites (Who in the family has the most "power" over him? Whom will he most likely refuse?); and so on, and then making a decision about which alternative is most likely to result in the Dependent's showing up, sober, at the right place at the right time.

Most interventions take place in the morning because that's the best time to catch the Dependent sober. The planned event may be a breakfast or brunch, an office meeting, or a lunchtime housewarming, birthday, or anniversary party. Once again, the details should be worked out by the family members, with the intervention counselor helping them to fit the pieces together into a cohesive and coherent whole. The family members know the Dependent intimately and thus they are the best judges of which plans will work and which won't. They must be allowed to make the final decisions and then take the responsibility for these decisions; otherwise, they may feel manipulated and confused, and if anything goes wrong with the intervention, they will be tempted to pin the blame on the counselor or turn on one another. If this happens, they're back where they started: divided, angry, filled with hopelessness and despair, and confused about what to do next. If, on the other hand, the family makes the decisions and assumes the responsibility for those decisions, they have begun the process of determining their own fate, refusing to see themselves as victims and setting their own health and recovery as a priority. With such an approach, the intervention can be considered a success even before the actual face-off with the Dependent.

What if. What if the Dependent doesn't show up? What if he takes one look at you and walks out of the room? What if he blows up and threatens to cut everyone out of his will? What if he says he'll quit on his own?

The "what ifs" are the most terrifying part of the entire intervention process, for within these questions lie all the unspoken fears, insecurities, and anxieties of the family members. The "what ifs" can stop an intervention before it ever really gets started, leaving the family paralyzed with anger and guilt and terrified of giving up a secure if miserable present for an unknown and precarious future.

If the "what ifs" can be surmounted, the family members' fears can also be overcome, for they have made the decision to proceed for themselves as much as for the Dependent. They accept the fact that they deserve more than what they've had in the past, and they can face the risks without flinching. They can say to the Dependent, "I care too much for you to continue to be a part of your slow but sure death; I will be part of the solution, but I will not go back to being part of the problem."

But what, exactly, does that mean? If you are the parent of a teenage Dependent, do you threaten to cut off your child's allowance, take away the car, or kick him out of the house? If the Dependent is your parent or parents, do you deny them access to their grandchildren, refuse drunken phone calls, or threaten to cut ties completely unless they get sober?

Intervention may mean none of these things, or it may mean all of them. Every family will have to develop their own plan, depending on their situation. The only necessary requirement is that you be ready, this time, to back up your threats with actions. If you tell him you'll leave if he doesn't get help, then you have to be prepared to pack your bags. *This* time has to be different from all the other times you've said to him, "I can't take it anymore," and then when nothing changed, you set the dinner table as usual, went to bed as usual, woke up in the morning as usual, and put up with him as usual. The Dependent has to understand that this time you mean what you say; you are determined, resolute, and absolutely firm in your commitment to your own health and happiness, regardless of what the Dependent does or doesn't do. You are past the stage of simply reacting to him; now you're initiating actions of your own, and, through your knowledge and understanding of the disease, you're finding the courage to see these actions through.

Your message to the Dependent must be gentle, loving, and absolutely clear: "If you continue to drink or use drugs, I won't be there for you anymore because it hurts too much." Only you can decide what it means to "not be there anymore"—it could mean that you'll stay with the Dependent but attend Al-Anon meetings regularly; or that you'll go back to school, get trained for a new job, or begin to explore your problems and potential solutions with a counselor, social worker, or psychologist. Or you might decide to cut yourself off from the Dependent completely through separation or divorce, leaving town, or withdrawing financial support. Again, whatever you decide must come from a deep understanding within you that change is essential for your own health and happiness, and not from any pressure that you might feel from your family, friends, or counselor.

It may be that the Dependent will reject your established plans and offer his own compromise. He might, for example, refuse to enter the treatment center you have selected and insist on choosing his own treatment, or he may state his intention of quitting on his own. You should be prepared for such a contingency and decide among yourselves beforehand exactly what your response will be. In most cases, it's a good idea to agree to give him one last chance to try to quit on his own. *However:* as part of this agreement, it must be understood that if the Dependent starts drinking or drugging again, he will immediately and automatically enter treatment. He must agree to this in front of everyone; many intervention counselors insist that the agreement be put in writing and that the Dependent be required to sign it. The consequences of breaking this agreement should be carefully laid out so that the Dependent understands them and is convinced of the family's commitment to carry through on them.

What if he makes a pledge to "cut down" on his drinking or drug use? This is the one "what if" that has a firm and unshakable answer: *no.* Abstinence must be the only option available to him, the only goal you can or will accept. A Dependent who "cuts down" is still feeding his addiction and allowing it to control his life. There must be no bartering with the addiction. The Dependent's answer must be "yes" or "no"; "maybes" are not acceptable. This is a life-and-death struggle you are engaged in, with the addiction pulling from one end and you tugging mightily from the other. If you give the addiction any slack whatsoever, you've lost your advantage. Stay firm, hold tight to your carefully elaborated plans, and know that what you are doing comes from love and concern and offers the best and, perhaps, the only chance for happiness and peace of mind in the future.

TWENTY-THREE

Getting the Facts Down

Facts are the heart of the entire process known as intervention, because they document the progression of the disease and its impact on the Dependent and his family. Confronted with the hard, cold realities of the addiction, the Dependent has no room to maneuver or manipulate. When the facts of the disease are presented one by one in a steady stream by the people who care most about him in the world, the addiction's protective armor is quickly broken down. Reality, at long last, can shine through, allowing the Dependent to see clearly where the addiction has brought him.

Your intervention counselor will ask you to put together a list of precise, accurate, nonjudgmental facts based on your firsthand knowledge of incidents, behaviors, and personality changes related to the Dependent's drinking and/or drug taking. What, exactly, makes you believe the Dependent has a problem with alcohol and/or drugs? What, specifically, has happened in the past to make you feel that this intervention is necessary? What are your feelings—fear, sadness, loneliness, guilt, anger—about these events?

Your written statements or letters will serve three important purposes:

1. They will give you the security of knowing exactly what your role will be in the intervention. With a carefully prepared list of facts, each family member knows ahead of time what he will be expected to say and what every other participant will say. Thus, there are no surprises or possible points of contention or disagreement between the participants that the addiction could use to sabotage the intervention.

2. Your written statements will allow the intervention counselor to maintain control of the intervention. Because she knows exactly what will be said to the Dependent, the counselor is assured that everyone understands his role and that no one participant will "grandstand" or be carried away by anger or other potentially volatile emotions.

3. Factual documentation conveys to the Dependent that the intervention team is prepared, organized, and confident in what they are doing. The Dependent is faced, in other words, with a united front rather than a collection of confused, anxious, and fearful individuals.

In compiling a list of facts about the disease, your intervention counselor will ask you to keep seven essentials in mind:

1. Give specific examples of behaviors that are symptomatic of alcoholism or drug addiction and are abusive, uncharacteristic, dangerous, or embarrassing.

2. Include the exact date and, if possible, the time of the specific event. Make sure the event is as recent as possible; something that happened last week or last month will be a lot more effective than an event that occurred five years ago.

3. Make sure that you have witnessed these events or have absolute confidence that they've happened. You should not include speculative or secondhand information.

4. Emphasize the harmful consequences that occurred because of the chemical consumption, and, if possible, mention the actual amount consumed (a case of beer, a quart of vodka, a gram of cocaine, two marijuana joints, et cetera).

5. Point out the contradictions or conflicts in values or behavior caused by the drinking or drugging. For example: "You're so gracious and loving when you're sober, Mom; but when you drink, you change completely. You would never even think of hitting me when you're sober. But last Wednesday you got so drunk that you slapped me several times; I still have the bruises on my neck."

6. Comment on your feelings about this behavior, being careful to stay nonjudgmental, while at the same time making it clear to the Dependent that the addiction has had a profound negative effect on you and other members of the family.

7. State your concern about what is happening to the Dependent and repeatedly emphasize your love and concern for him.

Following are "scripts" based on these general principles, written by people involved in actual interventions. Names and certain descriptive events have been changed to preserve anonymity.

"Last Saturday you drank so much before dinner that you were unable to eat. Your head was practically on the dinner table. Mother had to wipe the food off your arms and face. I was so sad for you and for all of us. I had never seen you that drunk before."

*

"Mom, I was really excited while preparing everything for Father's Day dinner last month. When you and Dad returned from Vermont, I was looking forward to an enjoyable evening. Then as you finished off almost a half-gallon of wine, you began to insult Sam's girlfriend to the point where she almost started crying. It seared my heart to see how you upset Sam and consequently ruined the fellowship of a family dinner."

*

"Martha, I love you and want desperately for you to get help. Your current drinking pattern—you drink almost a fifth of vodka a day—has become a hazard to your health and the health of others. I remember following you home from the Fergusons' party two weeks ago. Your driving was erratic, and once you came within inches of sideswiping the guardrail on the side of the highway. The magnitude of your problem was very depressing to me that evening."

*

"Mom, I went to the Rialto Theatre with Joey Jensen last summer and saw you in the bar across the street. I felt awful and embarrassed and confused. I go to Miss Ellis to help me control my stuttering. I want you to get help for your drinking. We will be happier. I love you, Mom."

*

"Maggie, I love you very much. You're my big sister and while growing up I respected and admired you for your clever wit, intelligence, and beauty. Now I'm afraid of you. Last winter, when I was a senior in high school and you were working at the restaurant, you came home around dinnertime. I was sitting in the living room when you came home from work and immediately sensed that you'd been drinking. Apparently I gave you a "dirty" look, although I didn't say anything. You called me "arrogant" and slugged me across the head, full force. I am always sickened when I know you've been drinking. I can't hide this from you. I love you and want you to get well."

*

"Jake, I love you as much as I did twenty-seven years ago, when we were married. But I am worried sick about your drinking and am so afraid you will be in a car accident or even be the cause of one. It's upsetting when I see large and small bruises on your body and cuts on your head. You seem surprised when I mention them to you and you don't seem to know how they got there. I'm afraid that maybe you might have fallen. It's scary for me when you started mentioning you were getting forgetful. This happened last October: you came in drunk and said you didn't know if you'd taken your medicine or not. You decided to take it anyway. Then when you were not drinking, you couldn't remember if you had taken it or not and would take it anyway—just in case. I was so afraid of your double-dosing and mentioned to you to tell me when you take it or write it down. This went on for quite some time— three or four months. I notice that you are now writing it down. But the fear is still with me that you will forget."

*

"Last month when I took you to have your teeth out, you asked me to buy you wine right after we left the dentist in the morning. As soon as we got home, you had several glasses. You finished up the bottle in a few hours and slept. When you woke up a few hours later, you opened another bottle and drank again so you could put yourself out. I empathized with your pain and sadness, but it hurt me to see you drinking like that."

*

"Dad, I'm here because I love you and care about you and worry about your drinking problem and I want you to stop. I also am scared to come home to you because you have such unpredictable behavior. Sometimes you're nice and sometimes you yell. I was also very embarrassed when you hit a parked car, and I didn't know why. Then we went home and I found vodka in your milk. I also was going to pour out all of your alcohol but when I went to the cupboard all of about ten bottles were empty. I also get very scared because you drink at night and you could fall and hurt yourself. And nobody would be there to help you. And I want you to get professional help because I need a healthy dad."

*

"Last February on a Monday night about 2:30 A.M. I woke up to hear the car horn honking. I went to the car and you were asleep inside and kept bobbing back and forth on the horn. The motor was still running, so I banged on the doors and windows to wake you up, but you didn't wake up. I got my keys and opened the door. A big gush of heat came out of the car as you had the heat on high and you started to fall out of the car. I pushed you back inside by the shoulder but you still did not wake up. I then shook you hard and started yelling your name over and over and finally slapped you. You looked up at me with unfocused eyes and said "Go back in the house—I'm all right." You shut off the motor, and I went back in the house. I went in the bathroom and threw up because of the scare. Four weeks ago, again on a Monday night, I woke up hearing little beeps on the horn. I sat straight up in bed, full of fear. I looked out and thanked God the motor wasn't running. But I already am dreading the next time. Len, you do this every winter—you sleep in the car with the motor running. I pray after today there won't be a next time. I want so much for you to be well and free of alcohol—for both of us."

*

"Remember two years ago, Dad, when you came home and Bobby asked you a question and all you could do was kick him and tell him to go to his room? You then came into the kitchen and told me to clean up my dinner. I told you as soon as I was finished eating I would clean it up right away. Then you told me not to talk back to you and I asked if you were going to kick me, too, and that's when you took a swing at me. I was so upset with you. But anytime I would talk about it, it would make me cry because this was my dad, who had been my buddy ever since I could say it, and my buddy was trying to hurt me. I am not saying all this just to hurt you. I just want my buddy and best friend back. And I lost him because of the drugs. I love you."

*

"Late one night last week you came home drinking. You told Mom you would be home early to fix my bike. I was in my bedroom when you came home, and I asked you when you would fix it. You said, "Shut up, stop bugging me about it or I might never do it." You were very drunk. I felt scared and sad. I covered my head with the blanket so you couldn't see me cry. I felt alone."

*

"Before I was married Dad, and still living at home, you called from downtown in the middle of the night. The police had stopped you because you were drunk and you wanted me to come get you. When I picked you up, you cried in the car, and I held you. I was heartsick. A week later the police stopped you again. You were drunk again. You called me again. I had to rescue you again. I felt angry and sick. You always said as I was growing up, "Honey, I'm going to do what's best for you. If you hate me for a time, I will sacrifice your feelings for me to do what's best for you." I'm here in that same spirit. If you go to treatment, I'll do whatever I can to help. I'll be there."

*

In each of these examples, facts are intermingled with deep feelings of love and concern. The facts give an unblinking look into the damage inflicted by the addiction; the feelings confirm that there is still something left to salvage from the devastation. Without the facts, the feelings are raw and confused; without the feelings, the facts leave no hope. When facts and feelings are used together, however, the message comes across strong and clear: You need help, and we're here to support you because we care about you.

Faced with such powerful statements, the Dependent is left defenseless. He cannot deny the undeniable. He *can* turn his back on love, but for the first time, perhaps, he understands how much that will cost him. He's been given a choice: love or loss, hope or despair, life or death. Hands are stretched out, waiting. The alternatives are clear, the consequences well defined. The choice is his.

TWENTY-FOUR
—

The Rehearsal

When you meet for the final rehearsal before the intervention, you will probably feel frightened and overwhelmed. *This is real! We're actually going to go through with it,* you may think, with a sinking heart. This sudden realization can be so terrifying, the fear it draws forth so vivid, that many family members balk by showing up for the rehearsal totally unprepared. They tell the intervention counselor that they "forgot" their fact sheet or that they didn't have time to work on it. They look around nervously, wondering if anyone else is feeling the same naked terror. They seriously consider calling off the whole thing. Hearts are pounding, mouths are dry, hands are nervously clenched, and minds aren't working properly.

This is the theater of the real, and there's no denying how terrifying it can be to face the reality of your situation full force, no holds barred, with your family and friends as witnesses. The feelings that come uncorked during the rehearsal can be raw and extremely painful. But they are also healing and unifying. As you listen to what others have written about their experiences with the Dependent, you will find yourself thinking with a heart-thumping jolt, *I didn't know that!* or, *I never knew you felt that way!* It never fails that during the rehearsal the

195

participants are shocked and distressed to learn of the depth and breadth of the experience of others who have lived with or known the Dependent—even though these are people who have known one another intimately for years. Events will be recalled that you never knew about; feelings that have been buried for years will finally be brought out into the open. For most families, the rehearsal is a time of coming together as never before; of understanding, for perhaps the first time, the enormity of the problem; and of uniting, at long last, to put an end to it.

During the rehearsal the intervention counselor will ask each person to read his letter to the group. It often happens that the words need to be toned down or edited slightly to put the emphasis where it belongs—on the addiction rather than on the addict himself. In one rehearsal, the son of a fifty-five-year-old alcoholic recalled one of his father's drunken episodes, ending with, "You were disgusting." The family agreed that the word *disgusting* was too strong, carrying a sense of moral judgment. After talking it over, they agreed that the son should emphasize his feelings about his father's drinking rather than his disapproval. By changing the sentence to "I felt angry and sad, and I was embarrassed for you," the son emphasized the impact his father's disease had on him—an effect the father couldn't deny—and avoided the potential pitfall of making his father feel judged and therefore alienated.

In another rehearsal, the husband of a woman addicted to pills and alcohol had concluded his fact sheet with, "You have made my life a misery." The intervention counselor asked him to think about how, exactly, the disease had made his life miserable and try to express his feelings about the addiction and what it had done to his life. With feedback from the group, the concluding words were changed to, "I love you, and your drinking hurts me because I know you are sick, but I don't know what to do to help you." Words such as *revolted, disgusted, terrible,* or *awful* should be toned down so that the Dependent isn't put on the defensive but instead feels the love and concern of the people gathered together.

It is also critically important that participants in the intervention avoid using definitive labels such as *alcoholic* or *drug addict* and refer instead to the fact that they believe there is a "problem" with alcohol and/or drugs. The purpose here is not to downplay or deny the addiction, but to avoid getting into an argument with the Dependent about exactly what an alcoholic or drug addict is and stick instead to the undeniable fact that the drinking or drug taking has had a negative impact on each of the family members. The extent of that drug problem can be determined later, in treatment.

Last-minute details will also need to be worked out at the final rehearsal. Who will be responsible for making sure the Dependent arrives on time? Who will read through his list first? Where will everyone sit? Again, there are no set rules to this process; your intervention counselor, relying on her experience and intuition, will help you to work out the best possible course of action.

Some people are "cooler" under fire than others and during the rehearsal the counselor will be able to assess which members of the intervention team are likely to stay calm and, perhaps more important, emotionally "connected." The primary emotions conveyed to the Dependent must be love and concern. A family member whose love for the Dependent is buried underneath layers of anger, resentment, shame, and fear will probably not be the best person to convey a message of caring and concern. The spouse, for example, may seem like the best person to initiate the intervention because she has had the most hands-on experience with the addiction. But the day-to-day battle with the addiction, waged over many years, can leave terrible scars, transfiguring love into pity or even hatred, making a mockery of hope, and creating a smoldering sense of injustice and resentment. Furthermore, the addiction has gained in knowledge and strength over the years and it "knows" how to manipulate the spouse's emotions to further its own ends.

For all these reasons, the spouse often is not the best person to speak first; sometimes the spouse is so emotionally fragile that he or she is present at the intervention only for support and does not speak at all. Once again, each family is different, and every family member will need to look into his own heart, admit what he sees there, and be willing to share his deepest feelings with the group. This is not the time to put on a false front of bravery or attempt to bluff your way through your emotions; this is the time to face your feelings and fears honestly, admit to both your strengths and weaknesses, and accept the group's decisions about the best way to proceed.

It frequently happens that the person who is selected to start off is actually the least emotionally involved with the Dependent of all those assembled. A boss, co-worker, neighbor, or friend, for example, may be the best choice to start the process by establishing a calm, no-nonsense approach to the problem. Such a person typically finds it easier to keep his emotions under control, to present the facts without becoming distracted or overwrought, and to convey a sense of caring and concern without the accompanying baggage of "look what you've done to my life." Nevertheless, in the heat of battle even the bravest are known to crumble, and your counselor may reserve the right to decide the final order of who goes first, second, and so on, during the actual intervention.

The family should be prepared for the fact that the Dependent might crumble after just one or two people speak. Some interventions take several hours to complete; others are over within a few minutes. In one intervention, the Dependent walked in, sat down on a chair, looked around at the group, held his hands up in mock surrender, and, with a sad smile, said, "Okay. Whatever you want, I'll do it." Nobody had said a word.

During the rehearsal, the counselor will also want to make some decisions about seating arrangements. Those people with the most positive connection to the Dependent should be seated closest and within direct view; those who have had an emotionally charged, volatile history with the Dependent should be in more distant seats; and the intervention counselor should stay in the background, peripheral to the rest of the participants.

The doors should not be blocked because the Dependent

may feel trapped and thus spend all his energy trying to figure out a way to escape. It's critically important that the Dependent not feel confined or imprisoned by too many people in a small room or by people sitting too close, talking too loud, or in some other way threatening his personal space and privacy. Barely concealed anger or resentment can also undermine the ultimate success of the intervention; if one person in the room visibly smolders, the entire event can go up in flames.

The rehearsal often unlocks feelings and emotions that have been repressed for years, and the intervention counselor must be on the lookout for family members who are unprepared to deal with the pain of facing and acknowledging these feelings. This crucial aspect of the counselor's job is hampered by the fact that everyone who has lived with the addiction for any length of time has also become extremely skilled at covering up his emotions. During the rehearsal, family members may quickly clamp down on the raw emotions that begin to surface and attempt to stuff them back inside.

An astute and observant counselor can often identify those people who are in pain and help them to work through their feelings rather than hiding them once again. If complications do arise during the rehearsal, listen to your counselor and follow her advice. She will make sure that your health and recovery are given top priority.

For no matter what the Dependent decides to do, your life must go on. How you live your life after the intervention must not be left to chance or fate. You must be able to take responsibility for yourself, for your feelings, and for the rest of your life. Only then will you cease to be a puppet of the addiction and begin, instead, to pull your own strings.

TWENTY-FIVE

Barbara Johnson

*The carpets are more important to Mom than her grandchildren,
Debbie thought angrily. As she washed the breakfast dishes, she
remembered her conversation that morning with her mother,
Barbara Johnson. Debbie had asked her mother to watch the
girls for the afternoon, hoping that baby-sitting might give her a
reason not to drink for part of the day. But, of course, her
mother had thought up an excuse; this time, she said she had to
clean the carpets.* What's she going to do, *Debbie thought,* get
down on her hands and knees and scrub the entire five rooms
of wall-to-wall carpet?

She's always thinking up an excuse, *Debbie thought bitterly.
She could count on one hand the number of times her mother had
asked to be with her grandchildren. And Carole, Debbie's oldest
child, was eleven years old.*

*A glass slipped from Debbie's hand and crashed to the floor.
She just looked at it for a moment; then she sat down on the floor
in the middle of the broken glass and started to cry. All the
doubts and fears, the feelings of powerlessness and frustration,
flooded over her.* Maybe it's my fault that she has no relationship with the kids, *she thought for the hundredth time.* I've
purposely kept the girls from her because I didn't want them

around her when she was drinking. But she's always drinking! So when is there any time to talk or to be with the kids? Doesn't she care? Why does she do this to herself, to us?

Sitting on her kitchen floor, Debbie thought about the weekly family dinners at The Homestead restaurant. They had been meeting every Wednesday for almost eleven years. The evenings used to be fun and full of laughter, sharing, and love. But now these dinners seemed to Debbie a trial and a farce.

We're not a family anymore, *she thought.* We don't laugh anymore. We don't even talk anymore. Everyone sits in their place and watches Mom, with fear and horror, even with disgust. *Debbie thought back to four weeks ago, when her mother walked into the restaurant, already tipsy at five o'clock. After two martinis, her facial expressions changed, and everything she said was negative:* "I don't like your new haircut," *she told her daughter Maureen.* "These martinis are too sweet," *she complained, making a face.* "Those people," *and she actually pointed to the corner table,* "are obnoxious."

Then her head started to bob, almost hitting the table at one point. It seemed to take all of her mother's concentration just to keep her eyes open. When the dinner arrived, she couldn't hold a conversation, let alone chew her food. She kept leaning to one side and ended up supporting herself against Carole, her eleven-year-old granddaughter.

Debbie cringed, thinking about what happened next.

Carole moved her chair next to Debbie, being careful to move gently so her grandmother wasn't thrown off balance.

"Is Grandma drunk?" *Carole whispered.*

"Yes," *Debbie answered, more ashamed of lying than of telling the truth.*

"I'm afraid of her," *Carole said.*

Debbie squeezed her daughter's hand. "I know," *she said.*

"Is she going to die?"

Debbie didn't have an answer for her daughter then. But now, as she sat on her kitchen floor with broken glass scattered around her, the answer seemed clear: "Yes, she's going to die—unless we help her." *Debbie knew what she had to do. Months before she'd seen a television program on alcoholism and drug interven-tion. She had written down the intervention counselor's name and phone number: Lois Martin, intervention specialist. Quickly, hands shaking, Debbie dialed the number.*

Debbie had no difficulty convincing her younger sisters, Maureen and Stacey, to come to the first meeting with the counselor, but her brother Joel was furious.

"What do you think you're doing, Debbie?" he practically screamed at her. "Mom can't be an alcoholic—she's too much of a lady! She's gentle and quiet—she doesn't bother anyone! Maybe she's got a drinking problem, but she's no alcoholic!" Joel tried to calm himself down, but his next question upset them both: "Have you thought about Dad, Debbie? How do you think Dad's going to take this? What's he going to say?"

Dad, Debbie had to admit, was a big problem. Dave Johnson was a heavy drinker himself, and Debbie was convinced that he, too, was an alcoholic. His disease was not as obvious as his wife's, but he drank every day, he had a high tolerance, he experienced periodic blackouts, and his moods changed dramati-cally when he was drinking. Whenever anyone in the family had mentioned the need for help for their mother, Dad had stopped listening. Once he'd started yelling at Debbie, calling her a busybody and a gossip. "I know my wife," he'd said, his tone cold as ice, "and she doesn't need any help from you or anyone else." Even more frightening for the children was the fact that their father owned the business that employed them and their spouses. They feared that by risking his anger, they might lose their jobs.

"I don't know what to do about Dad," Debbie said finally. "But, Joel, we have to do something about Mom. I don't know if she's an alcoholic or not, but you have to admit she drinks too much. She almost choked on her food again the other day! Please, Joel—just come and talk with the counselor. Maybe she can help us."

Joel finally agreed to attend the counseling sessions. At the first meeting he sat apart from the rest of the group, his arms folded across his chest, and looked defiantly at Lois. She appeared not to notice.

"You've all described to me a very painful situation. I think you've done a superb job dealing with your anger and frustration. I can tell how much you love your mother—she's very lucky to have a family like you who care enough about her to get help." Lois went on to explain about the disease concept, the many misconceptions about alcoholism and its victims, and the need for the family to learn about the disease and the emotional problems that come from living with a chemically impaired person. She asked each family member to attend Al-Anon meetings and gave them several books to read before the next session.

In the next nine weeks of counseling, dramatic changes began to take place in the family. John, Debbie's husband, stopped drinking after reading the books Lois had recommended. "My father was an alcoholic," he explained, "and I could see some of the early-stage symptoms in myself. It's just not worth the risk." Stacey, the youngest daughter, moved out of her parents' house and into an apartment of her own. Joel began to accept the fact that his mother was an alcoholic. All the children faithfully attended Al-Anon meetings and Debbie's daughter, Carole, went to Alateen meetings twice a week. The family's fear and confusion were gradually being replaced with a calm determination to defeat the disease and make the family well and whole again.

But one towering fear remained: Dad. At the first meeting, the family had decided to exclude their father from the intervention. There was simply too much to lose by risking his anger: their jobs, his love, and his emotional support for their mother's recovery. They were also afraid that he might sabotage the intervention in an attempt to protect his own drinking. But conducting the intervention behind his back made them all nervous and edgy.

Three days before the scheduled intervention, they held a rehearsal in which they prepared for the event. It was decided that Joel's wife, Elizabeth, would not talk at the intervention because she and her mother-in-law argued frequently and heatedly. Eliz-

abeth would attend the intervention not as a participant but as a support person for her husband.

During the final moments of the rehearsal, Randy, Maureen's husband, got cold feet. Randy was a born-again Christian and expressed the fear that the intervention violated the Christian tenets of love and devotion to your family no matter how much they might hurt you.

"Isn't this a betrayal of both Mom and Dad?" he asked. "They'll both end up hating us. They'll never forgive us for ganging up on her."

"Randy," Lois said, "I know how difficult this can be, and how frightened you are about the outcome. But think about this: when Jesus said to turn the other cheek, he didn't mean to get hurt again—he meant to find another way. What you are all doing is the ultimate act of love. You are showing Barbara that you love her so much that you're willing to risk everything— her anger, her hatred, even her rejection—to get help for her."

Randy slowly nodded. "I understand," he said after a moment. He held his trembling hands out in front of him for a moment and laughed nervously. "It's just that I'm scared to death."

Maureen took his hand. "We all are," she said.

The intervention took place on a Saturday morning, when Dave Johnson was out of town on a business trip. Stacey had asked her mother to come over for an "apartment warming" brunch. Maureen and Randy were picking Barbara up at nine o'clock. Maureen's best friend, Janice, had a key to the Johnsons' house and a list of clothing and other items that Barbara would need at the treatment center. Janice would wait outside until the house was empty and then pack Barbara's suitcases.

Everyone else was meeting at Stacey's apartment at 8:30 A.M. The seating arrangements were all worked out, with everyone sitting in an elongated circle, Debbie directly across from her mother, and Lois seated slightly apart from the group. Cars were hidden, the treatment plans were repeated, and everyone took some long, deep breaths to calm themselves.

At 9:45 A.M., Maureen, Randy, and Barbara Johnson walked

*into the apartment. Barbara just stared at everyone, clutching
her purse to her breast; it struck Debbie that her mother looked
like a deer she had once seen, frozen by the approaching head-
lights of her car, incapable of flight.*

*"Hello, Mrs. Johnson," Lois said, introducing herself. "Your
family has come together this morning because they love you and
are concerned about your drinking. Would you be willing to just
listen for fifteen or twenty minutes?"*

*Barbara Johnson nodded numbly. "Certainly," she said, sit-
ting down in the empty chair.*

*"Mrs. Johnson," Lois continued, "I've rarely worked with
such a concerned and loving family. You are very lucky. As I've
listened to your family, it became apparent to me, as it has to
them, that drinking is becoming more and more of a problem in
your life. And it's because of this awareness that they would like
to share their love and concern with you. Debbie, would you
share your concerns with your mother?"*

*Debbie held several sheets of paper in her hands. She began to
read from them in a halting voice. "Mom, I love you very much.
I know how much you love me. That's why I need to tell you how
your drinking has affected me.*

*"When I visit you in the afternoons, it's difficult to maintain a
conversation with you, since you keep repeating things over and
over again. During these conversations I find myself staring out
the window or at the television because your face becomes so
mean-looking and hostile. I know that's not the real you, because
when I visit you in the mornings you're so concerned about people
and so loving. I know it's the alcohol that turns you into a
different person."*

*Debbie kept her head down, trying hard to stay in control, and
forced herself to continue reading from her list.*

*"Watching you at The Homestead lately has been so sad. I
watch you closely because I'm terrified that you'll choke. One
night Joel had to pound you on the back because you were so
drunk you couldn't chew your food properly."*

*Debbie paused and wiped her eyes with the back of her hand.
John handed her his handkerchief.*

"*Christmas of 1984,*" she continued, "*you sprained your ankle trying to put the lights on the tree. You had been drinking again.*

"*When I was twelve years old, you took me to Kathy Farley's birthday party after school. You had been drinking. You drove into the ditch on the side of their driveway, and I crushed my thumb in the car door. It's still misshapen. No one has ever talked about that.*"

Debbie's shoulders began to shake. She looked up at her mother, who was looking at Carole, her granddaughter. Carole had her hands over her face and was sobbing silently. Debbie pulled herself together and continued reading.

"*Lately it's your attitude that worries me. I need your approval for what I do, and I value your input. But when you start drinking, your personality changes, and you become cranky and short-tempered. I used to blame myself for your crankiness. I never knew what I had done, but I knew I had to try to make you happier somehow.*

"*When I was growing up, if there was something I wanted to do in the afternoons, you would say 'no' without further discussion, or without telling me your reasons.*"

Debbie read quickly now, keeping her head down, her hands tightly clutching the pieces of paper. "*One evening last fall I called you. I hung up crying, thinking you were mad at me—you had a sarcastic laugh that made me feel sick to my stomach. I called the next day to see if everything was okay, and you didn't recall any of the conversation.*

"*When you were hospitalized last Christmas, and stopped drinking for a few weeks, it was wonderful talking with you. You were so alert and receptive to things around you. You were very faithful in not drinking. But whenever I heard the freezer door open and the ice cubes clinking into your glass, I couldn't help but cringe, even though you were just drinking Pepsi.*

"*The moment I knew you were drinking again wasn't because I saw you drinking . . . it was because of your sarcastic smile, and the way you grab your bottom when you walk, as if you're trying to hold yourself in balance. I felt sick when I saw that—and worse was that you denied you were drinking again.*"

Debbie raised her head, took a deep breath, and looked directly at her mother. "Mom, I love you more than anything. And it's because of my love for you that I'm willing to do anything to help. I understand that this is a disease you have, just as some people are diabetic. I want so much for you to get well again. I love you, Mom."

Everyone in the room was silent; it was as if they were all holding their breath. "Mrs. Johnson," Lois said after a moment, "are you willing to get some help?"

Barbara Johnson smiled slightly and looked directly at her granddaughter Carole. "Of course I am," she said softly.

EPILOGUE

When Dave Johnson returned from his business trip, his children gathered to tell him that Barbara was in treatment. He quietly accepted the news and said that he was glad she was finally getting some help. After Barbara was released from treatment, Dave began to spend longer hours at the office. He continues to drink, daily and heavily.

Barbara Johnson is ten months sober. She is alert, energetic, and her sense of humor has resurfaced. Her blood pressure is down from 170/100 to 120/80. She attends A.A. meetings three or four times a week. Every Saturday she invites her grandchildren over to her house to play cards or help her bake bread or cookies.

Barbara Johnson's recovery is the first priority for her children. As time goes on, the family knows that Dave Johnson's drinking will have to be confronted. But right now, the children understand that they need to give their mother's recovery time to solidify and strengthen. In the future, they will encourage their mother to go to Al-Anon meetings with them so that she can share her fears and concerns about her husband's drinking. When the time is right, the family will do what they can for their father.

TWENTY-SIX

Looking Ahead

The time you spend in an intervention, telling your Dependent how much you love him and how concerned you are for his life, will undoubtedly be the most emotionally intense experience of your life. Inevitably you will come down to earth, and the transition may be bumpy. You may feel utterly drained and exhausted. You may burst into tears. You may start shaking and find it difficult to stop. You may feel completely exposed and vulnerable.

After the intervention, you will need to "come down" by getting back together with the group, talking over what happened, discussing how you felt about it, listening to what others have to say, reinforcing one another in your decision to conduct the intervention, and making plans for the future. Follow-up sessions are an essential part of the intervention process; without them, you'll feel at loose ends: lost, lonely, and uncertain about what to do next.

After one intervention, for example, the Dependent's wife collapsed on the couch. She confessed that she felt like a tree in the middle of a violent lightning storm. The branches of the "tree" were her exposed nerves; she felt as if her nerve endings were on fire, absorbing the electric jolts and carrying the current to the tree's heart—her heart. "I'm just a throbbing bunch of protoplasm!" she said, laughing through her tears. "What am I going to do with myself?"

What does happen next? If everything worked, your Dependent is on his way to treatment. But what about you—what should you do?

Let go . . . of fear, anger, guilt, sadness, and grief. You did what you did for love. It was the right thing to do.

Take care of yourself. Make sure your needs are being met. If you need to talk, talk. If you need to sleep, sleep. If you need to run ten miles, run. If you need a good cry, cry. If you need a long hot bath, take one. If you need to be with someone, don't be alone. If you need some time alone, don't feel you have to be with others all the time. Act on your feelings. Take care of your needs. Love yourself.

Reach out. Never feel afraid to ask for help. Immediately after the intervention, turn to your intervention counselor; tell her your concerns, ask for her advice. And understand that she had a specific job, which was to prepare you for the intervention. Now that the intervention process is over, she must turn you over to other sources of support—family, friends, Al-Anon, involvement in the family treatment program, and, perhaps, ongoing individual counseling. These support systems will help you through the rest of your recovery.

Be selfish. You are responsible for your life; no one else is going to take care of you the way you can take care of yourself. Being selfish isn't bad; it's loving yourself enough to take care of yourself. That can only be good for you and the people who love you.

Be honest . . . with yourself and others, at all times.

Be patient. Recovery takes time. People who have been through it claim that for every year you have lived with a

Dependent, you will need a month in recovery—six years, six months; ten years, ten months. Time is your ally now. Take each day as it comes, know that the bad times will be followed by good times, and that, as time goes by, the good times will outmuscle the bad.

Support your Dependent. He may be in for some rough times now. Be understanding. Don't expect miraculous changes to happen in days or weeks. Don't try to change things immediately. Don't overprotect. Don't be judgmental. Ask how you can help and support him, where you can fit into his new life. Be willing to talk with him about treatment and recovery, to ask what's happening and what he's feeling. If he wants to talk, listen; if not, willingly share his silences. Let him know you're there if he needs you. Trust him; he must take responsibility for his life, just as you are taking responsibility for your life.

Be open to life. Remember the story of the Little Prince and the Tippler:

"Why are you drinking?" demanded the little prince.

"So that I may forget," replied the tippler.

"Forget what?" inquired the little prince, who already was sorry for him.

"Forget that I am ashamed," the tippler confessed, hanging his head.

"Ashamed of what?" insisted the little prince, who wanted to help him.

"Ashamed of drinking!" The tippler brought his speech to an end, and shut himself up in an impregnable silence.

Let there be no more impregnable silences in your life.

Instead, let your silences be open to sound.

Let your speech leave room for others to talk.

And let your heart, freed of its invisible chains, believe in love, again.

Appendix:
Drug Facts

Know your enemy. Your Dependent is a prisoner of the particular drug or drugs he uses. While the "cage" of addiction is similar for all addictive drugs, the quality of life within that cage will vary from one drug to another.

Every drug has its own distinct chemical makeup and specific effects on the body and on the addict's behavior. Learning about these drugs, how they affect the user's psychological, emotional, and physical health, how long the effects of the drug last, and the characteristic symptoms associated with addiction and withdrawal will help you to react calmly, sensibly, and effectively to the deadly disease threatening your Dependent's life and your mental and physical health.

ALCOHOL

General facts: The most widely used drug known to man, alcohol is a relatively simple chemical with extraordinarily complex effects on the human body. Its simple molecular structure allows it immediate entrance to the brain—the site of many of its most harmful effects—and to every major organ in the body. Within minutes of taking a drink, you feel the effects: euphoria, lowering of inhibitions, and lessening of anxiety and tension.

In low doses, in fact, alcohol acts as a stimulant, increasing blood flow, accelerating heart rate, exciting the brain and spinal cord reflexes, and stimulating the transmission of nerve impulses. After two or three drinks, however, the average drinker will begin to experience the sedative effects of alcohol: a slowing of mental and physical reactions, delayed reflexes, slurred speech, mental sluggishness, and physical incoordination. In large doses, alcohol is a central nervous system depressant, leading to disorientation, sleepiness, and respiratory depression.

Medical uses. Alcohol is contained in many over-the-counter and prescription drugs, including cough syrups, elixirs, and expectorants. Before the advent of modern anesthetics, alcohol was used as a painkiller; its painkilling effects, however, are experienced only after drinking very high doses. The Civil War soldier who drank a bottle of whiskey before his leg was amputated may have been drunk, but unless he was unconscious, he still felt the knife entering his body.

Primary effects. Effects of alcohol are dose related, with low doses creating euphoria, a sense of well-being, and decreasing tension, and moderate to high doses causing intoxication, drunken behavior, and physical and mental incoordination. The effects are also related to the individual taking the drug. The more the drinker weighs, for example, the more water there is in the body to dilute the alcohol and lessen the effects. Women have less water in their bodies than men and more fatty tissue, which is not easily penetrated by alcohol, and thus they typically get drunk faster than men. The BAL—blood alcohol level, a measure of the percentage of alcohol in the blood—will also rise faster just before a woman menstruates, due to fluctuating hormone levels. Alcohol taken on an empty stomach will be more rapidly absorbed into the bloodstream, contributing to a more rapid rise in BAL. Warm alcohol is absorbed more quickly than cold, liquor enters the bloodstream faster than wine or beer, and carbonated mixers such as quinine water speed up absorption.

The phenomenon of tolerance (see p. 52) is important to understanding the drinking behavior of the early-, middle-, and late-stage alcoholic. An early-stage alcoholic experiences an increased tolerance to alcohol's effects: he can drink a great deal without becoming visibly intoxicated. This is due to cellular adaptations in the brain and liver, which actually lead to improved functioning when alcohol is present in the body. Over the years, however, alcohol and its toxic byproduct, acetaldehyde, actually damage the cells so that they can no longer handle large amounts of alcohol. The late-stage alcoholic often gets visibly drunk on just one or two drinks, an obvious sign that his body's cells have been damaged by the poisonous, long-term effects of alcohol.

Addiction potential. An estimated 10 to 15 percent of the people who drink alcohol become addicted to it. Studies have conclusively proved that people with a family history of alcoholism run a four times greater risk of becoming addicted. Certain ethnic groups—Native Americans, Irish, Scandinavians—are also extremely vulnerable to alcohol's addictive effects, while other ethnic groups—Italians, Jews, Asians, for example—appear to be more resistant.

Dr. Bert Vallee and colleagues at Harvard Medical School have isolated fifteen different forms of the alcohol dehydrogenase (ADH) liver enzyme and discovered that the number and variety of these enzymes vary widely from person to person, with certain characteristic patterns evident in various ethnic groups. These different enzyme combinations are apparently responsible for an individual's specific physiological response to alcohol (flushing, nausea, headaches, sleepiness, for example) and may be related to an increased vulnerability to alcohol's addictive effects.

One compelling theory for the difference in ethnic susceptibility is that the longer an ethnic group is exposed to alcohol, the lower the rate of alcoholism. And this relationship does appear to hold true: Jews, Italians, and Asians, for example, have been exposed to alcohol for thousands of years and have low alcoholism rates, while Native American Indians and Eskimos, who have been exposed to the drug for only several hundred years, have extremely high rates of alcoholism.

Symptoms of addiction. Alcoholism progresses from an early, hidden stage through the middle stage, when most alcoholics begin to suffer both physically and psychologically from their drinking, into a final, late stage, when the alcoholic's mental and physical health rapidly deteriorate.

In the early stage the symptoms of addiction are difficult to "see" unless you are familiar with the disease's impact on behavior. Obvious physical and psychological damage is not yet apparent, but the early disease does affect its victims' thoughts, feelings, and actions. The early-stage alcoholic, for example, will show an enjoyment of drinking that is more pronounced than the typical drinker's periodic desire to get "high." The early-stage alcoholic becomes preoccupied with alcohol to the point where a social occasion without the drug may seem like a waste of time. As the disease progresses, the early-stage alcoholic will experience changes in his drinking patterns: drinking more, drinking more often, switching to stronger drinks, gulping the first drinks, drinking earlier in the day, finding excuses to drink, et cetera. He may begin to experience hangovers, slight tremors, and periodic bouts with remorse and guilt over his drinking.

In the middle stage, the behavioral symptoms progress into increasingly obvious psychological, emotional, and sometimes physical problems. *Behavioral* symptoms include rationalization and denials; attempts to quit or cut down; the making and breaking of promises; hiding bottles and protecting supplies; drinking more than intended; et cetera. *Emotional/psychological* symptoms include mood and personality changes, irritability, depression, nervousness, anxiety, guilt, despair, self-pity, loss of self-respect, and unreasonable resentments regarding others' attempts to criticize behavior. *Physical* symptoms include increased tolerance, tremors, and alcohol-related illnesses or disorders such as high blood pressure, ulcers, gastritis, nausea, and diarrhea.

In the late stage, all these early- and middle-stage symptoms combine and increase in intensity to create an agony of emotional, mental, and physical distress and deterioration. The late-stage alcoholic experiences an overwhelming craving for alcohol and will continue to drink despite the loss of everything of value in his life. Loss of control is evident in the late-stage alcoholic's desperate need to drink to control the ever-worsening withdrawal syndrome, combined with his mental inability to judge how much alcohol his body can handle and his physical inability to tolerate the large amounts of alcohol needed to relieve withdrawal.

The late-stage alcoholic typically drinks in the morning, often goes on prolonged binges, suffers from malnutrition, drinks alone, pays no attention to personal hygiene, suffers from accidents such as falling down stairs, requires frequent hospitalizations for physical complications and alcohol-related disorders, is haunted by recurring episodes of paranoia, unreasonable fears, and suicidal thoughts, and may experience the more serious and life-threatening withdrawal symptoms such as convulsions and delirium tremens.

Withdrawal symptoms. In alcoholism, as in addiction to other drugs, there are generally two distinct categories of withdrawal: *acute* and *protracted.* For alcoholics, the *acute* withdrawal syndrome lasts anywhere from several hours to several days, with the duration and intensity of symptoms increasing from early to late stage. In the early and middle stages, acute symptoms include a shaky and agitated feeling, nervousness, weakness, nausea, diarrhea, excessive perspiration, loss of appetite, memory impairment, vivid dreams, insomnia, hangovers (headaches, eyeaches, and dizziness), gastrointestinal distress, and psychological anguish (guilt, anxiety, self-accusation, sense of hopelessness and despair). In the late stage, these symptoms worsen and more serious symptoms emerge: convulsions, hallucinations, and D.T.s (delirium tremens). D.T.s is a particularly dangerous condition: without medical treatment, 10 to 15 percent of D.T.s sufferers die.

The *protracted* withdrawal syndrome can last for days, weeks, even months after the last drink. Symptoms include anxiety, depression, nervousness, agitation, moodiness, insomnia, and a recurring craving for alcohol. This syndrome is caused by (1) the direct, often slow-to-heal effects of alcohol on the central nervous system and (2) the lesser-known, indirect effects of malnutrition and fluctuations in blood sugar levels. Chronic alcoholism causes nutritional deficiencies by interfering with the body's ability to absorb and use various nutrients.

In an informal study described in *Eating Right to Live Sober,* Dr. Ann Mueller reported that 93 percent of recovering alcoholics suffer from hypoglycemia, a chronic condition of low blood sugar responsible for numerous symptoms including exhaustion, depression, insomnia, anxiety, irritability, headaches, difficulty in concentrating, mental confusion, and a craving for sweets and/or alcohol.

Death. Alcohol is a very effective killer, and death can come in a number of ways. Acute alcohol poisoning caused by drinking too much too fast is one way. Cases exist of teenagers who drink a quart of whiskey in half an hour on a dare and die of respiratory shutdown—the alcohol-poisoned brain simply stops relaying the message to breathe. Addictive drinkers (alcoholics) know how to pace their drinking and will usually die of alcohol-related illnesses such as heart disease, liver disease, pancreatitis, cancer, pneumonia and other respiratory-tract diseases, or of suicide, accidents, drownings, et cetera.

In combination with other drugs, alcohol can be deadly. Karen Ann Quinlan, Dorothy Kilgallen, and Marilyn Monroe all died after combining alcohol with other drugs, and thousands of others die every year from such combinations. The effect of two drugs taken together is known as *synergism:* 1 + 1 doesn't equal 2, but 4, 5, even 10 or more. Synergism describes a chemical chain reaction that is capable of overwhelming the body's ability to metabolize and dispose of drugs, which can lead to respiratory shutdown, convulsions, coma, and death.

COCAINE

General facts. Cocaine (flake, rock, crack) is a product of the coca plant, which thrives in the Andes Mountains in Peru, Columbia, and Bolivia. For thousands of years, natives of these countries have chewed the leaf of the coca plant to relieve hunger and fatigue. Today the leaves are mixed with an organic solvent such as kerosene or gasoline, then treated with acid and crystallized, leaving a white powder worth approximately $100 per gram on the street.* Cocaine is a valuable export product to many impoverished South American countries. In Bolivia, for example, cocaine brings in $450 million per year—about the same amount as legal exports.

Sigmund Freud was an advocate for cocaine use, insisting that it was effective for treating psychosis, digestive disorders, alcohol and morphine addiction, and asthma, and proclaiming its wonders as an aphrodisiac and local anesthetic. In 1886, Coca-Cola, which contained cocaine, was promoted as "a brain tonic and cure for all nervous infections, sick headache, neuralgia, hysteria and melancholy." But cocaine was not to remain legal for long; in 1914 the Harrison Narcotics Act prohibited the use of cocaine in tonics or patent medicines, and for almost sixty years the drug lost popularity and its perceived respectability.

Experimentation with drugs by an increasingly affluent population combined with police crackdowns on amphetamine production and distribution led to a resurgence of interest in cocaine in the late 1960s and early 1970s. Today cocaine use is

---

*The price of cocaine fluctuates according to supply and demand; in 1986, for example, a gram of cocaine was available in many cities for $60 to $80 per gram because of the large supply available.

considered an epidemic, with over 22 million Americans reporting that they have used cocaine at least once, and 5,000 teenagers and adults using it for the first time each day. About 5 million people use the drug at least once a month, and more than 2 million of these users are believed to be in trouble with the drug. Experts estimate that one of every ten users (the same percentage as for alcoholism) will become addicted to the drug.

Dealers commonly mix or "cut" pure, flake cocaine with a number of substances that do not change the drug's appearance. Thus, the person who snorts or injects cocaine usually has no idea what he's got when he buys cocaine, or what toxic effects the substance might have. Purity generally ranges from 10 to 70 percent, depending upon the number of "cuts."

Free-base cocaine is another story. Free-base is the chemical base of cocaine, a pure, concentrated form of the drug—and while the user doesn't have to worry about adulterants, he is more susceptible to toxic reactions or overdoses and to addiction.

Medical uses. Cocaine is legally—and incorrectly—classified as a narcotic. Chemically, it has the characteristics of both anesthetics and sympathomimetics. As an anesthetic, cocaine is a mild euphoriant similar in structure to Novocain or Xylocaine, but it is the only local anesthetic that produces both anesthesia and vasoconstriction of the mucous membranes, making it a potentially valuable aid in surgery in the nose, throat, larynx, and lower respiratory passages. As a sympathomimetic, it dilates the pupils, increases heart rate, blood pressure, and body temperature, and acts as a powerful central nervous system stimulant, similar to the amphetamines.

Cocaine's potential for abuse and its possible toxic effects severely restrict its medical uses. People who have hypertension, seizure disorders, or heart problems are at high risk for potentially serious side effects; and as a stimulant and vasoconstrictor, cocaine increases the risk of spontaneous abortion in pregnant women.

Primary effects. Most recreational users chop up their cocaine into lines or columns arranged on a piece of glass or a mirror and then "snort" the powder through the nose with a rolled-up dollar bill or a straw. An increasingly popular method of administration is free-basing, in which the active part of the drug is "freed" from its base, a hydrochloric salt, and then smoked. The extraction process involves dissolving the cocaine and adding a chemical catalyst, which causes the free base to separate. The active ingredient—about one-half gram from each gram of "cut" cocaine—can then be filtered out and dried. The user heats the rock-candy-like granules in a special pipe and inhales the vapors. A cocaine solution can also be injected intravenously.

Crack, which originated in the early 1980s on the West Coast as "rock," is actually free-base cocaine. The chips of cocaine, which are cut from a brittle cake of cooked cocaine and baking soda, were renamed "crack" by Harlem pushers because they resembled pieces of cracked plaster from the ceiling and because of the crackling sound when the cocaine pellets are heated. A chunk of crack is sold for as little as $10 per dose; an equivalent dose of flake cocaine may cost $30 or more. Thus, while a "hit" of crack is relatively cheap, it represents for the dealer a return of $250 to $400 for each gram; or double to triple the profit of flake cocaine. And the instant jolt to the brain—a delay of only seven seconds and a powerful high that lasts up to twelve minutes—creates an explosion of energy, alertness, confidence, and euphoria that quickly brings the user back for more—and more and more. Crack may be the most addictive drug known to man—more compelling even than heroin.

Three to five minutes after snorting, fifteen to thirty seconds after injecting, or seven seconds after smoking free-base, cocaine reaches the brain, where it excites the neurons of the sympathetic nervous system, which is responsible for regulating blood pressure, heartbeat, and respiration. Cocaine lodges within the molecular makeup of these neurons, preventing them from lapsing into a nonactive, resting state and thus speeding up the blood pressure, heartbeat, and respiration. Cocaine also causes blood vessels throughout the body to constrict, or close in upon themselves, requiring the heart to pump harder and faster, an additional cause of high blood pressure.

The key to understanding cocaine's addictive potential, however, is in its activation of nerve cells in the brain that release a chemical messenger or neurotransmitter called *dopamine.* Dopamine creates sensations of pleasure, alertness, confidence, euphoria, and motor control—and these sensations are so compelling that they override the brain's interest in food, sleep, or sex.

But then comes the crash. Approximately twenty to thirty minutes after snorting, fifteen minutes after injecting, and twelve minutes after smoking the drug, the user begins to experience feelings of depression. The body, in its cocaine-induced, hyperexcited state, uses up its ready supply of neurotransmitters, and cocaine saturates the nerve synapses in the brain and chemically blocks the neurotransmitters from returning to their storage places. Thus, these essential chemicals are depleted more rapidly than they can be replaced, causing feelings of irritability, restlessness, and depression. After cocaine use stops and the brain has a chance to manufacture more dopamine, the nervous system bounces back, usually within a few hours.

Most people who use cocaine with any regularity tell of a powerful urge to keep using the drug. This is related, in part, to cocaine's stimulation of certain parts of the brain—the amygdalae and the hypothalamus—which are considered compelling reinforcing areas; heroin and other opiates stimulate these same brain areas. Combined with its ability to control the use and manufacturing of essential neurotransmitters responsible for life-protecting and life-producing signals—the needs for sex, food, water, and flight—cocaine can become, for the regular user, the most important function in life. The drug actually becomes more important than any of the primary, life-sustaining drives it controls. The cocaine addict stops eating regularly, loses interest in work, family, friends, and sex, and becomes wholly focused on one overpowering need: more cocaine.

Addiction potential. Experts estimate that 10 to 20 percent of regular users will become addicted to cocaine. Like alcohol, cocaine appears to have a selectively addicting effect: Some people can use it with no compelling urge to increase the frequency or quantity of use, while others appear to be captured in a sort of quicksand effect. For these users, the drug provides such compelling effects that they feel an overwhelming need to keep using the drug and are unable to stop or control their use, despite the drug's catastrophic effects on their lives.

But while the problem of getting hooked is different for different people, the risk is greatly increased if the user freebases. The instantaneous high is more intense and the soon-to-follow crash is more powerful. While addiction to regular cocaine develops after three to four years, crack users can become full-blown addicts after only six to ten weeks.

Heredity also plays a role. Dr. David Smith of the Haight-Ashbury Free Medical Clinic and others who work with cocaine addicts report a fascinating statistic: 70 to 80 percent of the addicts they see have a family history of alcoholism. This clinical finding provides further proof that cocaine and alcohol addiction are related phenomena: the drugs apparently interact with a person's specific brain and body chemistry to create addiction. Todd Wilk Estroff, a psychiatrist, described it this way in the March 1985 edition of *Discover* magazine: "The brain and cocaine may be like a lock and a key. Some people say, 'That's what's been missing from my life to make me feel wonderful,' while others remain unaffected . . . [cocaine addiction] is a result of the drug's interaction with a person's brain chemistry."

Symptoms of addiction. As with all addictions, the symptoms of cocaine addiction can be split into three groups, all of which increase in severity as the addictive process continues: (1) behavioral; (2) emotional/psychological; and (3) physical.

Behavioral symptoms include regular use on a chronic or frequent basis; infrequently, if ever, turning down an offer of the drug; financial problems related to use; social life revolving around cocaine use; the development of an elaborate system of denial and rationalization to explain increased use and dependence on the drug; minimizing of negative effects and insisting that cocaine is a "great," "safe" drug; previous priorities in life (marriage, relationships with children, work, sex) lose their meaning; marital problems increase; a continual effort to "seek the high"; use of other drugs (alcohol, sedatives or tranquilizers, marijuana, heroin) to dull the "crash" of withdrawal; and compulsive, continued use of the drug despite negative consequences.

Psychological/emotional symptoms of addiction include frequent mood swings (up, then down, with no warning between), depression, irritability, guilt, remorse, self-pity, paranoia, uncontrollable rages, and violent outbreaks.

Physical symptoms include enlarged pupils, runny nose with watery discharge, chronic sinus problems, sleep disturbances, nervousness, appetite loss, weight loss, malnutrition, sexual dysfunction, heart palpitations or fibrillations, angina (severe pain in the chest), irregular heartbeat, patches (or flashes) of white light in the field of vision, difficulty in focusing the eyes, hypersensitivity to light, double vision, hyperactivity, tremors, dizziness, dryness of mouth and throat, sensitivity to heat and cold, and changes in body temperature.

Certain physical symptoms are also associated with the way in which cocaine is taken into the body. Snorters will develop chronic sinus problems, including frequent sniffling, a constantly drippy or runny nose (the addict will typically blame these problems on persistent colds or allergies); difficulty in breathing through the nose; disintegration of the wall (septum) dividing the nostrils; and, eventually, a collapsed septum, which must be rebuilt with plastic surgery. Free-basers often develop a sore chest, neck, and cheeks; asthma-type symptoms; swollen glands in the mouth; a hoarse, scratchy voice with possible permanent damage to the vocal cords; and lung irritations leading to deterioration of lung tissue. Injecting cocaine can lead to infections such as open, pussy sores, or more serious diseases, such as viral hepatitis or the deadly AIDS, caused by using dirty, infected needles.

Withdrawal symptoms. Cocaine has, in the past, been considered a nonaddictive drug because of the absence of severe, identifiable withdrawal symptoms such as D.T.s in the alcoholic or two to three days of retching, sweating, and shaking in the heroin addict. But while the withdrawal symptoms related to cocaine addiction are not as obviously physically debilitating as those of other addictive drugs, they are nevertheless both powerful and overwhelming. And the epidemic of crack use is rapidly changing people's minds about cocaine's addictive potential.

Acute withdrawal symptoms include sleep disturbances, nervousness, tremors, difficulty in controlling anxiety, and "cocaine psychosis," a hair-raising phenomenon that progresses in stages. The first stage involves the irritability and depression— the "crash"—that most users experience when the drug effects wear off. In the second stage, the addict experiences erratic mood swings and often terrifying feelings of paranoia. These symptoms become more exaggerated in stage three, when the addict may have auditory, visual, or tactile hallucinations (for example, a sensation of bugs crawling under the skin), and uncontrollable, violent rages or outbursts.

Protracted or long-term withdrawal can be seen in persistent "drug dreams," in which the addict dreams he used or refused cocaine and awakens frightened and deeply upset; and in the often overwhelming sensation of "drug hunger," which can continue for months after drug use has stopped. In *One Step Over the Line,* author Joanne Baum describes this potent hunger as an "involuntary craving for the drug often accompanied by strong images of purchasing and using the drug."

The crash of withdrawal is crushing, reducing the addict to

one throbbing need that overwhelms all others: more cocaine. "Flesh wrapped around the drug" is the way one cocaine addict described the addiction. The experts agree. "It's impossible for the nonaddict to imagine the depth and viciousness of depression that an advanced cocaine addict suffers from," said Dr. Arnold Washton of the National Cocaine Hotline.

Death. Between 1970 and 1980 a 600 percent increase in cocaine deaths was reported, and the death rate continues to increase at an alarming rate. Cocaine-related emergency room episodes tripled from 1981 to 1985.

The epidemic of crack use is quickly making even these alarming statistics obsolete. With crack, the risk of potentially deadly brain seizures, lung damage, and heart strain is considerably higher because of the drug's intense concentration. And the paranoia and psychosis produced by heavy crack use are leading to a rash of brutal crimes: seven crack-related homicides were reported in New York City in one month in 1986.

Death from cocaine can come in a variety of ways. The rapid rise in blood pressure can blow out weak blood vessels in the brain, leading to *cerebral hemorrhage* and *strokes*. Large doses of cocaine can overwhelm the brain's ability to keep the nervous system functioning, causing *respiratory failure*. Cocaine can cause *epileptic seizures* in people with no previous signs of epilepsy, or heart fibrillations leading to *cardiac arrest* in people with no history of heart problems. A small percentage of users lacks the necessary enzyme to metabolize cocaine and may experience a *fatal reaction* to the drug. Some people die from *allergic reactions* to the drug or from *bad "cuts."* Free-basers may, if they last that long, die of *cancer of the lungs*.

Acute overdose can lead to death in five to fifteen minutes, progressing from confusion, dizziness, fever, convulsions, irregular breathing and heartbeat to respiratory and cardiac arrest. The risks of overdose are dramatically increased when the addict combines different drugs. John Belushi, for example, died from an overdose of a potent mixture of cocaine and heroin known as a "speedball." Alcohol, narcotics, barbiturates, sedatives, and tranquilizers can all react with cocaine in potentially deadly ways.

A surprising number of cocaine addicts and dealers die violently. Cocaine psychosis can lead to deranged behavior, including intense paranoia and violent outbursts against others who the addict believes are plotting against him: one sixteen-year-old addict stabbed his mother to death after she caught him smoking crack. Suicide is another cause of death, and it can occur when addicts experience the crash of withdrawal or, in a more "rational" state, when their lives seem totally unmanageable and death seems like a release from the emotional pain of living.

MARIJUANA

General facts. Marijuana has been perceived by most users as a low-key, low-impact, nonaddictive drug with temporary, minor, insignificant effects. In other words, a *safe* drug. But the facts argue otherwise.

Marijuana, sensimilla (a potent version of marijuana), and hashish, which is made by crushing and boiling the cannabis plant's leaves and stems to produce a water-insoluble resin, are all derived from the cannabis sativa plant; marijuana is processed from the leaves and flowering tops of the plant. Cannabis contains 421 known chemicals, making marijuana the most chemically complex of all the illegal drugs. When "the weed" is smoked, its 421 chemicals combust into over 2,000, and when these 2,000 chemicals are metabolized, or broken down in the body, hundreds *more* chemicals are produced. Researchers have concentrated the great majority of their studies on one particular group of chemicals known as the *cannabinoids,* which contain the chief mind-altering chemical, delta-9-tetrahydrocannabinol, or simply THC. THC by itself breaks down in the body into 35 known metabolites.

Marijuana's chemical complexity makes it an extremely difficult drug to study. Two further complications confuse researchers: (1) the chemical content of one batch of marijuana can vary significantly from that of a neighboring batch (and, in fact, the chemical content of the same plant varies significantly from one hour to the next), and (2) a particular person's body chemistry interacts with the incredible variety of chemicals in marijuana, creating a uniquely different psychological and physical reaction in every person who uses the drug.

Nevertheless, since 1971 the federal government has conducted a broad range of studies using the marijuana grown on its own NIDA (National Institute on Drug Abuse)-funded plantation near the University of Mississippi. Because human subjects are used in these government studies, the THC potency of the NIDA marijuana is restricted to approximately 2 percent: the "impairing impact" of marijuana is dose related, meaning that the higher the quantity and "quality" or potency of the marijuana, the worse the effects. Thus, the findings reported in the research journals show only the low-dose impact of marijuana. The real impact of marijuana currently sold on the street can be inferred to be much more severe and pronounced.

In the past twenty years, in fact, selective harvesting techniques have increased the THC potency from 1 to 2 percent to as high as 20 percent. Thus, the average marijuana being sold and smoked today is five to twenty times more THC-potent than that sold just ten to twenty years ago and five to ten times more potent than the marijuana used in federal research studies.

In addition to its chemical complexity, marijuana has one other characteristic that makes it unique among most drugs: its chemical components, particularly the cannabinoids, are fat soluble. Alcohol and most other drugs are water soluble, and since our bodies use a water-based disposal system of blood and urine, these drugs are easily excreted from the body within a few hours. The cannabinoids in marijuana, however, settle into the fatty tissues of the body and collect there for days, weeks, even months before they are finally broken down and eliminated. A regular marijuana smoker will continue to excrete cannabis in the urine for three to four weeks *after* all marijuana intake has stopped.

The primary settling grounds for the cannabinoids include fatty organs such as the brain, gonads (testes and ovaries), adrenal glands, and liver; the protective cushion of fat surrounding many major organs such as the heart and kidneys; and the surface and internal membranes of every cell in the body. The cannabinoids, in other words, can and do settle everywhere in the body, but particularly around the major organs, and their effects continue long after the user stops smoking.

Medical uses. The THC in marijuana has a beneficial effect for some cancer patients suffering from nausea and vomiting produced by chemotherapy. Capsules containing a synthetic, pure form of THC, standardized for potency, have been made available to cancer patients through the National Cancer Institute. Unfortunately, even this synthetic form of THC has been shown to have harmful physical and psychological side effects including incoordination, dizziness, ataxia (unstable gait), and paranoia; drowsiness, hallucinations, anxiety, and rapid heartbeat are also common side effects.

In general, studies show that 30 to 50 percent of cancer patients report beneficial effects from using THC; most of these are younger patients, many of whom are regular users of the drug. While some cancer patients claim that smoking marijuana is more effective in lessening nausea than the synthetic THC pill, researchers warn about the fungus content of "natural" marijuana, which in people with weak immune systems (cancer patients treated with chemotherapy, for example) can lead to serious, even life-threatening infections.

Glaucoma is an eye disease characterized by increasing pressure within the eye, causing damage to the optic nerve, impaired vision, and leading, in some cases, to blindness. Smoking marijuana can lower the pressure within the eye, but, according to researcher Frank Newell, M.D., a marijuana cigarette would have to be smoked every two hours, day and night, to be effective. Furthermore, glaucoma is particularly common among the elderly, who often cannot tolerate marijuana's side effects. THC eyedrops are being developed for use by glaucoma patients, but, again, researchers worry about the possible harmful side effects, including difficulty in focusing, decreased tearing, pupil abnormalities, and "dancing eye" (nystagmoid movements). Researchers are currently hoping to develop a THC-related drug that would be effective in treating glaucoma but would not produce the unpleasant side effects of THC.

Cannabidiol, a nonpsychoactive cannabinoid found in marijuana, elevates the seizure threshold and has been found helpful in treating grand mal epilepsy. Scientists believe this is a promising area for further research, although cannabidiol has also been found to enhance tumor growth in cancer patients.

In general, marijuana is considered by researchers to be a "crude" drug with a hard-to-control and unstable chemical complexity. While some of its chemical constituents have been shown to be effective in treating certain medical disorders or diseases, the side effects are significant. The search for other, more effective and less potentially toxic drugs continues.

Primary effects. The mind-altering chemicals in marijuana are activated by heat, and the most popular method of "getting high" is by smoking. (Boiling marijuana in tea or baking it in brownies or, like oregano, on top of pizza are also effective methods of ingestion.) Marijuana, then, usually enters the body through the lungs, where its particles are deposited on the walls of the air passages and air sacs adjacent to the capillaries; the chemical components are then absorbed into the bloodstream and cardiovascular system. Within minutes the mind-altering cannabinoids are transported to the brain and other vital organs of the body. The three major organs affected by smoking marijuana are the *lungs,* the *heart,* and the *brain.*

• *The lungs.* Smoke from marijuana and tobacco contains many of the same compounds—ammonia, hydrogen, cyanide, actolein, benzene, N-nitrosamines, dimethyl, and methylethyl, for example—that have been proved to have harmful effects on the lungs and heart. Marijuana smoke, in fact, contains significantly higher amounts of proven carcinogenic compounds called "polynuclear aromatic hydrocarbons" (PAHs) than tobacco smoke. Since the typical marijuana smoker holds the smoke in his lungs for ten seconds to one minute, and the typical cigarette smoker inhales for only two to three seconds, the harmful effects of these compounds are believed to be increased in marijuana smokers. As former Surgeon General Dr. Julius B. Richmond, quoted in *Marijuana Alert,* said in a 1979 report:

> From the total body of experimental evidence accumulated to date, it appears that daily use of marijuana leads to damage similar to that from heavy cigarette smoking. Although, thus far, there is no direct evidence that smoking marijuana is correlated with lung cancer, it must be remembered that it takes lung cancer twenty to thirty years to grow. Therefore, there is very good reason for concern about the possibility of pulmonary cancer resulting from extended use of marijuana over ten or twenty years.

Commonly seen complications involving the pulmonary tract of chronic marijuana smokers include colds, allergies, sore throat, increased nasal secretions, irritation and inflammation of the nose and pharynx, chronic, persistent cough, sinus problems, wheezing sounds or rales in the chest, chest pain, chronic bronchitis, and laryngitis. In the respiratory tract, marijuana affects everything from the sinus cavities around the nose to the tiny, secluded cells of the lung. In studies reported in *Marijuana Alert,* rats exposed to one to six marijuana joints per day showed extensive lung inflammation, tissue debris blocking the deepest air passageways, and potential, precancerous lesions, and healthy young male marijuana smokers showed significant impairment in lung function, similar to that found in moderate to heavy cigarette smokers.

A famous study of hashish- and cigarette-smoking soldiers by pioneer marijuana researcher Dr. Forest S. Tennant, Jr., reported numerous respiratory problems—chronic cough, abnormal sounds in lungs and air passageways, excessive sputum production, coughing up blood, inflammation of lungs, short-ness of breath, and atypical, possibly precancerous cells. As reported in *Marijuana Alert,* Tennant concluded his years of marijuana studies with this startling statement:

> It seems clear that the lungs are simply not strong enough to withstand the assault of both tobacco and cannabis. The harmful effects are synergistic. One plus one equals far more than two. And most cannabis smokers do seem to use tobacco cigarettes as well.
>
> A further worrying factor: Early emphysema and chronic bron-chitis are normally not seen unless you've smoked a pack a day of tobacco cigarettes for twenty to twenty-five years. But among the many hundreds of soldiers I treated . . . I sometimes saw those conditions in eighteen-, nineteen-, and twenty-year-old men.

• *The heart.* The heartbeat speeds up after marijuana use, often doubling within fifteen to thirty minutes and persisting at high rates for two hours or more. More varied and less pro-nounced is marijuana's effect on blood pressure. Marijuana is known to decrease the force with which the heart can pump blood, the amount of blood pumped, and the overall volume capacity of the heart, but the effect varies with individuals and the amount of marijuana smoked.

How does marijuana exert this influence on the heart? Through the brain. The cannabinoids, in particular, act on certain parts of the brain that control the workings of the heart and blood vessels. While major cardiac symptoms have not been re-ported in healthy people smoking moderate doses, the effects become critically important in individuals who already have heart disease—and fully one-fourth of the people with heart disease have no idea that their heart is functioning abnormally until it suddenly stops working. Furthermore, the effects of long-term exposure to marijuana have not been adequately studied. Researchers don't yet know what effects marijuana may have on the chronic smoker's heart ten to twenty years down the road.

• *The brain.* The behavioral symptoms associated with chronic marijuana use include abrupt mood swings, impaired short-term memory, abnormal irritability and hostility, lack of motivation, panic reactions, paranoia, depression, and, in some cases, suicidal feelings. Researchers have presented alarming evidence showing that these symptoms have their origins in physical alterations to the brain caused by smoking marijuana. "Animal data confirm what many of us have suspected from clinical experience with marijuana users, namely that this drug produces distinctive changes in the brain," summed up Dr. Robert Heath, a neurologist who has conducted research on both humans and monkeys, as reported in *Marijuana Alert*.

The brain is composed of a number of distinct regions, each of which is responsible for specific, enormously complex tasks. Marijuana appears to affect just about every one of these regions. The limbic area, for example, is the center of such emotional and physical symptoms as pleasure, hostility, and hunger. As reported by Dr. Heath, electrodes implanted in the limbic system of rhesus monkeys exposed to marijuana showed brain wave abnormalities that did not return to normal for six months or longer *after* marijuana use was discontinued. Autopsies of the monkeys' brains showed cell damage in forty-two different sites in the brain, with the most dramatic damage evident in the "pleasure center" of the brain—the limbic center. Distinct abnormalities were noted in the synaptic vessels, small sacs that contain the brain's chemical messengers, the neurotransmitters, and in the synaptic clefts, or spaces, between the nerve connections. Researchers speculate that in humans these changes could be related to the short-term memory impairment, apathy, lack of motivation, and periodic emotional flareups (irritability, hostility, paranoia) so often reported by chronic marijuana smokers.

EEGs of human marijuana smokers show a marked slowing of alpha and theta rhythms; these rhythms are a measure of the intellectual functioning taking place in the cortical-cerebral complex of the brain. Slow rhythms are commonly found in moderate to severe brain injuries, infections, and traumas, and they indicate reduced functioning, a lowering of "alertness" and arousal, lessened awareness of events, wandering of attention, and a decreased complexity of thought processes.

In other words, marijuana smokers show chronic brain impairment while smoking.

How much of the damage to the brain is reversible? Brain cells, unlike other body cells, are not regenerated. While billions of "extra" cells are available to take over the function of dead or damaged cells, the point comes when the damage is severe enough and has been going on for long enough that permanent abnormalities may be present. Once again, while the studies noted here report chronic brain damage only while smoking marijuana and therefore cannot be extended to conclusions about long-term damage, the possibility of permanent damage is of grave concern to most researchers.

Addiction potential. Marijuana is generally considered psychologically addicting but of a degree unknown in terms of physical addiction. Nevertheless, chronic, heavy users of marijuana display each of the three cardinal symptoms of physiological addiction: *compulsion* to use the drug; *loss of control* over the ability to cut down or stop using the drug; and *continued use despite adverse consequences.* Furthermore, there is an identifiable *progression* of symptoms in chronic marijuana smokers, from seeking the high to preoccupation with obtaining the drug and getting high, to needing the drug just to "get by" and function every day. Marijuana smokers definitely experience physiological *tolerance,* needing larger amounts or more potent varieties of the drug in order to achieve the same effects. Researchers speculate that the toxic effects of THC on the brain may actually suppress the body's natural "pleasure" chemicals and eventually injure the chronic user's ability to achieve a natural, nondrug-induced sensation of pleasure or euphoria.

The hallmark of physical addiction is withdrawal symptoms; because stopping the intake of marijuana does not lead to severe withdrawal, the drug has been labeled "soft." Marijuana's effect on the brain, however, is both more subtle and more insidious than that of the "hard" drugs such as heroin or alcohol. Unlike these drugs, marijuana is not readily broken down and eliminated from the body; instead, it accumulates in the brain, breaking down only very slowly and resulting in altered brain functioning and changes in cell structure. This is one reason why marijuana smokers don't suffer dramatic symptoms of withdrawal when they stop using the drug: the drug is literally being time-released and is still present in the body weeks, even months, after use has stopped.

Strict definitions of physical addiction would bar marijuana from the ranks of the "hard" physically addicting drugs. But the known facts about its actions on the body and, in particular, its physically induced psychological symptoms, would tend to argue for its inclusion with alcohol, heroin, cocaine, and other drugs as a potentially dangerous, physically addicting drug. Furthermore, clinical experience with marijuana users shows that they cannot return to "normal," moderate use of the drug, with the ability to start or stop at will. The marijuana addict, like the alcoholic, can be off the drug for years when just one or two joints will set him back on a binge and, within days, bring back all the psychological and physiological symptoms associated with chronic abuse.

Symptoms of addiction.

Emotional/psychological. Ego deterioration (lack of self-worth, dislike of self, et cetera); depression; long-lasting feelings of inadequacy; psychotic reactions (disorientation, hallucinations, paranoia); increased irritability; increased stubbornness; confusion; abrupt mood swings; suicidal feelings.

Behavioral. Promises to quit or cut down; chronic lying; denial (failure to recognize or admit the drug's negative impact on psychological and physical health, work, family, relationships, et cetera); guilt; suicidal feelings or attempts; deterioration of relationships with family and friends; academic or job deterioration; increased social isolation; inappropriate behaviors; aggressive behavior; hyperactivity; apathy; passivity; lack of interest in personal hygiene.

Physical. Tolerance to the drug's effects; headaches; impaired short-term memory; complaints of fatigue; inability to perform complex tasks; alterations in time perception; poor concentration.

Withdrawal symptoms. Irritability; sleep disturbances; flashbacks (a spontaneous, involuntary recurrence of the feelings and perceptions associated with using the drug); chronic headaches, persisting in some users for days; panic attacks (racing heart, sweating, palpitations, heavy breathing, and severe anxiety); loss of memory and, in some cases, blackouts.

Death. The long-term effects of marijuana on the cardiac and respiratory systems are, as we've noted, unknown. Research into the drug began less than two decades ago and the facts are not yet in. Because marijuana smoke contains so many of the same components as tobacco smoke, however, researchers speculate that long-term effects may include such life-threatening diseases as cancer, emphysema, and heart disease.

The risk of an acute, fatal reaction is greatly increased when marijuana is combined with other drugs; and an estimated 50 percent of marijuana users also regularly use one or more of the other illegal drugs (and an even higher percentage use the legal drug, alcohol). Suicide is a known and documented cause of death among chronic marijuana users, particularly adolescents. Because marijuana cuts down on reflexes and thinking ability, fatal automobile accidents are increasingly being tied to drivers under the influence of marijuana. Finally, the lives of many thousands of innocent people are jeopardized by marijuana smokers who try to perform their jobs as airplane pilots, air traffic controllers, mechanics, or military personnel, while under the influence of the drug.

NARCOTICS

General facts. Narcotic drugs have a quadruple whammy effect: they produce pleasure, kill pain, dull fear, tension, and anxiety, and induce sleep or insensibility. They are also highly addictive.

The term *narcotic* generally refers to opium and drugs made from opium such as heroin, morphine,* and codeine. Morphine and codeine are naturally occurring drugs derived from the opium plant; heroin is a semisynthetic, a derivative of morphine; and Demerol and methadone are synthetic narcotics manufactured in the laboratory.

Morphine, codeine, and Demerol are available only by prescription; the law prohibits refilling a prescription containing a narcotic. Use or sale of heroin is prohibited in the United States. Because of its extreme potency, heroin is the most popular drug among addicts.

Medical uses. Narcotics are the most effective pain relievers (analgesics) known to man. Codeine acts on the cough center in the brain to decrease coughing and symptoms of the common cold; in higher doses it is used to relieve pain. Demerol is used to relieve moderate to severe pain, to make a person drowsy before an operation, to supplement general anesthesia during surgery, and to relieve the pain of childbirth. Narcotics have also been used for centuries as a remedy for diarrhea.

Primary effects. Narcotics cause drowsiness, apathy, lethargy, decreased physical activity, constipation, pinpoint pupils, and reduced vision. Larger doses may produce insensibility, nausea, vomiting, and respiratory depression: the skin becomes cold and clammy, breathing becomes slow and shallow, the body limp, the jaw relaxed. If respiratory depression is severe enough, convulsions, coma, and death may occur.

The chemical configuration of narcotics fits like a "lock and key" into the molecules of the brain that normally regulate the pain-pleasure circuits. Specifically, narcotics alter the beta

---

*Most of the morphine extracted from opium by the pharmaceutical industry is converted to codeine and other semisynthetic narcotics, which produce less intense, direct effects and also less harmful side effects.

endorphin neurotransmitter system. Beta endorphins are the body's natural source of pain relief and pleasure. When a narcotic drug is present in the body, the brain makes fewer endorphins on its own and becomes progressively less responsive to the narcotic itself. When the drug effects wear off, the body's pain-relief and pleasure centers are left high and dry, resulting in severe withdrawal symptoms while the brain attempts to replenish its own supply of the pleasure-pain molecules.

Addiction potential. Narcotics are highly addictive; if used regularly they will produce addiction in almost anyone. The high addiction potential of these drugs is related to the fact that they are chemical "twins" to the body's own pleasure-pain molecules. The brain is anything but dumb; it won't put its energy into producing substances that are already readily available.

Symptoms of addiction. Regular use of narcotics leads rapidly to abuse and addiction. Thus, the normal "stages" of the addiction process for alcohol and cocaine progress much faster with heroin, morphine, or codeine addiction. Obvious withdrawal symptoms, which often take years to develop in alcohol and cocaine addiction, may be apparent within months, even weeks after the user becomes addicted.

Withdrawal symptoms. Narcotics have a lulling effect on the brain and central nervous system; their withdrawal produces the opposite state of extreme excitability. Within eight to twelve hours after use of morphine or heroin has stopped, the addict is anxious, restless, yawning, unable to sleep, and beginning to get desperate for another dose of the drug. Within the next twenty-four to sixty hours, these symptoms increase in intensity and new symptoms are added: loss of appetite, gooseflesh, sweating, tremors, violent yawning or severe sneezing, depression, nausea, vomiting, stomach cramps, and diarrhea. Heart rate and blood pressure are elevated. Chills alternate with flushing and excessive sweating, and the addict complains of pains in the bones and muscles of the back and extremities. The addict may also become suicidal.

Without treatment, the syndrome eventually runs its course, with most symptoms disappearing in seven to ten days. In treatment, tapering doses of narcotics are typically used over a three- to four-day period to control the withdrawal symptoms and to make the patient as comfortable as possible. Long-term (protracted) withdrawal may continue for one to three months, with addicts experiencing depression, irritability, sleep disturbances, anxiety, and a persistent craving for the drug.

Death. Heroin causes less organ damage than alcohol, and even untreated withdrawal is rarely fatal. Yet, the death rate among heroin addicts between the ages of twenty-five and forty-four is ten times greater than that of the general population. Why? Addiction to narcotics, particularly heroin, carries with it certain lethal occupational hazards: sharing dirty needles can cause AIDS, a deadly and incurable disease, and viral hepatitis, a liver infection; impurities in heroin can cause acute fatal reactions (addicts have been known to die seconds after injecting a dose, the needle still imbedded in the vein); and dissolving heroin in dirty water can lead to subacute bacterial endocarditis (bacterial infection of the heart valves). Violent crime is an ever-present hazard for the addict, and suicide is not uncommon. Combining heroin with other drugs greatly increases the risk of fatal reactions.

STIMULANTS

General facts. Caffeine, nicotine, and amphetamines are all stimulants; cocaine has many of the properties of a stimulant.

Medical uses. The amphetamines and other stimulants are available by prescription for weight control and hyperactivity. Caffeine is an effective laxative. Cocaine is sometimes used as a local anesthetic.

Primary effects. Stimulants reduce fatigue, increase alertness, extend wakefulness, temporarily elevate mood, and increase the sensation of well-being. They may also cause hyperactivity, irritability, anxiety, and feelings of apprehension. Other effects include dilated pupils, increased pulse rate and blood pressure, insomnia, and loss of appetite.

Addiction potential. Cocaine, as discussed in the previous section, can be highly addictive, particularly in the form known as "crack." Amphetamines can also be physically addictive if used over long periods of time; tolerance develops rapidly, with large doses of the drug or a stronger drug required to produce the same effect. Even the relatively weak stimulant caffeine is considered addictive: when regular coffee drinkers try to quit or cut back, they may experience headaches, insomnia, and mood swings.

Symptoms of addiction. Large doses of amphetamines can cause agitation, increase in body temperature, hallucinations, convulsions, and even death. *Behavioral* symptoms include repetitive grinding of the teeth, touching or picking at the face and extremities, and performing the same task over and over. *Psychological* symptoms include hostility, paranoia, panic, suspiciousness, and preoccupation with self. *Physical* symptoms include dizziness, tremors, agitation, headaches, flushed skin, chest pain, excessive sweating, vomiting, and abdominal cramps; these are also, it should be noted, symptoms of overdose.

Withdrawal symptoms. Apathy, depression, disorientation, fatigue, and disturbance in sleep patterns are acute symptoms that may last for several days. Protracted symptoms, which may persist for weeks or even months, include anxiety, tenseness, and suicidal tendencies.

Death. Overdose, which is not uncommon due to the rapid development of tolerance to these drugs, can lead to high fever, convulsions, and cardiovascular collapse. Because stimulants raise body temperature, physical exercise and outside temperature can greatly increase the risk of toxic and fatal reactions. Cases of athletes who take moderate amounts of stimulants and then collapse under the strain of exertion are not uncommon. The combination of stimulant drugs with other addictive drugs can also lead to toxic and sometimes fatal reactions.

DEPRESSANTS

General facts. Types of depressant drugs include sedatives, hypnotics, and tranquilizers. Sedatives reduce nervousness, anxiety, irritability, and excitability, and cause relaxation. Tranquilizers calm or quiet anxious patients without causing the drowsiness or suppressed body reactions common to sedatives. Hypnotics induce sleep.

Major tranquilizers. Mellaril and Thorazine, for example, are typically prescribed for severe mental problems. *Minor tranquilizers* are usually prescribed for complaints of stress, nervousness, anxiety, and tension. The benzodiazepines, a class of minor tranquilizers that includes Librium, Valium, and Dalmane, have dominated the tranquilizer field; they are not only the most heavily prescribed of the psychoactive drugs but the most heavily abused as well.

Primary effects. The depressant drugs exert their specific effects by slowing down or depressing various functions of the brain and spinal cord (the central nervous system). Drowsiness, dizziness, lightheadedness, unsteadiness, and clumsiness are common side- or aftereffects of these drugs. Headaches, slurred speech, unusual weakness or tiredness, stomach upsets, nausea, and diarrhea are other not uncommon side effects.

Addiction potential. The depressants as a group are highly addictive, even when taken as prescribed by a physician. These drugs should never be taken for long periods of time or in larger amounts than prescribed. The addiction potential is greatly increased when other drugs, including alcohol, are taken simultaneously. The combination is not addictive but *explosive* and can lead to dangerous, even fatal reactions. Dorothy Kilgallen died after taking moderate doses of barbiturates and alcohol; Karen Ann Quinlan lapsed into a coma and eventually died from the combination of several gin-and-tonics and Quaaludes (methaqualone, a sedative and hypnotic drug); Betty Ford became addicted to both alcohol and prescription pills after taking painkillers and muscle relaxants as prescribed by her physician.

All drugs that exert similar effects on the central nervous system (CNS)—including alcohol, painkillers, sedatives, and tranquilizers—can lead to cross-tolerance and cross-addiction when combined with other CNS drugs. An alcoholic, for example, is instantly tolerant to other CNS drugs and needs more than the prescribed amount to experience the effects of the drug. The body's cells, having adapted to one drug, are also tolerant to the effects of pharmacologically similar drugs— that's *cross-tolerance*. It's a lesser-known fact that regular exposure to CNS drugs can cause a speeded-up addiction process to all CNS drugs taken, a phenomenon known as *cross-addiction*. Once addicted to one drug, the "pathway" of addiction is already paved and use of other CNS drugs will quickly lead to addiction to these drugs, too.

Withdrawal symptoms. Withdrawal from depressant drugs typically begins four to five days after drug use is stopped, reaches its greatest intensity by the sixth to seventh day, and subsides within eight to twelve days; this is a withdrawal course more than *twice* as long as that endured by most alcoholics. For people addicted to both alcohol and prescription depressants, withdrawal is greatly intensified.

Certain "long-acting" depressants such as Valium cause increasing symptoms for up to ten days and then continued, fluctuating symptoms that come in waves of varying intensity for two to four weeks. Acute withdrawal symptoms are similar to those experienced by alcoholics—tremors, elevated blood pressure and pulse, nervousness, nausea, diarrhea, excessive perspiration, agitation, mental confusion, and paranoia. But sedative addicts also experience a feeling of "pounding inside" and overwhelming sensations of helplessness and hopelessness during withdrawal. For the polydrug addict—someone who is addicted to more than one CNS drug—the symptoms are intensified, the course of withdrawal is often unpredictable, and seizures and hallucinations are common.

Protracted withdrawal for people addicted to CNS depressants can continue for weeks or even months. Depression, anxiety, nervousness, sleep disorders, suicidal feelings, mood swings, and persisting feelings of helplessness and despair are common, particularly for polydrug addicts. The "drug hunger" of these addicts can be overwhelming, even after weeks or months of abstinence. Special care and handling in treatment are required if these patients are to become committed to a lifelong recovery program. (For detailed information on the care and handling of the polydrug addict in a treatment situation, see *Recovering: How to Get and Stay Sober,* by Mueller and Ketcham, chapter 13, pp. 186–93.)

Death. The greatest danger of death with depressant drugs is when they are combined with other drugs. Unfortunately, this is not an uncommon practice. Astonishing numbers of middle-aged men and women regularly drink alcohol and take prescription pills—treatment centers are reporting that 80 to 90 percent of their patients are cross-addicted to both alcohol and prescription drugs. Teenagers often sneak a few prescription pills from their parents' medicine cabinets to increase the intensity of an alcohol or marijuana high. And the elderly are at a high risk for accidental overdose and death because of the different drugs they take for medical and psychological problems and their reduced ability to metabolize these drugs.

Symptoms of an overdose include slow and shallow breathing; cold, clammy skin; dilated pupils; and a weak and rapid pulse. Death can come slowly, from a drug-induced coma, or quickly, from respiratory or cardiac collapse.

HALLUCINOGENS

General facts. Hallucinogens distort the perception of objective reality, producing sensory illusions and making it difficult to distinguish between fact and fantasy. The most commonly used hallucinogens include LSD, mescaline, psilocybin, MDA, and PCP.

While not physically addictive and generally not death-dealing, these drugs are included in this appendix because they are often used in combination with other drugs, generally by adolescents, and their use can signal a potential problem.

Medical uses. None, except for PCP, which is used as a veterinary anesthetic under the trade name Sernylan.

Primary effects. Illusions and hallucinations (with the exception of MDA); disoriented perception of time, direction, and distance; restlessness and sleeplessness. Intensity and duration of effects vary with the individual drug and amount used.

Addiction potential. The hallucinogens produce no documented withdrawal symptoms and are not considered physically addictive.

Death. The greatest hazard associated with using these drugs is that their effects are unpredictable, and each "trip" will differ from the last. Toxic reactions are common, leading to acute psychotic episodes, convulsions, and, in rare cases, death. Suicidal thoughts and feelings are not uncommon reactions to hallucinatory drugs, and preoccupation with death is a common reaction to PCP.

Selected Reading List

Hundreds of books about alcoholism, drug addiction, and co-dependency crowd bookstore and library shelves. These are our favorites:

A MUST READ

Under the Influence: A Guide to the Myths and Realities of Alcoholism. James R. Milam and Katherine Ketcham. Seattle: Madrona Publishers, 1981 (Bantam Books paperback edition, New York, 1983). If you were to read just one book on alcoholism, this is the one you should read. A comprehensive and controversial look at the physiological factors determining alcoholism, with specific recommendations for treatment, recovery, and prevention of alcoholism.

CO-DEPENDENCY

Co-Dependent No More. Melody Beattie. New York: Harper & Row, 1987. A practical, action-oriented book that avoids preachiness and focuses on understanding what co-dependence is, who's got it, and how to recover from it. The best book available on co-dependence.

The Family. John Bradshaw. Pompano Beach, Fla.: Health Communications, 1988. An insightful and illuminating look at dysfunctional families with numerous self-help exercises and case histories.

Women Who Love Too Much. Robin Norwood. New York: Pocket Books, 1986. A fascinating and revealing look at why women seek out and stick with relationships that are hurtful, unhappy, even destructive.

ADULT CHILDREN OF ALCOHOLICS

Adult Children of Alcoholics. Janet Woititz. Pompano Beach, Fla.: Health Communications, 1986. Thirteen characteristics of adult children of alcoholics are described in detail, with advice on how to break out of the mold.

Another Chance: Hope and Health for the Alcoholic Family. Sharon Wegscheider. Palo Alto: Science and Behavior Books, 1981. Provides a detailed look at the disease of dependency, its impact on the family, and the "survival roles" adopted by family members.

It Will Never Happen to Me. Claudia Black, Ph.D. Denver: MAC Publishing, 1981. A classic work that shares the experiences of children of alcoholics from childhood to adulthood.

INTERVENTION

I'll Quit Tomorrow. Vernon E. Johnson. New York: Harper & Row, 1973. The first book to detail the concept of "intervention." Excellent sections are included on the symptoms of alcoholism; especially useful are the descriptions of rationalization and denial.

How to Stop the One You Love from Drinking. Families in Crisis, Inc., and Mary Ellen Pinkham. New York: Putnam, 1986. A personal look at the process of intervention by the author of *Mary Ellen's Helpful Hints.*

ADOLESCENT PROBLEMS

Not My Kid: A Family's Guide to Kids and Drugs. Beth Polson and Miller Newton, Ph.D. New York: Arbor House, 1984. A straightforward approach to identifying drug problems in adolescents, working through both the family's and the teenager's denial, and reaching out for help.

Getting Tough on Gateway Drugs: A Guide for the Family. Robert L. DuPont, Jr., M.D. New York: American Psychiatric Press, 1984. Focusing on the three "gateway" drugs used most frequently by adolescents—alcohol, marijuana, and cocaine—Dr. DuPont offers a hard-line approach for families.

FOR YOUNG CHILDREN

My Dad Loves Me, My Dad Has a Disease. Claudia Black, Ph.D. Denver: MAC Publishing, 1982. A workbook for children of alcoholics, ages seven to fourteen, to help them understand such concepts as addiction, tolerance, and relapse and learn how to deal with their own feelings about the disease.

An Elephant in the Living Room: The Children's Book. Jill Hastings and Marilyn Typpo. Minneapolis: CompCare Publications, 1984. Helps children from age seven to early adolescence understand the disease of alcoholism and find emotional support outside the family.

TREATMENT

Recovering: How to Get and Stay Sober. L. Ann Mueller, M.D., and Katherine Ketcham. New York: Bantam Books, 1987. The best book available on all aspects of treatment, with clearly written, sensible advice on how to get the reluctant alcoholic or drug addict into treatment, how to select a good treatment center, what to expect in treatment, and how to prevent relapses and ensure a stable and happy recovery.

Bibliography

Adult Children of Alcoholics. Janet Woititz. Pompano Beach, Fla.: Health Communications, 1986.

Alcohol and the Brain. Ralph Tarter and David Van Thiel (eds.). New York: Plenum Publishing, 1985.

Alcoholics Anonymous. New York: A.A. World Services, 1955.

Alcoholism: The Nutritional Approach. Roger J. Williams. Austin: University of Texas Press, 1959.

The All-American Cocaine Story: A Guide to the Realities of Cocaine. David R. Britt. Minneapolis: CompCare Publications, 1984.

Another Chance: Hope and Health for the Alcoholic Family. Sharon Wegscheider. Palo Alto: Science and Behavior Books, 1981.

Chocolate to Morphine: Understanding Mind-Active Drugs. Andrew Weil, M.D., and Winifred Rosen. Boston: Houghton Mifflin, 1983.

Cocaine: A Drug and Its Social Evolution. Lester Brinspoon and James Bakalar. New York: Basic Books, 1976.

Cocaine: Seduction and Solution. Stone, Fromme, and Kagan. New York: Crown Publishers, 1984.

Doing Drugs. Bruce Jackson and Michael Jackson. New York: St. Martin's Press, 1983.

Drug and Alcohol Abuse: A Clinical Guide to Diagnosis and Treatment. Marc Schuckit, M.D. New York: Plenum Publishing, 1984.

Eating Right to Live Sober. Katherine Ketcham and L. Ann Mueller, M. D. Seattle: Madrona Publishers, 1983 (New American Library paperback edition, 1986).

Getting Them Sober. Toby Rice Drews. S. Plainfield, N.J.: Bridge Publishing, 1980.

Hypoglycemia: A Better Approach. Paavo Airola, Ph.D. Phoenix: Health Plus Publishing, 1977.

I'll Quit Tomorrow. Vernon E. Johnson. New York: Harper & Row, 1973.

Is Alcoholism Hereditary? Donald Goodwin, M.D. New York: Oxford University Press, 1976.

Marijuana Alert. Peggy Mann. New York: McGraw-Hill, 1985.

The Natural History of Alcoholism: Causes, Patterns, and Paths to Recovery. George Vaillant. Cambridge: Harvard University Press, 1983.

One Step Over the Line: A No-Nonsense Guide to Recognizing and Treating Cocaine Dependency. Joanne Baum, Ph.D. New York: Harper & Row, 1985.

Peoplemaking. Virginia Satir. Palo Alto: Science and Behavior Books, 1972.

Under the Influence: A Guide to the Myths and Realities of Alcoholism. James R. Milam and Katherine Ketcham. Seattle: Madrona Publishers, 1981 (Bantam Books paperback edition, 1983).

Women Who Love Too Much. Robin Norwood. New York: Pocket Books, 1986.

National Substance Abuse Resources

Addiction Research Foundation
33 Russell Street
Toronto, Ontario
M5S 2S1 Canada
416/595-6056

Al-Anon Family Groups World
  Services
P.O. Box 862
Midtown Station
New York, New York 10018
212/302-7240

Alateen
(Same as above)

ADPA
Alcohol and Drug Problems
  Association of North America,
  Inc.
444 North Capitol Street, N.W.
Washington, D.C. 20001
202/737-4340

A.A.
Alcoholics Anonymous
General Service Office
P.O. Box 459
Grand Central Station
New York, New York 10163
212/686-1100

American Council on Alcohol
  Problems, Inc.
3426 Bridgeland Drive
Bridgeton, Missouri 63044
314/739-5944

American Council for Drug
  Education
204 Monroe Street, Suite 100
Rockville, Maryland 20850
(formerly American Council on
Marijuana & Other Psycho-active
Drugs)
301/984-5700

AMSA
American Medical Society on
   Alcoholism & Other Drug
   Dependencies
12 West 21st Street, 8th Floor
New York, New York 10010
212/206-6770

AHHAP
Association of Halfway House
   Alcoholism Programs of North
   America
786 East 7th Street
St. Paul, Minnesota 55106
612/771-0933

ALMACA
Association of Labor-Management
   Administrators and Consultants
   on Alcoholism, Inc.
1800 North Kent Street, Suite 907
Arlington, Virginia 22209
703/522-6272

CSPI
Center for Science in the Public
   Interest
1501 16th Street, N.W.
Washington, D.C. 20036
202/332-9110

COAF
Children of Alcoholics Foundation,
   Inc.
200 Park Avenue, 31st Floor
New York, New York 10022
212/351-2680

Families in Crisis
715 Green Valley Drive
Bloomington, Minnesota 55437
612/893-1883

Hazelden Foundation
Box 11
Center City, Minnesota 55012
800/328-9000

ICAA/American
American International Council
   on Alcohol and Addiction/
   American Foundation
P.O. Box 489
Locust Valley, New York 11560
516/676-1802

ICAA
International Council on Alcohol
   and Addiction
Case Postale 189
1001 Lausanne, Switzerland

The Johnson Institute
7151 Metro Boulevard
Minneapolis, Minnesota 55435-
   3425
612/341-0435

MADD National
Mothers Against Drunk Driving
669 Airport Freeway, Suite 310
Hurst, Texas 76053-3944
817/268-6233

NAATP
National Association of Addiction
   Treatment Providers, Inc.
2082 Michelson Drive
Irvine, California 92715
714/476-8204

NACOA
National Association for Children
    of Alcoholics, Inc.
31582 Coast Highway, Suite B
S. Laguna, California 92677
714/499-3889

NADAC
National Association of Alcoholism
    and Drug Abuse Counselors
3717 Columbia Pike, Suite 300
Arlington, Virginia 22204
703/920-4644

NALGAP
National Association of Lesbian
    and Gay Alcoholism
    Professionals, Inc.
204 West 20th Street
New York, New York 10011

NASADAD
National Association of State
    Alcohol and Drug Abuse
    Directors, Inc.
444 North Capitol Street, N.W.
Washington, D.C. 20001
202/783-6868

NBAC
National Black Alcoholism
    Council
417 South Dearborn Street,
    Suite 700
Chicago, Illinois 60605
312/663-5780

NCALI
National Clearinghouse for
    Alcohol and Drug Information
P.O. Box 2345
Rockville, Maryland 20852
301/468-2600

NCA
National Council on Alcoholism,
    Inc.
12 West 21st Street, 7th Floor
New York, New York 10010
212/206-6770

NCA/Washington Office
National Council on Alcoholism,
    Inc.
1511 K Street, N.W., Suite 320
Washington, D.C. 20005
202/737-8122

NIAAA
National Institute on Alcohol
    Abuse and Alcoholism
Parklawn Building Room 16-105
5600 Fishers Lane
Rockville, Maryland 20857
301/443-3885

NIDA
National Institute on Drug Abuse
Parklawn Building
5600 Fishers Lane
Rockville, Maryland 20857
301/443-4577

NNSA
National Nurses Society on
    Addiction
2506 Grosse Pointe Road
Evanston, Illinois 60201
312/475-7300

National Safety Council
444 North Michigan Avenue
Chicago, Illinois 60611
312/527-4800

National Self-Help Clearinghouse
  Graduate School & University
  Center
City University of New York
33 West 42nd Street, Room 1222
New York, New York 10036
212/840-1259

RID
Remove Intoxicated Drivers
P.O. Box 520
Schenectady, New York 12301
518/372-0034

Center of Alcohol Studies Library
P.O. Box 969
Piscataway, New Jersey 08855-
  0969
201/932-4442

The Christopher D. Smithers
  Foundation, Inc.
P.O. Box 67
Mill Neck, New York 11765
516/676-0067

SADD
Students Against Driving Drunk
P.O. Box 800
Marlboro, Massachusetts 01752
617/481-3568

DOT
U.S. Department of
  Transportation
National Highway Traffic Safety
  Administration
Office of Alcohol and State
  Program
NTS-21
400 Seventh Street, S.W., Room
  5130
Washington, D.C. 20590
202/366-9581

Women for Sobriety, Inc.
P.O. Box 618
Quakertown, Pennsylvania 18951
215/536-8026

Index

cocaine (*cont.*)
  "drug hunger" and, 223
  free-basing, 18, 148, 218–219,
    222–223
  Freud and, 217
  general facts about, 217–218
  Harrison Narcotics Act, 217
  heredity and, 221
  injecting, 219–220
  medical uses, 218
  medicine containing, 217
  multiple-addictions, 42–44, 224–225
  packaging of, 148
  primary effects, 219–221
  side effects, 218
  snorting, 219–220
  source, 217
  stimulant, as a, 237
  symphomimetic, as a, 218
  symptoms of addiction:
    behavioral, 222
    physical, 222–223
    psychological/emotional, 222
  usage statistics, 217–218
  withdrawal symptoms, 223–224
    acute, 223
    protracted, 223–224
codeine, *see* narcotics
Co-Dependent No More, 243
co-dependency (term), x
combining drugs, *see* multiple addictions
coping behavior, 15–16
counselors, *see* intervention counselors
crack, 44, 217, 219, 223, 224, 238; *see
  also* cocaine
craving, 43
crisis line, 154
cross-tolerance, 240
  as a term, 42
  dangers, 42
  effects, 42
cross-addiction, 240; *see also* multiple
  addictions

D.T.'s, *see* delirium tremens
Dalmane, 239
Dan (case of addiction-inspired guilt),
  87–90
data base, 128–129
delirium tremens, 29–30, 215, 223
Demerol, *see* narcotics
denial, 98–99, 132–134
  statements used by family members,
    98–99, 133
depressants, 43, 239–242
  addictive potential, 239–240
    cross-addiction, 240
    cross-tolerance, 240
  CNS (central nervous system) drugs,
    240–241

death from, 241–242
general facts, 239
hypnotics, 239
Librium, 239
Melaril, 239
primary effects, 239
sedatives, 239
Thorazine, 239
tranquilizers, 239
Valium, 239, 240
withdrawal symptoms, 240–241
  protracted, 241
  Valium, 239, 240
detoxification centers, 152
Discover magazine, 221
Doing Drugs, 52
DuPont, Robert L., Jr., 244

EAP, *see* Employee Assistance Program
Eating Right to Live Sober, 216
early-stage addiction, 25, 31, 38, 46,
  213, 214–215
ecstasy, 44
*Elephant in the Living Room, An: The
  Children's Book*, 245
Employee Assistance Program, 117, 157
Enablers, 77, 158
Estroff, Todd Wilk, 221
Exorcist, The, 45, 48

facial signs of addiction, 49
Family, The, 243
family questionnaire, 126–127
Families in Crisis, 117
fear, 5, 74, 97–99, 101–104, 134, 137,
  176
  definition of, 97
  kinds:
    change, 101
    concrete things, 102
    conscience, 102
    Dependent's reactions, 102
    loneliness, 103
    loss of identity, 102–103
    moral disapproval, 101
    the unknown, 101
feelings, 5–6, 10–14, 19, 24, 72, 77–79,
  83–87, 98–99, 130–131, 136–138,
  168–171, 175; *see also* anger,
  guilt, fear, and love
  being indispensable, 20
  self-esteem, 71–72, 78, 97, 171
  trust, 138
  unable to determine, 6, 12
  untrustworthy, 18
fetal alcohol syndrome, 154
flake, *see* cocaine
Ford, Betty, 240
free-base, *see* cocaine
Freud, Sigmund (and cocaine), 217

Garland, Judy, 42
Getting Tough on Gateway Drugs: A Guide for the Family, 244
glaucoma, *see* marijuana
Goodwin, Donald, 39
guilt, 86–94, 97, 98, 169–171
  steps in getting rid of, 91–94

Haight-Ashbury Free Medical Clinic, 221
Hal (adolescent/multiple addictions), 45–46; *see also* case histories
hallucinogens, 43, 242
  addiction potential, 242
  death and, 242
  general facts, 242
  LSD, 242
  MDA, 242
  medical uses, 242
  mescaline, 242
  PCP, 242
  primary effects, 242
  psilocybin, 242
  Sernylan, 242
Harrison Narcotics Act, 217
Hastings, Jill, 245
Heath, Robert, 231
Henry (case of roles in alcoholic family), 81–85; *see also* case histories
heredity, 39, 221
heroin, *see* narcotics
Hypoglycemia, 216
hypnotics, *see* depressants

I'll Quit Tomorrow, ix
insurance (for treatment), 151–152, 155, 157
intervention, 3, 115–138, 179–187, 188–194, 195–199, 200–207
  awareness structure, 162
  Brian (case history/adolescent intervention), 139–150
  costs, 151–152, 155
  crisis, 153–154
  education for:
    keeping a journal, 130
    reading, 130
  employer in, 156–157, 180; *see also* Employee Assistance Program
  factual documentation, 188–194
    seven guidelines, 189–190
    scripts, 190–194
  families:
    abstinence in, 134–135, 187
    children present at, 159–160
    denial of, 132–134
    drinking and drug use in, 134–135
    fears of, 134, 185
    motives of, 137–138
    needs of, 136
    post-intervention needs, 208–210

role, 124–138, 179–187
  Families in Crisis, 117
formal, 115, 132, 181
how to get dependent to, 184–185
insurance coverage of, 151, 155, 157
Johnson, Barbara (case history/ intervention), 200–207
letter of support, 136
love factor, 137–138
miniintervention, 132
minister and, 160–161, 180
participants in, 180–181
physician and, 158
preparation for, 63–64, 179–185
problems, 151–162
rehearsal for, 195–199
relapse, 161
secrecy, 157
soft, 116
surprise in, 132
three steps to, 79–80
  accept, 79
  acknowledge, 79–80, 162
  recognize, 79, 162
threats and, 185–187
timing, 123, 153, 181–182, 184
treatment (planning for), 154–156
trust, 138
where to hold, 182–184
who to tell, 157–158
intervention counselor, x, xi–xii, 10–12, 115–122, 124–138
  choosing a counselor, 117–118
    qualities to look for, 118–119
    questions to ask, 119–120
  cost, 151–152
  crisis line, 154
  data base, 128–130
  Families in Crisis counselors, 117
  family questionnaire, 126–127
  first meeting, 124–127
  physicians and, 158–159
  predominant emotions of families, 130–131, 136–138
  rehearsal for intervention role, 195–199
  roles of, 120–122
  treatment options, 154
  ways they help, 116–117
intensified withdrawal, 43; *see also* multiple addictions
Is Alcoholism Hereditary?, 39
It Will Never Happen to Me, 244

Jackson, Michael, 52
Jessica (life with alcoholic father), 6–8; *see also* case histories
John (child of alcoholic), 72–74; *see also* case histories

Thorazine, 239
tolerance as a characteristic of addiction, 30, 213, 214
 cellular adaption, 42
 loss of, 43
tough love, 47
toxic reactions, 42
tranquilizers, 43, 239; *see also* depressants
treatment:
 aftercare, 156
 ages, 43–44
 in-patient centers, 152, 155–156
  choosing, 117–118, 154–156
  costs, 151–152, 155
  detoxification, 152
  intervention counselor, 125
  polydrug addict in, 241
  questions to ask, 119–120, 155–156
 out-patient, 152
 relapse, 161
Tree Grows in Brooklyn, A, 100

Twelve Steps, The, 156, 164–165
Typpo, Marilyn, 245

Under the Influence: AA Guide to the Myths and Realities of Alcoholism, ix–x, 130, 243
University of California, San Diego, 39
University of Mississippi, 226

Valium, 239, 240; *see also* depressants
verbal expressions characteristic of addiction, 49
viral hepatitis, 223, 237

Washton, Arnold, 224
Wegscheider, Sharon, 76–79, 244
withdrawal syndrome, 37
women (pregnant), 154, 218
Women Who Love Too Much, 95, 243

xenophobia, 60
Xylocaine, 218

ABOUT THE AUTHORS

Katherine Ketcham is the coauthor of *Under the Influence: A Guide to the Myths and Realities of Alcoholism; Eating Right to Live Sober;* and *Recovering: How to Get and Stay Sober.* Currently at work on her fifth nonfiction book, she lives in Walla Walla, Washington, with her husband, a college professor, and their three young children.

Ginny Lyford Gustafson, a certified chemical dependency counselor, has worked for ten years in the drug/alcohol field. For three years she has taught a course on intervention at the Alcohol Studies Program, Seattle University in Seattle, Washington. She is a drug/alcohol consultant to the North Shore and Lake Washington school districts, the Impaired Doctors Board, and the Impaired Dentists Board. She is also substance abuse counselor for O'Dea High School, Seattle. The mother of four, she lives in Kirkland, Washington.